REFORMING
ASIAN LABOR
SYSTEMS

REFORMING ASIAN LABOR SYSTEMS

ECONOMIC
TENSIONS
AND WORKER
DISSENT

FREDERIC C. DEYO

CORNELL UNIVERSITY PRESS
Ithaca and London

First published 2012 by Cornell University Press
First printing, Cornell Paperbacks, 2012

Printed in the United States of America

Library of Congress Cataloging-in-Publication Data

Deyo, Frederic C.
  Reforming Asian labor systems : economic tensions and worker dissent / Frederic C. Deyo.
    p. cm.
  Includes bibliographical references and index.
  ISBN 978-0-8014-5051-8 (cloth : alk. paper) —
ISBN 978-0-8014-7807-9 (pbk. : alk. paper)
  1. Labor—Asia.   2. Labor policy—Asia.   3. Industrial relations—Asia.   4. Working class—Political activity—Asia.   I. Title.
  HD8653.5.D49   2012
  331.1095—dc23   2011048714

Cornell University Press strives to use environmentally responsible suppliers and materials to the fullest extent possible in the publishing of its books. Such materials include vegetable-based, low-VOC inks and acid-free papers that are recycled, totally chlorine-free, or partly composed of nonwood fibers. For further information, visit our website at www.cornellpress.cornell.edu.

Cloth printing   10 9 8 7 6 5 4 3 2 1
Paperback printing   10 9 8 7 6 5 4 3 2 1

≋ CONTENTS

≋ ACKNOWLEDGMENTS

I am grateful to the following people for helpful comments on earlier chapters and versions of this manuscript: Kaan Ağartan, Teri Caraway, Peter Deyo, Rachael Deyo, Rick Doner, Leslie Gates, Kanishka Jayasuriya, Bob Jessop, Sarosh Kuruvilla, Kwangkun Lee, and two anonymous reviewers, as well as to faculty participants in two seminar presentations at the City University of Hong Kong, in which I presented early versions of my work. Factory visits in Guangdong Province, China, were generously arranged by the Asia Monitor Resource Centre in Hong Kong.

I am grateful as well for the hospitality, research support, and scholarly feedback I enjoyed while working on this book as a research fellow at Cornell University's Polson Institute for International Development, Department of Development Sociology. I have also benefited from the support and assistance of Roger Haydon, executive editor at Cornell University Press. Finally, and most important, I am grateful to my wife, Judy, my life partner and best friend, for her years of patience and support as I worked to complete this book.

REFORMING
ASIAN LABOR
SYSTEMS

Introduction

How has market-oriented economic reform affected the economic livelihood of East Asian workers? How have workers responded politically to the pressures of reform? How have governments sought to pursue economic agendas of reform and development while at the same time addressing the political challenges of worker dissent? What can we say of the policy impact of labor politics in a region where workers are typically marginalized in causal accounts of social change? And how may we explain the diverse trajectories of institutional change in East Asian labor regimes over the past three decades of market reform?

In this book, I address these questions through the prism of a labor systems view that embraces theoretical discussions of economic institutions, elite economic strategies, political conflict, and the labor process. I argue that a labor systems perspective offers an integrative conceptual framework for understanding a range of intellectual debates on market reform that are too often guided by preexisting or ideologically driven assumptions and conclusions, and for explaining long-term trajectories of change in regimes of labor and social regulation. While this framework may in principle be applied elsewhere, my focus here is on East and Southeast Asian developing countries.

Since the early 1980s, the ascendency of neoclassical orthodoxy and neoliberal policies has to varying degrees liberated markets; transformed states and diminished their economic role; scaled back state enterprises; removed a host of regulatory restraints on private firms; created new opportunities for financial innovation; energized private entrepreneurship; and greatly augmented the free flow of goods, services, and investment across national boundaries. These and other outcomes of the neoliberal "turn to markets" has consolidated what some have viewed as the emergence of a stable new economic order, one that seemingly has replaced an ossified and increasingly dysfunctional ensemble of statism, market rigidity, growing fiscal deficits, and economic stagnation with a new regime that encourages renewed efficiency, flexibility, competitiveness, and growth.

But to the varying extent this new institutional order has been successfully implanted, it has brought with it new tensions and politically consequential outcomes. Among the more visible and widely debated of these tensions are heightened financial instabilities, most dramatically seen in periodic regional and world financial crises; an undermining of the institutional capacity of governments to support economic growth and technology development; threats to agricultural producers and local manufacturers from foreign imports; growing currency and trade imbalances; and growing political challenges from opponents of new global policies. For some, these policies seem not only to hinder development and threaten environmental sustainability but also to delegitimate and undermine efforts by governments to cushion their own populations against market risks and economic instability, and to respond to the social disruptions resulting from growing economic inequality and social marginalization within and across national boundaries, disruptions that are often seen as closely linked to the reform process itself.

I attend to those reform-driven tensions that relate most specifically to the sphere of work and employment, and to the adequacy and security of the economic livelihood of workers. Employment-related tensions impinge on both social and economic agendas: the former relating to requirements of livelihood adequacy, employment stability, and social protections; the latter to the sometimes opposed requirements of competitiveness and growth. If social agendas predominate in the discourses and politics of workers, economic agendas find their natural home among economic elites. States, by contrast, must seek to reconcile these two agendas, or to manage the conflicts they conjointly create, through a variety of institutional and political strategies. That states are rarely fully captured by the interests of capital, even in neoliberal regimes, follows from and encourages their attentiveness to both social and economic agendas, as they seek to secure both political legitimacy and economic growth. For this reason, states play a critical role in addressing a common disconnect between the narrow and often short-term microlevel focus of firms on competitiveness and profitability and the longer-term, macrolevel goals of economic growth and development.[1]

From the standpoint of *social* agendas, market reforms have brought new benefits to some workers,[2] but for many others they have undermined both livelihood security and the organizational capacity of workers to push for progressive social policies. Reform has thus more generally reduced labor's influence in national policymaking; reduced the scope and depth of social safety nets and citizen entitlements; variably privatized and marketized a range of social services previously guaranteed by government; and heightened the economic dependency of workers on ever-more-volatile labor markets and ever-less-stable employment. From a larger perspective, these changes have eventuated in a dramatic tilting of the political landscape against labor and to the advantage of capital.

From the standpoint of *economic* agendas, reform has been associated with two related tensions: those impinging on the competitiveness of firms and those relating to the requirements of national growth and development. Firm-level competitiveness and national development are in turn associated with opposed—if often stylized—understandings of the relationship between markets and market-regulating institutions, a debate (primarily among economists) focused on the appropriate degree of institutional or regulatory guidance necessary to enhance economic efficiencies and growth. Here, the primary theoretical and policy divide is between a neoclassical insistence on minimal regulatory interference in labor and other markets and a rejoinder that pervasive and disruptive market failures necessitate robust institutional guidance and restraint by regulatory states if markets are to function adequately and if long-term growth is to be achieved (Stiglitz 2000).

A third economic tension, that relating to the *relationship* between economic and social agendas, typically opposes two general positions: the neoclassical argument that social policy, employment regulation, and support for trade unions create labor market rigidities and inefficiencies that impede competitiveness and growth, and a counterargument that emphasizes the economic importance, not only of generalized political and social stability, but—more specifically in the realm of employment—of social protections, livelihood security, stable labor-management relations, active labor market policy, education and training, and other regulatory interventions that may in

---

1. Neoliberal discourse typically and erroneously conflates these microlevel and macrolevel economic goals.

2. That is, skilled and technical workers in economically dynamic sectors, regions, and industries.

fact increase, rather than reduce, the flexibility, efficiency, and developmental outcomes of labor markets.

In this book I address these reform tensions as they relate specifically to Asian industrial workers and employment under the growing pressures of globalization, privatization, and labor market deregulation. I offer a conceptual framework within which to locate and characterize the tensions, understand their economic and political consequences, and explain efforts to mitigate them in order to sustain economic growth and to address major social dislocations. The framework addresses these matters through the conceptual lens of labor systems: those variably institutionalized, socially regulated, and politically contested strategies and processes of labor transformation through which workers are adapted to and integrated into the accumulation strategies of domestic and transnational elites and that, conversely, define the material structures and conditions within which workers and their families seek their livelihood. In part, the tensions I identify relate to an institutional undermining of economic agendas of competitiveness and growth. And, in part, they are manifest in political conflict and social instability flowing from a growing insecurity of employment and livelihood. As governments have sought to resolve these tensions, they have confronted the difficult task of building on existing institutions and structures in constructing new institutional modalities through which simultaneously to address economic and sociopolitical agendas. It is the problematic and seeming incompatibility of these two agendas—making markets work, and protecting society and ensuring social order—that drives the continuing and incessant change in trajectories of social and economic regulation.

In this context, I examine the experience of four Asian countries that present widely differing contexts within which market reform has been pursued: China, a case of postsocialist market reform in a low-income country; South Korea, a higher-income country transitioning from export manufacturing into information and service-based industries; the Philippines, an economically more stagnant country whose early and more sustained market reform has been driven in larger measure by the conditions of external debt and economic vulnerability that are so apparent in Latin America; and Thailand, a lower-middle-income developing country now seeking to transition into higher-value niches of world markets. This choice of country cases is intended less to offer a cross-national comparative study of reform than to explore diverse institutional trajectories and dynamics of change within dramatically differing socioeconomic situations of regional reform. In each case I examine the interplay of institutional legacies, elite interests, economic requirements, and political conflicts in shaping government responses to the tensions of reform. Since my emphasis is less on the national experiences of these particular countries per se than on the alternative and intermixed reform pathways they present, I selectively draw as well on the experiences of other countries in the region and beyond. In this way I explore the diverse and often contentious courses, outcomes, and redirections of reform as seen in recurrent and renewed efforts to contain or address its sometimes economically disruptive, socially destabilizing, and anti-developmental effects. My focus here is on the manufacturing sectors in these countries. This choice is dictated by the critical role this sector has played in the developmental "miracle" presented by the region. Indeed, even today manufacturing growth rates continue to exceed overall growth in gross domestic product (GDP) in China, Korea, and Thailand (but not in the Philippines), despite rapid growth in the service sectors of these countries (WB, *WDR* 2010).[3]

The policy trajectories of East Asia offer a unique vantage point for the study of market reform in developing countries. Because in Latin America and elsewhere the social dislocations and tensions of reform were so often rooted in external debt crises and in the economic stabilization policies imposed by external creditors as a condition for debt relief and rescheduling (McMichael 2008), the question arises whether it was the programs of market reform and restructuring or the austerity budgets and procyclical policies wrung from insolvent states that caused the real distress. In the economically dynamic East Asian countries, by contrast, reform was less often linked to debt-driven austerity and stabilization.[4] For that reason, the study of market reform in this economically dynamic region affords the opportunity to explore the tensions and institutional accommodations of reform in relative isolation from the relentless pressures of debt, austerity, and economic stabilization, thus offering a less-obscured view of the institutional and social tensions of reform itself.

A second rationale for the study of the East Asian reform experience relates to the continuing importance of this region in defining new international models of development. In this instance we see a synthesis of market reform, social accommodation, and developmentalism that is adaptive to the constraints of continuing integration into an evolving regional and world economy and that explores new social-reform initiatives that are more difficult

---

3. As a percentage of world manufacturing, Asian manufacturing value-added increased from 11.2% in 1995 to 20.1% in 2008 (UNIDO 2009) and to 24% in 2010 (UNIDO 2011).

4. Except, of course, in the Philippines and during the relatively brief regional financial crises of 1997–98 and 2008–10.

to institutionalize in other developing world regions.[5] Reference, punctuated only briefly by the 1997–99 Asian financial crisis, to the possibility of a "Pacific Century," marked by growing hegemonic conflict between an economically stagnant West and an economically resurgent (China-centric?) East, has suggested to many the importance of understanding development lessons to be learned from the region, especially regarding new economic and social roles of the state in an era of reform (Tipton 1998; Jessop 2002; Weiss 2003). Indeed, as in the earlier experience of state-led, export-oriented industrialization, the Asian reform experience after the late 1990's regional financial crisis has increasingly influenced the globalization agendas of the World Trade Organization (WTO), the World Bank, and to a degree even the International Monetary Fund (IMF).[6]

Given the important role of the East Asian Tiger economies (notably Taiwan, South Korea, Hong Kong, and Singapore) in redefining international development agendas over several decades,[7] and in suggesting new ways of managing the social tensions so often generated by market reform, it is not surprising that so much is now being written about the social economy of postcrisis developing Asia (see, e.g., Ramesh 2000, 2004; Tang 2000; Wong 2004; Jayasuriya 2006).

In the context of this larger literature, my more modest goal is first to suggest a conceptual framework that engages and integrates that literature and the evolving experience it reflects in a way that foregrounds the foundation of all capitalist social economies: the labor systems that harness human populations to the economic strategies and projects of corporate and governmental elites and to the requirements of national and global economic accumulation. My second, derivative, goal is to describe and explain the changing macrolevel regulatory regimes and policies through which dominant elites at national and transnational levels have sought to shape and influence labor

---

5. See Iyanatul Islam and Anis Chowdhury (2000, 209) on an emerging paradigm shift in development thinking that embraces a more inclusive social model. Earlier discussion of Asian developmentalism has included substantial social emphasis: Roger Goodman's (Goodman, White, and Kwon 1998) "welfare orientalism" and Frederic Deyo's (1993) "developmental paternalism."

6. This was the case in the belated acknowledgement that midcrisis capital controls may well have had their intended positive outcome of economic stabilization in Malaysia (World Bank 2002a). For more recent ILO–World Bank collaborative work on social and labor issues, see Gordon Betcherman and Rizwanul Islam (2001). Note, too, the strong emphasis on development issues in the current, Doha Round of WTO negotiations that began in 2001.

7. This was dramatically seen in the independent stance taken by Malaysia in regulating foreign-capital flows following the initial shock of the financial crisis of 1997; this stance was at first condemned and later reluctantly accepted by the IMF.

systems, and to address the socioeconomic tensions inherent in those systems in ways that balance the often conflicting pressures of political contestation, class interest, and the requirements of economic growth.

My primary intellectual debt is to Karl Polanyi, whose 1944 account in *The Great Transformation* of the social dislocations wrought by the attempted instituting of unregulated markets, initially in nineteenth-century England, defines an important point of departure for discussion of capitalist restructuring in our own time. For Polanyi, misguided efforts to transform labor, money, and land into what he termed "fictive" commodities to be bought and sold in markets created social tensions and cultural and institutional dislocations that threatened the social fabric and elicited a societal countermovement that sought, through means sometimes progressive but as often disastrous, to reinstitutionalize and socialize markets in ways supportive of economic growth and renewed social cohesion. The resurgence of interest in Polanyi's work (e.g., Buğra and Ağartan 2007; Joerges, Strath, and Wagner 2007) reflects the social tensions and dislocations of the round of market reform beginning in the early 1980s. In this study, I explore those tensions and the institutional and policy accommodations through which they have been addressed as it relates to one of Polanyi's fictive commodities: labor.

In part 1 I present the conceptual framework of the book, centering on labor systems and their regulatory governance, as well as a theoretical overview of the labor implications of market reform. In part 2 I discuss the deregulatory face of reform in China, Korea, Thailand, and the Philippines, including both the de facto deregulation generated by economic structural reforms and the de jure deregulation flowing from labor market and social policy reform. In part 3 I identify some of the disruptions and tensions generated by deregulatory reform, as relating both to the economic and developmental agendas of elites and to the social and livelihood needs of workers. Finally, in part 4 I discuss some of the major policy initiatives and institutional accommodations made by dominant elites in trying to manage or contain these emergent tensions, as well as the roles of path dependence, elite economic agendas, and labor politics in influencing the nature of those accommodations in different national and sectoral contexts.

PART I

Labor Systems, Economic Development, and Market Reform

CHAPTER 1

Labor Systems

Social Processes and Regulatory Orders

Labor systems comprise those variably institutionalized social processes and activities through which potential labor is mobilized and transformed into actualized labor, useful services and products, and—in capitalist economies—profits. Labor systems may be differentially understood from the vantage point of their contrasting meaning to employers, state agents, and workers. From the standpoint of employers, these systems define a core institutional foundation of competitiveness, profitability, and growth. For states, they define as well an institutional milieu for ensuring social stability and political legitimacy. And, for workers, they comprise a primary means through which to procure a variably stable economic livelihood beyond that attainable through subsistence production or through the state-mediated or community-based social wage. It is clear that these three somewhat disparate meanings and agendas often clash, thus creating policy dilemmas and divergent political pressures to which states must somehow attend.

Inasmuch as labor systems are initially and primarily constructed by economic and governmental elites, my starting point in defining and identifying them centers on their economic role for firms and national economies. I distinguish in this regard among four critical transformative phases:[1] social

---

1. The term "phases" tends to imply temporal sequencing, especially that defined by the transition from social reproduction and labor market allocation to the labor process itself. While the logic

reproduction, social protection, labor allocation and the labor process (see figure 1). Corresponding to these four phases are four domains of government policy: human resource development, social policy, employment policy, and labor relations.[2] While the very close relationships among these phases imply a degree of overlap and interpenetration, their analytical differentiation and articulation affords a useful framework for identifying the internal tensions and dynamics of labor systems during times of reform and crisis.

If processes of labor transformation define labor systems structurally, their institutional or regulatory dimension refers in the first instance to the terms of employment, formal and informal, that specify the mutual rights and obligations relating sellers and buyers of labor power. These terms of employment, whether imposed or agreed on, are in turn embedded in larger sectoral and national regimes of social and labor regulation that define, constrain, sanction, and legitimate both terms of employment and the actual transformative processes of particular labor systems. National labor institutions variably influence most economic activities irrespective of sector, especially in the formal sector. Sectoral institutions,[3] by contrast, are more attentive to

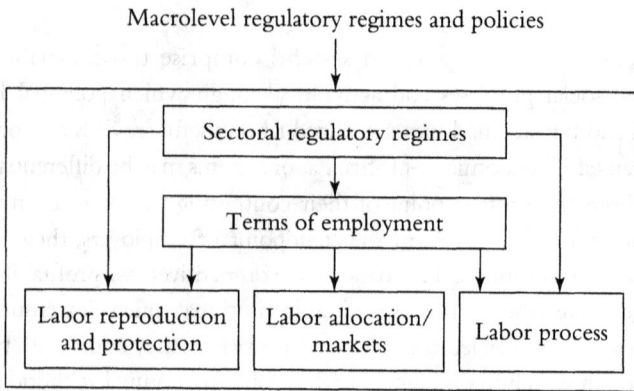

Macrolevel regulatory regimes and policies

```
                    ┌───────────────────────────────────┐
            ┌───────┤   Sectoral regulatory regimes      ├───────┐
            │       └───────────────────────────────────┘       │
            │                       │                            │
            │       ┌───────────────────────────────────┐       │
            │       │       Terms of employment          │       │
            │       └───────────────────────────────────┘       │
            │           │           │            │               │
    ┌───────────────┐ ┌──────────────────┐ ┌──────────────────┐
    │ Labor reproduction │ │ Labor allocation/ │ │ Labor process   │
    │ and protection     │ │ markets           │ │                 │
    └───────────────┘ └──────────────────┘ └──────────────────┘
```

FIGURE 1.1. The labor system.

of labor transformation is consistent with such sequencing, it should be recognized that the relationships among the phases may be recursive, as, for example, the situation in which earlier education and training prove inadequate to the requirements of the labor process, or where increased work contingency forces workers continually to seek re-employment. In addition, the phases may occur simultaneously or in reverse order. Despite these ambiguities, I have retained the term "phases" to signal their underlying analytical ordering.

2. Each of these policy domains influences more than one phase of labor systems. Social, human resource, and employment policy, for example, all clearly influence labor markets and the labor process.

3. Sectoral institutions are here understood as referring to the nature of the products or services produced.

the influence of policy and contextual differences rooted in the nature of sector-specific productive arrangements, technologies, and product markets. Thus, while labor systems may be specified at multiple analytical levels, from the workshop and firm to national and transnational economies, I here attend largely to their constitution within the industrial and economic sectors of national economies.

It may be useful at the outset to explain my preferred reference to *labor* systems in lieu of a more common usage, that of *employment* systems (e.g., Fligstein 2001). First, employment systems refer largely to situations of paid employment, thus ignoring multiple alternative situations of labor, including self-employment, petty-commodity production, household and unpaid family labor, communal or cooperative labor, and the like. While this book does focus most heavily on paid employment in manufacturing, it reaches beyond this category to other labor situations as well. Second, the literature on employment systems centers mainly on labor markets and their outcomes in formal or informal contractual agreements that define what may be viewed as the market-derived external terms and conditions of employment (pay, benefits, job tenure and security, work hours, etc.) within which the less-studied labor process is situated. Research in this tradition tends to ignore nonmarket labor allocation, and, more important, places relatively less emphasis on other phases of labor transformation.[4] It is precisely my intent in this book to explicate the relationships among the primary phases of labor transformation, and thus to offer an analytically coherent account of the implications of development and reform for labor systems.

By examining the dynamic relationships and interplay among these transformative phases and scalar dimensions of labor systems, I suggest an approach to understanding the diverse changes in the circumstances of livelihood and employment among Asian manufacturing workers over the past three decades of industrialization, globalization, and market reform.

Social Reproduction and Protection

From the standpoint of employers, the social reproduction of labor entails an investment in education, training, health, and other areas of human resource development that ensure the availability of a pool of workers suitable or adaptable to the work requirements they are likely to face. Labor reproduction

---

4. Similarly, reference to the "wage-labor nexus" in Marxist writings tends to conflate labor allocation and the labor process, two phases of labor systems whose interdependence is a key focus of this book.

includes, as well, adequate compensation for currently employed workers so as to maintain their necessary levels of availability and productivity.

Social economies present a variety of means through which social reproduction is organized. In casual labor markets the costs of social reproduction and protection are largely assumed by families, social networks, and communities. Among formal-sector workers, governments may mandate to firms a variety of social reproductive functions, including minimum compensation, training, and social insurance. Alternatively, governments, trade unions, or nongovernmental organizations (NGOs) may assume some of the costs of social reproduction in such areas as primary health, education, and training.

Closely related to social reproduction is the social protection of labor, itself comprising two interlinked functions. The first is economic, centering on the need for the labor force to be protected from such risks and uncertainties as those of short-term unemployment and temporary health problems, so as to ensure the continuing availability of unemployed workers for subsequent employment. The second element of protection is seemingly only social in nature: centering on the need to protect the livelihood of workers and their families in the face of market risk or loss of employability due to such contingencies as disability or old age. From a narrower economic standpoint, this latter social mandate is a critical underpinning of the willingness of workers to commit to full-time paid employment, a willingness partly contingent on the assumption that livelihood support will continue during periods of income loss.

A number of critical questions emerge in discussion of these two phases of labor systems. First, who pays for and who provides the necessary social reproduction and protection of labor: families, communities, employers, or states (Itzigson 2000)? Second, and relating especially to wage and benefit compensation,[5] social reproduction as consumption in part consists of an inverse reflection of its twin, market demand, the ultimate guarantor of continued accumulation at both national and global scales. But what is the level of acceptable adequacy in this regard—normative standards of livelihood and economic security, or only that level and distribution necessary to sustain labor and to foster and economic expansion? Given the export orientation of many Asian economies, and a corresponding strong reliance on world

---

5. Pay and benefits, as key elements in the terms of employment, link the four elements of labor systems: social reproduction (sustaining work effort and motivation); social protection (social security and health benefits); labor markets (terms of employment); and the labor process (the conflictual negotiation of the allocation of profits to workers and owners). These alternative perspectives on work compensation are noted in later chapters.

markets, this distinction is sharpened by a relative lack of economic dependence on domestic markets and by intensified international market pressure for cost reductions in the sphere of production (Robinson 2004; Palat 2010). Conversely, the long period of class compromise that permitted a balancing of production and consumption in the United States and Europe during the thirty years following World War II was based in large measure on the strong dependence of industry on domestic markets, a conjuncture that came unraveled during subsequent years of world market integration.

One important though contested and uneven outcome of globalization and economic reform has been an externalization of the costs of social reproduction and protection from employers and states to families and communities. This partial decoupling of social reproduction from other phases of labor systems reflects a corresponding delinking at the national level of production from consumption. However, it also flows from growing competitive demands for flexibility and cost reduction that have increasingly driven a wedge between the related mandates of livelihood security and the level of workforce readiness and stability, as firms have been pressed to rely increasingly on contingent labor, both in-house and through subcontracting.

Labor Markets and Allocation

The mobilization and allocation of labor are typically equated with functioning labor markets. For this reason, I hereafter follow convention in referring to 'labor markets' in lieu of the more general term 'labor allocation.' The allocative function is broader in scope, encompassing all those social processes (e.g., social networks, internal labor markets, personal sponsorship) through which workers are moved to available work sites and then inserted into and moved among productive activities within organizations.

Labor mobilization, the initial stage of allocation, becomes especially important during periods of rapid economic change, when the entry of new workers into the labor force lags behind the growth of new sectors, or in the context of the movement of workers from declining to expanding sectors. The actual insertion of workers into new productive activities is in the first instance based on agreement on or imposition of terms of employment between sellers/providers and buyers/users of labor, which entails variably formalized commitments relating to work hours, mutual rights and obligations, compensation, benefits, job security, recognition, autonomy, and advancement opportunities.

A variety of labor market typologies have been suggested in the literature, most based on some combination of the production process and associated skill requirements, the way markets allocate workers, and the terms of employment through which labor is secured by employers. In their classic account, for example, Gordon, Edwards, and Reich (1982) distinguish among primary independent, primary subordinate, and secondary labor markets. Primary independent and primary subordinate workers correspond respectively to professionalized workers enjoying job security, career progression, self-directed work, and adequate pay and benefits; and to skilled or semi-skilled blue-collar workers with job security, job benefits, and (sometimes) union protections, but lacking work autonomy, career prospects, and social mobility. Secondary labor markets, by contrast, do not offer these advantages and tend to be populated by economically disadvantaged groups. While this typology was developed mainly for the United States and other industrialized economies at an early stage of the structural changes associated with neoliberal reform, it does provide a useful starting point for distinguishing among various segments of the nonmanagerial industrial labor force that is the focus here. In the context of the substantial structural changes that followed publication of Gordon, Edwards, and Reich's *Segmented Work, Divided Workers,* subordinate primary markets/workers must now be further differentiated into primary contractual and primary stable labor markets, both of which transform and utilize the labor of skilled and semiskilled production workers but within quite different terms of employment. Primary contractual workers rely on formally specified (and thus legally sanctioned) terms of employment for limited durations of time that are binding on both worker and firm. Examples of primary contractual labor include the increasing numbers of engineers, technicians, and computer software developers hired to participate in specific time-delimited projects and R & D activities. By contrast, workers in primary stable labor markets comprise semiskilled, skilled, technical, and professional employees hired on a regular or more permanent basis within the core activities of firms. Although both contractual and stable primary-sector workers enjoy relatively good compensation levels, contractual workers must typically build careers through personal networking, occupational associations, and job mobility, as they move from firm to firm. This is in contrast to organizational and seniority-based career building or job progression found among primary stable workers.

Similarly, for Gordon, Edwards, and Reich (1982, 225–26), secondary labor markets, often populated by less-skilled production, service, and white-collar workers, may be further divided into casual and primary-supportive categories. Casual workers provide work as and when needed in firms seeking an inexpensive, numerically flexible workforce for a variety of relatively unskilled or standardized jobs requiring little organizational training or worker commitment. Traditionally, these workers were disproportionately employed in informal-sector firms. To the extent labor market deregulation has afforded firms increased discretion in employment policy and practice, however, casualized labor is increasingly found inside formal-sector firms as well. This indeed is an argument often made in support of labor market deregulation, one that justifies flexible labor markets as drawing larger numbers of vulnerable informal-sector workers into (partially deregulated) formal-sector employment. Finally, primary-support workers, not a primary focus of this book, provide essential, if lower-skilled, services in support of primary-sector and managerial workers in core organizational activities. The relatively more regular and secure employment of these workers reflects both their fuller social integration into the work activities of their supervisors and their job-specific and experience-based tacit knowledge—human assets that firms seek to retain and enhance.

Although this expanded version of the Gordon, Edwards, and Reich typology, defined by reference to the characteristics of work, skills of workers, and external terms of employment, is largely applicable to larger, formal-sector firms in industrialized countries, rather than to smaller, informal-sector firms in developing countries, it does provide a useful starting point for the study of changing labor markets in industrial Asia.

The Labor Process

This phase of labor systems comprises processes and practices of managerial efforts to coordinate, motivate, and control workers at the site of production, and to capture the economic surplus they produce. A substantial literature on the labor process is rooted in Marxian analysis,[6] which emphasizes the conflictual relationship between employers and workers as employers seek to go beyond the *formal* subordination of labor (obtaining labor under conditions specified by the external terms of employment) to labor's *real* subordination (the actualization of potential labor in the labor process) (Jaffee 2001, 42–43).

My understanding of the labor process is most strongly informed by the writings of Michael Burawoy and those subsequently influenced by his seminal 1985 work, *The Politics of Production* (e.g., Deyo 1989; Seidman 1994; Lee 1998; McKay 2006). Here, varying managerial agendas emphasizing work motivation, discipline, and initiative confront worker agendas relating to compensation, personal dignity, autonomy, and control in an ongoing

---

6. For current debates, see Thompson 2010.

negotiation of the work/reward balance. It is at this point that workers and employers build on and further elaborate the external market-derived terms of employment in constructing actual work relations. The labor process includes, as well, those practices through which employers increase the productivity of workers through labor enhancement, those practices through which employers increase the productivity of workers through capital investment, new technologies, and the reorganization of work.[7]

As in the other transformative phases, the labor process defines an arena of contestation, in this instance relating to control over work on the one hand, and, on the other, the contentious process of appropriating and allocating surplus or profits for redistribution to owners as profit, allocation to the wage fund or other forms of redistribution to labor, and reinvestment for further growth. In the unionized formal sector such appropriation is a major focus of collective bargaining, although it often takes less-regulated forms as well, including personal or informal negotiations both within and outside the place of production.[8] Since social contestation in the labor process is driven by and extends to patterns and agendas of conflict in other phases of labor systems and at higher regulatory levels, its study provides a further basis for understanding patterns of interdependence among the various elements of labor systems.

Regulating Labor Systems

As understood in this book, regimes of social and labor regulation (more specifically regulatory regimes and terms of employment as depicted in figure 1) relate to the construction, operationalization, and sanctioning of variably contested laws, rules, structures, and policies that seek to govern labor systems within delimited political jurisdictions.[9] Such regulatory regimes encompass three analytically separable but empirically linked elements: (1) formal and informal rules, policies, and norms, accepted practices, and underlying cultural logics (hereafter, *institutionalized rules*); (2) social actors, organizations, relations, networks, and groups, along with agencies of the state that embody, sanction, and channel regulatory rules (hereafter, *social structures* and

---

7. Training, a further element of labor enhancement, is here placed in the first phase of the labor system: the social reproduction of labor.

8. The field of labor relations most directly attends to the larger environment of contestation in the negotiated construction of labor systems, extending beyond the labor process itself to other phases of labor systems.

9. Some authors refer in this regard to cultural "logics," narratives, or paradigms (e.g., Fligstein 2001).

actors); and (3) social action on the part of dominant elites and state agencies that seeks to enact, interpret, administer, enforce, and defend institutionalized rules (hereafter, *regulatory social action* and *policy*). If institutional rules, authoritative policy, and regulatory social structures define the major elements of labor regulation, regulatory *action* shifts attention to the ways in which actors and collective agents seek to enact those rules and to utilize those elements in pursuit of their values, goals, and interests.

It is important to point out that this partial and static depiction of regulatory regimes must be balanced against recognition of the ubiquity of regulatory *change*, a primary focus of this book about trajectories of change in Asian regimes of social and labor regulation and in their associated labor systems. Such change is partly based on strategic policy innovation undertaken by dominant elites and partly on political action and social contestation (hereafter, *regulatory contestation*), wherein a variety of subordinated groups and classes (including both workers and non-incumbent elites) employ collective resources to alter economic policies, institutions, and outcomes in pursuit of their material and ideational interests—all within the constraints and opportunities offered by existing economic and political circumstances, including the capacity of workers to themselves influence or oppose elite strategies.

But if the discussion to this point identifies the elements of regulatory regimes and some sources of change in those regimes,[10] how may we characterize the more inclusive regulatory regimes themselves in a way that facilitates later discussion of trajectories of Asian regulatory reform? More specifically, what are the major analytical dimensions of social regulatory regimes that can guide such a discussion? Seven such dimensions are of particular importance here, four of which constitute formal or structural dimensions, while three relate to key dimensions of the substantive orientation or content of regulatory regimes.

The four formal dimensions are regulatory scope, depth, operative level, and extent of enforcement. The first of these, regulatory coverage or scope, refers to the extensiveness of state regulation and protection across the variety of labor and employment situations that make up national economies. Regulatory *depth*, by contrast, refers to the degree (vs. scope) of regulatory intrusion of state agencies and laws in the governance of employment, especially as it relates to substantive content. Regulatory *level*, perhaps as important as the first two but less often emphasized in reform studies, refers to the predominant scale at which effective regulation is organized. Reform-driven

---

10. Institutional change is discussed at greater length in chapter 2.

globalization has often eventuated in a regulatory rescaling to local levels (especially under governance devolution to local government) and at the same time to transnational levels (as in adherence to International Labour Organization [ILO] conventions or to the requirements of international lenders or multinational companies). Finally, regulatory *enforcement* refers to the extent to which regulatory regimes are actually sanctioned and applied. Even extensive de jure labor protections may be largely irrelevant to workers if they are not enforced (Caraway 2010). Indeed, differences in level of enforcement are typically greater than corresponding differences in the content of labor legislation itself, and thus they provide an important basis for cross-national or cross-sectoral comparison.

Regulatory regimes, of course, cannot be characterized by reference to form alone. Just as important is their *substantive orientation*. Here I identify three dimensions of orientation that are of particular importance in understanding the nature of economic reform. These dimensions are distinguished by reference to their relative emphasis on market efficiencies, on distributive or social outcomes, and on economic development (cf. Frenkel and Kuruvilla 2002).[11] The first of these emphasizes market conformance and the creation of incentives for rational market behavior. The second emphasizes distributive outcomes, both socially progressive (livelihood security and the narrowing of economic inequality) and regressive (reconcentration of wealth among dominant elites) (Evans 1989; Harvey 2005). The third is directed toward the imperatives of long-term economic development, even where this goal competes with market efficiencies and social equity. It is clear that these orientations are not mutually exclusive. Indeed, all modern governments pursue some combination of the three. But it is also clear that national regulatory regimes may be differentiated by reference to the relative emphasis they give to one or another dimension. In this regard, Anglo-American liberal market capitalism is often distinguished from European social capitalism and East Asian developmentalism.

These seven analytical dimensions of regulatory regimes together suggest a property space within which to characterize both regulatory regimes and the change trajectories of those regimes over time.

---

11. Relatedly, Frenkel and Kuruvilla (2002) suggest the influence on employment relations and labor policy of three governing 'logics': competition, industrial peace, and employment-income protection. The relative predominance of these logics, they argue, is influenced by such factors as globalization, labor markets, development strategy, union strength, and government responsiveness to workers. My own dimensions of regulatory content are similar to these except that I distinguish between economic efficiencies (the competitive focus of firms) and development (the competitive focus of states) and view industrial peace less as a goal in itself than as a means to competitive economic goals.

Sectoral Labor Systems and National Labor Regimes

Labor systems may be studied at multiple levels: from workshops and firms to sectors, nations, and global economies. The multiscalar nature of labor systems becomes most evident in considering the functioning of the individual phases of labor transformation. Labor markets, it is clear, can be studied at the level of the firm (e.g., internal labor markets) as well as at the level of sectoral, national, or global economies. Similarly, social reproduction and protection are often studied at the national level in recognition of the importance of the state in this domain. But the important roles of families, communities, and firms in the social reproduction of labor suggest a subnational focus as well. Finally, the labor process, while conventionally understood at the level of the firm, may be identified at both sectoral and national levels. Even if the firm would seem to define the most important and appropriate level of analysis for studying the labor process, commonalities in industrial and employment strategies among firms confronting the shared market, technological, and even regulatory conditions in a given sector, commonalities that variably differentiate one sector from another, often justify sectoral generalizations that ignore otherwise important differences in the labor practices of particular firms or groups of firms.[12]

In this study of Asian manufacturing employment, industrial sectors are seen as the most useful level for studying labor systems (Boyer 2005, 546). This choice is based on a number of plausible assumptions and credible observations—that sectoral markets and technologies influence the (several) types of labor required for production; that labor markets are most appropriately understood at the sectoral level; that organizational forms and labor practices are disseminated and shared across sector-specific networks of professionals and managers; that labor relations institutions, whether formal or informal, tend to follow the contours of sectoral differentiation; that states may differentially regulate the various economic sectors (especially in the context of active industrial policy); and that transnational production and financial networks are strongly differentiated along sectoral lines. Together, these considerations support the choice of the industrial sector as the most useful level at which to study labor systems (for discussion, see Kuruvilla et al. 2000, 2).

---

12. Such a sectoral view of the labor process adopts an aggregative view of sectoral labor systems that starts from modal differences in "typical" sectoral firms, rather than actually studying labor systems at the sectoral level.

When regulatory regimes are thus specified at sectoral levels, they are viewed as constitutive elements of labor systems themselves, systems that encompass major occupational groupings in specified industrial sectors of particular national jurisdictions. National regimes, by contrast, define a critical macroregulatory context within which sectoral labor systems are constructed and function. Such regimes both influence sectoral labor systems and respond to the changing tensions or requirements generated by those systems.

Much of the discussion of national employment institutions portrays them as relatively coherent, unitary influences on the competitive and labor strategies of firms. That is to say, national institutional complexes are seen as facilitating and encouraging firm-level outcomes regardless of sector, production contingencies, or competitive strategies. Such a view might suggest a clash between state-centric accounts, on the one hand, and sectoral or firm-centered accounts (where sectoral markets and technologies and managerial strategies play a relatively greater role), on the other.

Two analytical strategies may be suggested for articulating sectoral- and national-level regulatory orders in a way that recognizes the importance of each. The first sees state-linked national institutions as complex, sometimes varied and conflicted sets of agencies, rules, and policies that, far from defining a single, uniform influence on firms and labor systems, make up multiple sets of influence and opportunity along with multiple points of access. Here, firms acquire a degree of autonomy and choice in selectively targeting those institutional resources and locations most supportive of firm-level contingencies of production, markets, and strategic choice. In some instances, this institutionally differentiated understanding of macroregulatory regimes gains further credence in the context of sectorally targeted industrial promotion policies, encouragement of export-processing zones, and differential enforcement of labor and employment laws.

The second strategy for articulating the two approaches views macrolevel orders as being made up of institutional efforts to manage the tensions and the requirements of those sectors that are of particular strategic or developmental importance or that present the most formidable political pressures in national politics. Whichever of these two approaches one adopts, macroregulatory regimes are seen as neither displacing nor homogenizing the sectoral and microregulatory orders they so importantly influence.

National labor regimes and policies are of particular interest here insofar as they are the primary locus of those regulatory innovations that collectively define programs of market reform, as well as of regulatory responses to the tensions of that reform. As noted earlier, the influence of macrolevel social regulatory regimes on labor systems may be specified by reference to the major phases of those systems. Human resource policies (relating especially to primary health and education) have traditionally influenced processes of social reproduction, while social policy has influenced social protection, either by establishing a redistributive social wage attached to citizen entitlement or by mandating benefits and protections in contractual terms of employment. Labor markets are most directly regulated by administrative and legislative restrictions and proscriptions embodied in employment law. Labor markets are influenced as well by a broad range of administrative structures and institutions that facilitate, channel, and mediate flows of information and workers through the variably segmented networks that make up those markets.

Finally, the labor process, in which employers seek to motivate, coordinate, and control workers, is typically an area of relatively broad managerial discretion, apart from the constraints posed by employment law and by labor relations laws, institutions, and state interventions that regulate labor-management relations and that attempt to prevent or repress unlawful or economically disruptive worker action. Insofar as labor regimes seek to moderate and channel industrial conflict and disruption, those regimes encompass many of the issues and social processes typically addressed by research and debates within the field of industrial and labor relations. Viewed in this way, political contestation may itself be variably institutionalized within established regulatory regimes, even as other instances of contestation may occur outside of and in opposition to those regimes. It is this institutional divide between participation and opposition that defines a major political cleavage among unions and union federations in their multiple relationships with workers, states, and broader social groups.

From the standpoint of more proximate regulatory agents, microlevel and sectoral labor regimes are shaped most decisively by employers and their microlevel agendas of competitiveness and profitability, albeit within the political constraints of worker resistance and macroregulation. By contrast, national-level regulatory regimes are more reflective of the agendas of states, including those relating to national economic growth and reform, as well as to the requirements of sociopolitical stability and legitimacy. Insofar as state regulatory regimes are driven by economic agendas, I suggested earlier that they are most strongly shaped by the requirements of economic sectors that are viewed as developmentally or strategically important, or that present the most powerful political pressures to which states must attend. In this way, those labor systems that command ecological (structural) or political dominance in a particular national setting play a key role in shaping national labor regimes.

In contesting or trying to alter regulatory regimes, workers may seek out those collective modalities and scalar levels that most favor them. Thus, skilled and craft workers may negotiate most effectively at the workshop, factory, and firm levels, while semiskilled industrial operatives may turn to industry-level unions or union federations. Similarly, unskilled workers or workers in highly competitive sectors where worker bargaining power is weak may turn to social movements, political parties, or to other modalities to influence states. Indeed, recent research documents the ways in which local NGOs, trade unions, firms, and states pursue their interests and goals at multiple, often mutually reinforcing, levels (Trubeck, Mosher, and Rothstein 2000, 12), even as they are in turn influenced by the actions of other actors at all these levels. From this perspective, state regulatory regimes are influenced by multilevel action within arenas of trade, investment, social protection, labor relations, and so forth. Transnational coalitions and political actions among NGOs, trade unions, farmers' organizations, and other groups seeking to influence or oppose WTO-based trade liberalization offer a particularly dramatic example. I will show that these differences in worker strategies, and in the larger politics of labor with which those strategies are associated, may strongly influence trajectories of policy change and regulatory reform.

Interdependencies across Phases of Labor Systems

The disparate literatures on human resource development, social policy and social welfare, labor markets, and the labor process have generally evolved in relative isolation of one another. In some cases, analysts have emphasized one of these phases, bringing other phases in largely as contextual determinants or outcomes. For example, Burawoy's discussion of the labor process does refer to labor markets and social policy, but primarily as causal influences on factory regimes at the point of production, his real focus (Burawoy 1985, 141–48). Similarly, one may emphasize the ways in which labor (and product) markets shape employment markets and the labor process.

Other authors have pursued a different logic of integration, offering an inclusive definition of labor markets that itself embraces elements of the other phases. Gordon, Edwards, and Reich, for example, understand labor markets as encompassing the "behavioral rules governing task performance, the mechanisms through which their requisite skills are acquired and applied, and the labor market mechanisms mediating the allocation of workers among jobs" (1982, 202), three elements corresponding respectively to the labor process, social reproduction, and labor markets.

A labor–systems model pushes further in seeking a more explicit differ-entiation among the various elements of labor systems, one that gives equal determinative weight to each of the phases and that emphasizes the close functional interdependencies among the various phases of labor transforma-tion within and beyond the workplace.

Relationships among the phases of labor systems are in part conditioned by the institutional governance regimes that seek functionally to articulate those phases. And the employment strategies of firms play a further integra-tive role, especially in structuring the relationship between subprocesses of labor allocation themselves. When, for example, employers institute internal labor markets to enhance worker motivation and to retain the loyalty and services of valuable workers, those internal labor markets insulate structures of intrafirm labor allocation from external labor markets while at the same time fusing those intrafirm markets with the labor process itself. Alternately, employers may import external labor markets into the internal labor process by relying on hourly or piecework compensation, fines, and performance-based pay as primary means by which to motivate and discipline workers, a strategy Burawoy terms "market despotism."

Finally, the functional complementarities and conflicts among labor-system phases themselves often drive cumulative systemic changes. For example, labor market deregulation necessitates corresponding changes in social poli-cies and protections, while the growth of contingent labor in formal sectors has encouraged important changes in employment policy in the labor pro-cess. Indeed, an important theme in later chapters of this book is that labor market deregulation has created emergent economic and social tensions that have been met by compensating reregulatory changes in other phases of labor systems. Those compensating changes are essential elements of Asia's countermovement.

The Problematic Articulation of Different Labor Systems

Much of the labor-process literature adopts a simplifying view of labor sys-tems as functioning alone or at least in isolation of other such systems. Thus, for example, Burawoy's discussion offers a comparative typology of factory regimes or labor processes, but it does not seek to integrate the multiple labor processes (not to speak of the larger labor systems of which they are but one phase) that must typically be coordinated or integrated in real work settings or production systems. A more realistic, relational view of labor systems sees them as mutually articulated and integrated in actual situations of production.

It is clear, for instance, that unskilled, skilled, and technical workers interact with one another and with professional and managerial workers on a daily basis in the real world of production. Indeed, it has become clear that systems of lean and flexible production force firms more closely to integrate various production operations precisely to tighten their coordination and intercommunication in order to enhance quality and to foster greater organizational flexibility and adaptability. One consequence of this tighter systemic integration is that work teams now may encompass craft, semiskilled, technical, and unskilled employees who work closely together. Relatedly, Milkman (1998) suggests a blurring of different kinds of production work, as manufacturing firms seek to enhance organizational flexibility by negotiating with unions to reduce the number of job classifications, while Kalleberg (2007, 168-69) notes a growing tendency to employ temporary workers alongside skilled permanent workers in order to enhance capacity or "numerical" flexibility. This integration (vs. fusion) of diverse forms of work and associated labor processes poses a number of real-life problems and tensions to which companies and states must respond. To the extent different categories of workers within correspondingly different labor systems encounter different labor market conditions, expectations, and managerial controls, the experiences, interests, normative concerns, organizational and work commitments, and modes of self-expression and representation of these workers will likely differ. This outcome may create a conflictual or anomic work situation (Kalleberg 2007) that, while perhaps supportive of managerial efforts to diffuse, fragment, and disorganize worker opposition, may also undercut other organizational goals of coordination and collaboration that brought these various categories of workers together into heterogeneous teams in the first place.

Institutional conflict among different labor systems may take other, sometimes more consequential forms. Insofar as deregulatory elements of market reform encourage a shift from hegemonic modes of labor discipline to more market-disciplined forms, workers may invoke backward-looking traditional normative expectations to protest harsher employment relations, creating instability and dissent in the labor process. Similarly, as supply chains are more tightly integrated in the interests of flexibility and quality, divergent labor systems may collide as organizational boundaries blur.

CHAPTER 2

Explaining Regulatory Change

One of my primary goals is to identify and explain national trajectories of labor and social regulation over the past three decades of Asian development and reform. This goal is driven by a broader interest in the ways in which dominant elites have sought to respond to a variety of labor-related economic and sociopolitical pressures by reshaping labor systems through regulatory reform. It is thus important to begin by identifying some of the key influences on institutional change that must be addressed in this study. Four such influences are of particular importance here: path dependence, functional adaptation, strategic innovation, and social conflict.

Path Dependence

A prominent institutionalist perspective, historical institutionalism, emphasizes the importance of relatively stable complexes of values and institutions in influencing the strategic choices of firms and states. The stability of these institutional complexes is in turn rooted in the multiple ways in which established institutional patterns, policies, and practices embed themselves in society by cumulatively benefiting institutionally favored groups and classes over others, thus creating ever-more-powerful vested interests (Olson 1971); by shaping the public ideologies through which these favored groups and classes protect their status; by reinforcing and socially embedding regulatory structures and agents; by influencing educational systems, the media, and other agencies of socialization; and more generally by defining the taken-for-granted reality of daily life for most people.

Much of the institutionalist literature on path dependence, particularly that associated with the "varieties of capitalism" school (Hall and Soskice 2001), focuses on the influence of national institutions on firm-level behavior, including labor practices, noting ways in which the strategic choices of firms in responding to changing economic conditions and emergent sociopolitical challenges are themselves shaped by macroinstitutions. Such a view portrays national institutions as relatively static analytical starting points, albeit while recognizing that such institutions originate in major historical and political transitions and adaptively evolve over time (Fligstein 2001). This path-dependent view of national economic institutions leads some writers to a pessimistic view of the ability of some economies, as in Europe, to adapt effectively to the cumulative pressures of globalization (Hall and Soskice 2001).

While path-dependent accounts are often criticized as failing adequately to explain change, it should be noted that path dependence does not actually suggest *lack* of change so much as gradual or evolutionary change along divergent *pathways*. At the levels of both firm and state, these differentiated pathways result from strategic choices that are themselves shaped by existing institutions, sunken costs, and vested interests. In this book I acknowledge the path-dependent influence of preexisting institutions and social structures on elite strategies, and more specifically on the policies through which elites seek to manage the tensions of economic reform. Strategic innovations, according to this view, take advantage of, extend, elaborate, and adapt existing institutions and programs to meet new challenges and seize new opportunities.

Functional Adaptation: Market Pressures and Creative Destruction

Historical institutionalists often embrace a functionalist causal logic. Economies, and the stable social relations among firms, workers, suppliers, and customers that promote economic success, require institutional grounding. Institutions exist (and are created) because they are necessary for defining and securing property rights, governance structures, and rules of exchange (Fligstein 2001). Without these orienting rules and understandings, economic life degenerates into anarchy. Historical institutionalism thus lends itself most naturally to two explanations relating respectively to functionality and exogenous shocks: the first points to the tendency for institutions either to change or to be displaced in a gradual evolutionary manner as they adapt (or succumb) to changing circumstances; the second refers to the impact of major external events or changes (recessions, major technological changes, domestic or international conflicts, heightened competitive pressures associated with economic globalization, etc.).

A related functionalist insight on institutional change is suggested by an understanding of society itself as comprising systemic relations among a variety of interdependent social organizations and institutions. As discordant relations generate system imbalances and disequilibria, pressures mount to realign and re-equilibrate society. This view was most eloquently offered by Polanyi in his account of the way in which the attempted instituting of self-regulating markets in nineteenth-century England undermined established patterns of social organization and called forth new efforts to regulate markets in order to address broader societal requirements.

Whatever one's assessment of the sometimes problematic logic of a functionalist explanation, this approach does offer a useful framework for identifying systemic tensions to which societies must in some fashion attend, whether through strategic innovation or political contestation. As regards labor systems more specifically, such tensions may be identified across the phases of labor transformation, between labor systems and their macroregulatory regimes, and by reference to their problematic outcomes for economic growth and social stability.

Elite Economic Strategies

Building on the work of institutional economists, Hall and Soskice seek to understand how the strategic interactions through which firms stabilize and coordinate their relations with suppliers, states, buyers, and workers are influenced by macroinstitutional orders. This focus on the economically rational strategies of firms builds on a long tradition of writing by institutional economists (e.g., North 1990; Williamson 1975) and business historians (e.g., Chandler 1962 and 1977) who understand structures and institutions as outcomes of rational strategies through which firms resolve organizational dilemmas relating to uncertainty, transaction costs, and market failure. The resolution of these dilemmas takes the form of institutional and/or regulatory innovation (organizational divisionalization, vertical integration, etc.) at the enterprise level, the generalization of those innovations as "best practice" by enterprises more generally, and the emergence of sectoral legal and regulatory regimes supportive of those innovations by firms employing similar technologies and participating in similar sectors and markets.

This governance perspective differs from historical institutionalism in its greater emphasis on agency and in according a greater autonomy to elites in strategic innovation. It thus suggests a somewhat diminished role of path dependence in favor of a more dynamic model of strategic institutional change, flowing, as in the evolutionary accounts of some historical institutionalists, from both anticipatory and reactive institutional strategies as elites and strategic decision makers attempt to alter institutions in order to enhance efficiencies and organizational effectiveness.[1] While much of this strategic tradition focuses on corporate strategies, and thus on firm-level and sectoral regulatory regimes,[2] our discussion of market reform by necessity redirects attention to state strategies, and thus to national-level regulatory regimes.

An elite-centric strategic view embraces market reform directly and robustly, seeing macroinstitutional change as driven by the economically rational choices of politically and economically dominant coalitions and organizations. To take a prominent example, theories of the regulatory state (Majone 1997) and of regulatory capitalism (Levi-Faur and Jordana 2005) offer a succinct strategic-institutionalist view of market reform. In accounting for the post-1970's shift from what Majone (1997) terms the "positive interventionist state" focused on taxing and spending, to the regulatory state, centering on rule making ("rule of law") and the establishment of independent regulatory agencies, he discusses the "structural changes induced by a concatenation of several basic strategies: privatization, liberalization and deregulation" (140), strategies that he sees as adaptive responses to growing failures of market efficiency in the context of new pressures of globalization and market integration. While recognizing the path dependency of existing interventionist state structures, and of the political constraints on the creation of new regulatory structures, Majone emphasizes the primary, if sometimes delayed, structural and institutional outcomes of rational strategies of macroregulatory reform.

Social Conflict

If historical institutionalists emphasize the determinative role of institutionalized rules in influencing economic structures and action, while strategic

---

1. Reflective of this line of thought is Alfred Chandler's (1962) assertion that "structure follows strategy."

2. Human resource management, a scholarly field that has increasingly supplanted industrial relations, is a management-centered understanding of employment practices and institutions.

institutionalists give primacy to dominant corporate and government actors in regulatory innovation, social conflict approaches foreground the institutional outcomes of political contestation.

Of course, contestation is not entirely incompatible with institutionalist accounts. Of particular importance in this regard is the vast institutionalist literature within the field of industrial and labor relations. Beginning with John Dunlop's early "systems approach" introduced in his *Industrial Relations System* (1958) and again soon thereafter in an edited collection (Kerr, Dunlop, Harbison, and Myers 1960), many writers in this tradition have taken as their starting point the rules and norms that regulate employment and labor relations, rules seen largely as influencing and managing, rather than issuing from, industrial conflict (Bain and Clegg 1974). This institutionalist tradition, while increasingly attentive to broader issues of power and conflict, influenced later decades of research on how national institutions shape the interests and power of workers and employers, the employment strategies of firms, and the manner in which unions, firms, and states interact.

A less institutionally focused view of conflict is exemplified in Richard Hyman's influential and now classic work *Industrial Relations: A Marxist Introduction* (1975). Hyman takes as his starting point not the rules and institutions through which conflict is mediated and managed in a path-dependent fashion, but rather the social conflicts themselves as the driving force behind regulatory change. For Hyman, capitalism defines an economic order within which conflict between workers and employers is inherent and necessary, and that cannot sustainably be managed by regimes of social regulation. For Hyman and others working from a Marxist perspective, the analytical point of departure is not the determinate role of institutions so much as the source of those institutions in the play of interests and power.

A primary difference between elite-centric strategic views and conflict perspectives relates to a greater emphasis in the former on economic goals of competitiveness and efficiency and, in the latter, on competition among elite factions and across class lines. A social-conflict understanding of reform emphasizes the pursuit of material (and to a lesser extent political and ideational) interests as various social classes, groups, and organizations seek to realize their own goals by shaping national policies and institutions.[3] For this reason, the economically rational strategies of

---

3. It will be recalled that while disavowing a simplistic account of England's countermovement as driven by sectional economic interests, Polanyi did place importance on social conflict as the mechanism through which societal needs reassert themselves under market reform.

dominant policy elites are comingled in complex ways with considerations of material self-interest and the mobilization of power to pursue class interests in the face of intra-elite and cross-class contestation. Traditionally, states provide the institutional leverage for reconciling these varyingly disparate agendas.

David Harvey's work most usefully exemplifies this conflict-focused understanding of capitalist restructuring and regulatory change. For him, the 1980's transition to global neoliberalism is best understood and explained as a forceful state-mediated reassertion of capitalist class power in the context of economic stagnation and a growing profit squeeze associated with the institutional and political influence of organized labor (Harvey 2005). For Harvey and others working in this conflict tradition, what we have referred to as strategic policy choice is shaped only in part by economic requirements as defined by the realities of market competition and capitalist evolution. Just as important are social and class conflicts that both constrain and energize the historically contingent choices of dominant groups (2010, 128). This difference is significant and suggests an important question relating to the relationship between strategic and political influences on regulatory institutions. Are not these two sets of determinants, the one defined by the economic requirements of economic growth, the other by the changing balance of power and interests, often at odds with each other in influencing elite strategies? And, if so, is it possible to draw them into a common explanatory framework? The answer to this question flows in part from the observation that strategic and political (and indeed other) regulatory influences are not always or necessarily in direct conflict. This possibility follows from several important considerations.

First, it is true that in the short term, the factional interests of dominant economic groups may work at odds with even the most basic requirements of economic growth. Indeed, the globalization of corporate networks may create a growing wedge between national economic growth, the interests of ruling elites, and corporate profitability. But while, in the short run, economic interests, power, and economic rationality may collide as the pursuit of group interest impedes accumulation, in the long run, rational strategies and material conflicts tend to converge. This follows from the importance of economic efficiencies and growth in underpinning the material circumstances, social dominance, and political legitimacy of elites and of the regimes they establish. When ruling material interests effectively impede accumulation,[4]

---

4. As in the case of what Peter Evans terms "predatory elites" (1989).

economic stagnation ultimately forces the hand of elites. It is often argued in this regard that a critical source of regime legitimacy in many Asian countries is rooted in the positive economic outcomes of continued growth.

Second, economic imperatives may often be addressed in multiple ways (Fligstein 2001), thus yielding a degree of autonomy to states and dominant coalitions in shaping viable economic projects and policies in ways that also respond to the demands of self-interest, or even to political pressures from subordinate classes. In this regard, the range of alternative viable regulatory regimes, especially relating to social reproduction and the wage-labor nexus, is sufficiently broad to accommodate multiple possible outcomes of political selection, inter-elite conflict, and class struggle (Boyer 2005, 514–16). Harvey himself makes this point in his discussion of the multiple "activity spheres" constituting capitalist social formations. He identifies these spheres as technological and organizational forms, social relations, institutions, the labor process, relations to nature, social reproduction, and "mental conceptions of the world" (2010, 123).

> No one of the spheres [of economic and social life] dominates even as none of them are independent of the others. But nor is any one of them determined even collectively by all the others (123)....We now think of them as collectively co-present and co-evolving within the long history of capitalism....Something can also be said about the likely future development of the social order...given the tensions and contradictions between the activity spheres, even as it is recognized that the likely evolutionary dynamic is not determinant but contingent. (124)

Thus, insofar as these activity spheres, which include both economic drivers (technology, market, and organization) and political configurations (social relations and the labor process), would seem often to push in different directions from the standpoint of economic and regulatory policy (e.g., relating to the conflict between agendas of social legitimacy and of techno-economic efficiency), the loose coupling and complex interdependencies among these various spheres enlarges the space for strategic maneuvering within which elites can seek simultaneously to address conflicting imperatives.

Third, states themselves play a critical role in mediating the conflicts among divergent economic and political imperatives through the consolidation of new institutional orders that seek at least in part to *reconcile* divergent economic and political pressures. This mediating role offers the possibility of negotiated compromise among groups representing a variety of policy agendas and priorities.

There is, of course, the alternative possibility that successful regulatory regimes,[5] regimes that do manage to address the tensions and contradictions in capitalist social formations, may not fully emerge at all (Gordon 1994b), thus explaining cases of protracted political conflict amid economic stagnation.[6]

Critical Regulation Theory: Toward an Integrative Framework

A further theoretical perspective, critical regulationism, is also rooted in Marxist analysis but attends more fully to institutions than does either Marx or Marxist writers such as Harvey. From the standpoint of this book, this perspective offers an explanatory framework that usefully integrates the roles of path dependence, systemic functionalism, strategic innovation, and social conflict in influencing regulatory change. Critical regulation theory, best exemplified in the social structures of accumulation (SSA) school (Gordon, Edwards, and Reich 1982; Kotz 1994; Lippit 2010) and in French regulation theory (Leipitz 1992; Aglietta 1998; Jessop 2002; Boyer 2005), offers a variant of institutionalism that shares important assumptions with other institutionalist approaches. Like historical institutionalists, critical regulationists see macrolevel state-centered regimes as playing a critical economic role in fostering a supportive social environment for sustained economic accumulation by promoting social stability, the security of private property, the social reproduction of labor power, security of contracts, and other essential requirements that must ultimately be met, not within markets themselves but in the regulatory regimes in which those markets are embedded.

While regulationists also share with historical institutionalists a view that regulatory regimes are relatively stable over short-to-intermediate time periods, they depart sharply in their emphasis on the longer-term instabilities of such regimes as a variety of endogenous contradictions and pressures cumulatively grow or as regulatory regimes prove ever-more incapable of supporting continued economic accumulation. Such a view contrasts with the assumption in much historical institutionalist writing of systemic integration, and with the emphasis in that tradition on exogenous system shocks rather than endogenous sources of crisis and change. Ultimately, argue regulationists, these internal contradictions will bring accumulation to a halt, thus

---

5. Successful in the sense of addressing both economic and political requirements.

6. As in the Philippines, discussed in later chapters.

initiating a search for alternative regulatory orders that can promote renewed economic expansion (Piore and Sabel 1984). While a disclaimer is typically offered that this search may not always be successful, thus eventuating in continuing stagnation (Boyer 2005, 541), the assumption is usually made that the requirements of renewed accumulation will ultimately, somehow, be met through the consolidation of a new regulatory order within which social and economic conflicts and institutional tensions and contradictions can again be contained, externalized, or otherwise managed (though never fully resolved). As capitalist economies cycle through phases of consolidation, stagnation, crisis, conflict, and reconsolidation, they continually reinvent themselves through adaptive regulatory innovation, rather than giving way to a postcapitalist order as originally envisioned by Marx. It may be noted in this regard that it is precisely the path dependence and "stickiness" of consolidated regulatory regimes that permit tensions and imbalances to accumulate to the point of institutional crises and social conflicts that bring forth new institutional orders. Regulationists thus see new modes of regulation as emerging through institutional experimentation on the part of existing or ascendent elites that culminates in the consolidation of new regulatory regimes (Gordon, Edwards, and Reich 1982; Boyer 2005).

Of particular interest in more recent writings in the critical regulationist tradition, particularly among SSA writers, is the question of whether or not post-1980's global neoliberalism constitutes a successful social structure of accumulation or whether its failure to reignite rapid economic growth in its seedbed economies (especially the United States) suggests the *lack* of emergence of a successful new SSA. Here, Wolfson and Kotz (2010) argue that neoliberalism does in fact define a new SSA in a broad institutional sense, as stabilizing class relations through a reconsolidation of capitalist power over labor and dominance over the state (cf. Harvey 2005). Thus, while economic growth under the neoliberal SSA has been relatively sluggish, class power has been reestablished and a new basis for profitability and at least modest expansion have been established.[7] I take Wolfson and Kotz one step further and identify several institutional and social innovations through which the neoliberal order has been adapted to address emergent socioeconomic tensions and achieve renewed stability in the context of several dynamic East Asian economies.[8]

---

7. Also see Harvey (2005) on neoliberalism as the reestablishment of capitalist class power.

8. Wolfson and Kotz (2010) and Lippit (2010) assert in this regard that the neoliberal SSA entered a terminal crisis point during the 2008–10 financial crisis.

Framework of This Book

I take as a heuristic starting point the evolving economic strategies of dominant elites (see figure 2) as they confront and respond to ever-changing economic and political tensions and circumstances. These strategies are here viewed as flowing, not only from rational economic choice,[9] but as well from the collective material and ideational interests of elites, from the path dependence of existing institutions and social structures, and from interelite and class contestation.

The notion of ideational interests, rarely included in critical regulationist accounts,[10] has been emphasized in a number of accounts of the origins of both neoliberalism and of the regulatory innovations accompanying market reform.[11] Mark Blyth (2002), for example, writes that changing ideologies and understandings can drive dramatic strategic innovations, as in the case of the neoliberal revolution in economic thinking:

> Periods of institutional change thus follow a specific temporal sequence, with ideas having five different causal effects at different time points during periods of economic crisis (as in the 1970s): uncertainty reduction, coalition building, institutional contestation, institutional construction, and expectational coordination...it is worthwhile to make such distinctions analytically so that the importance of economic ideas in making institutional supply, stability, and change possible can be better understood. By seeing ideas as having different causal effects in different time periods as part of a sequence of change, we can explain both stability and change within the same framework. (35)

This emphasis on ideologies and ideational interests as influencing the ways in which governments chose in the 1980s to respond to new economic pressures and opportunities is prominent as well in Majone's (1997) discussion of the regulatory state (discussed in chapter 3).[12] In recognition of the

---

9. As in depictions of the Asian "developmental state."

10. Given their origins in Marxian thought, those perspectives typically emphasize material, rather than ideational, interests.

11. As noted, Harvey (2010, 123) includes "mental conceptions of the world" in his discussion of the seven activity spheres that comprise capitalist social formations. Also see Ho Lup Fung (2007) for his discussion of the influence of ideology on employment policy in China.

12. Asian-focused developmental state theory departs somewhat from Majone's understanding of institutional path dependency. His discussion emphasizes the negative role of existing institutions and structures in delaying the implementation of new regulatory strategies. Developmental state theory, by contrast, emphasizes the positive role of existing structures in endowing states with the

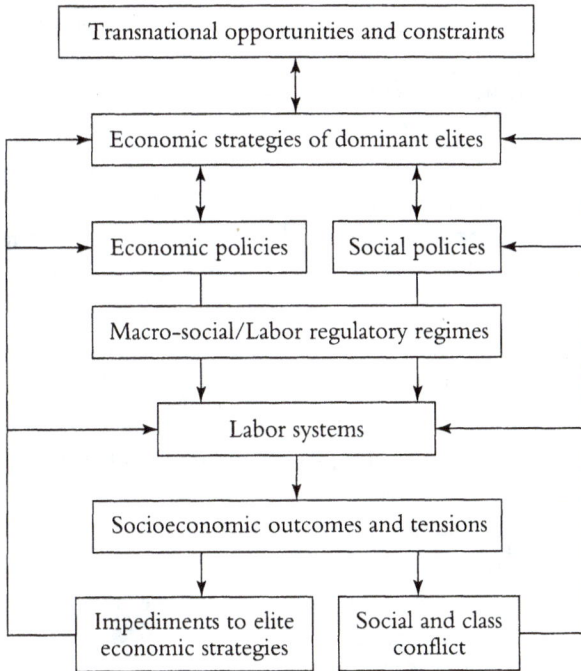

FIGURE 2.1.   The labor system in socioeconomic context.

near-hegemonic status of policies of market deregulation among many elite groups at national and international levels, I include reference to both ideational and material interests in influencing reform-oriented elite strategies.

Elite strategies are seen as influencing both economic and social regulatory orders, and economic and social processes, via policy changes and innovations. These macrolevel institutions and structures impinge in turn on the sectoral labor systems embedded in them, as indicated in the center of figure 2.1.

capacity to implement such new strategies as export-oriented industrialization and industrial upgrading. In the Asian context, historical institutionalist and structuralist versions of strategic institutionalism are to be found most prominently in the writings of Chalmers Johnson (1982), Alice Amsden (1989), Robert Wade (1990), and others. In partial reaction to conventional interpretations of the Asian economic miracle within the IMF and other international financial institutions, which mainly have emphasized the positive economic role of free markets, these authors have asserted the importance of developmental states in strategically directing national economic growth through industrial policy, targeted low-interest loans, and supportive social policy. In its more nuanced versions, developmental state theory has elaborated approaches that both link economic policy to markets and explain the varying effectiveness of developmental states in Asia and elsewhere by reference to their embeddedness in national economic networks.

At this point, the dynamic elements of the framework assert themselves as economic and social policies and structures and, more important, the labor systems they influence, generating a number of consequential outcomes. Inasmuch as some of those outcomes are seen as hindering elite economic strategies, they may evoke innovative regulatory responses that in turn alter labor systems. Alternately, the outcomes may more directly influence labor systems through the actions of firms and government agencies in responding to labor problems or disturbances at local levels. Just as important are ways in which negative social outcomes encourage regulatory contestation, policy opposition, or political instabilities to which local or national governments are impelled to respond through social-regulatory changes or even strategic redirections. Thus, strategic and policy change is seen as responding both to economic circumstances and outcomes and to political pressures and tensions in ways reflective of (1) rational-strategic considerations, (2) the self-defined material or ideational interests of elites, and (3) the imperatives of political accommodation of the demands of subordinate groups and classes.

It should be noted that the relationships among the elements in figure 2.1 are neither linear nor unidirectional. Indeed, it is the feedback loops from socioeconomic outcomes and their associated economic and social tensions that reorient policies, structures, macroregimes, and labor systems. In addition, the secondary, reciprocal, arrows between adjacent elements suggest the presence of interactive, rather than only unidirectional, causality. This figure is presented here in order to identify what I view as the dominant paths of influence and causality in shaping trajectories of market reform, and thus to anticipate the book's argument and the sequencing of topics in later chapters.

While this account foregrounds the role of strategic choice in determining regulatory change, path-dependent effects play an important role as well. First, some institutions and structures, whose origins are to be found in political, developmental, and other considerations and circumstances largely unrelated to and often preceding market reforms, may now function in new, unanticipated ways. Thus, for example, earlier established policies and institutions relating to social protections, labor relations, health insurance, and small enterprise development have come to play important ancillary roles in addressing the tensions of market reform in the countries included in this study. From the standpoint of elite strategies, these latent functions may increasingly be recognized, extended, elaborated, and adapted to meet the new challenges of economic reform itself.

Second, path dependencies are to be found as well in the reigning cultural logics and developmental commitments that continue to influence strategic choice, in part by defining ideational interests and ideologies. Similarly, existing institutions shape and augment the forces of social contestation by enhancing or undermining the political and organizational capacities of workers and other social groups.

Finally, and of particular importance during more recent reforms beginning in the mid-1990s, institutional learning increasingly provides the basis for anticipatory, rather than only reactive, institutional responses to emergent social and economic tensions. Such anticipatory responses to the tensions of market-oriented reform are now strongly embedded in the evolving "Washington consensus" (discussed in chapter 3) itself, as the hard political lessons of earlier-enacted market reforms have made themselves felt. For this reason, reform programs, particularly since the late 1990s, have typically combined and integrated polices of deregulation, institutional reregulation, and social compensation, as discussed throughout this book.

≋ CHAPTER 3

Reforming Labor Systems

Neoliberalism, Reregulation, and Social Compensation

> Within the developed countries themselves, this pe-
> riod [from the late 1990s] was marked almost every-
> where by a rejection of... the Reagan-Thatcher free
> market doctrines, in favor of "New Democrat" or
> "New Labor" policies.
>
> —Joseph Stiglitz, Foreword to Polanyi's *The Great*
> *Transformation,* Second edition, 2001 edition, xv

> [T]he neoliberal project itself gradually metamor-
> phosed into more socially interventionist and ame-
> liorative forms... in which new forms of institution
> building and governmental intervention have been
> licensed within the neoliberal project.
>
> —Peck and Tickell 2002, 387–88

The 1980's hegemonic consolidation of a new,
market-oriented, regulatory paradigm set in motion major global transformations in the nature of interstate economic relations and in the role of states
in national economies. Of particular interest here were associated changes in
regimes of social and labor regulation and in the labor systems through which
economic accumulation, economic livelihood, and social integration are secured
and mutually articulated. This new orthodoxy, usefully termed the Washington
Consensus by John Williamson (1990), came to define a dominant policy orientation among the International Monetary Fund, the World Bank and other
international financial institutions, and the executive branch of the United States
government. Subsequently dubbed by critics the "neoliberal" approach, the
major tenets of the Washington consensus were usefully summarized in the
2005 Asian Development Bank's annual issue of *Key Indicators* as follows:

liberalization of trade and inward foreign direct investment, privatization of state-owned enterprises, industrial deregulation, strengthening of property rights regimes, tax reform, liberalization of prices

(including interest rates), introduction of a competitive exchange rate, and fiscal discipline.... This package could be labeled "first generation reforms." (23)

If some market fundamentalists in the 1980s held an extreme and unrealistic view of the sustainability of unfettered markets, the actual trajectory of global reform suggests a quite different understanding. For, even as a new public discourse of expanded free trade, financial deregulation, privatization, and flexible labor markets seemed to herald an emergent emancipation of markets from the rigidities and constraints of governmental regulation, it quickly became apparent that social and political forces, institutional legacies, state and corporate agendas, and a vibrant complex of nonstate regulatory structures and institutions, both domestic and international, presented powerful constraints on the very possibility of wholly unleashing market forces. And even where market reforms were sometimes precipitously introduced without an appropriate accommodation of these constraints, as were several IMF agreements attached to economic bailouts during times of financial crisis, institutional and social tensions, along with institutional countermeasures taken to manage those tensions, soon reined in the excesses of reform.

Even at the height of influence of the original Washington consensus during the mid-1980s, the group of those most committed to radical market reform occupied a small, if strategically important, institutional and ideational niche in the economic thinking of the day. From the late 1990s, both academic and policy debates have further marginalized market fundamentalism and have stretched the consensus with which it was associated to embrace a variety of institutional and social accommodations of broader social forces. This latter aspect of reform, centered less on liberalization and deregulation and more on institutional *re*regulation and social compensation,[1] now defines a second major phase of reform that balances and constrains the first neoliberal phase.

Further, earlier neoliberal versions of the Washington consensus never really reflected the institutional architectures even of the national economies from which that consensus emerged. Despite the neoliberal, monetarist tilt of the Reagan and Thatcher administrations, in which the new economic doctrine was fashioned into a battering ram to remove states and other institutional obstacles to the spread of market capitalism in transitional Communist and developing economies, it is clear American and British market

---

1. By the late 1990s, for example, the World Bank had come to accept the importance of respect for core labor standards as formalized in ILO conventions (World Bank 2002a).

economies themselves remained embedded in regulatory institutions that, while significantly transformed, continue to establish, albeit with varying degrees of success, the conditions for social stability and economic growth.[2]

In the Introduction I suggested that the past three decades of economic reform may most usefully be understood from the standpoint of the dynamic relationship between two critical dimensions. The first is a freeing of markets from institutional and social encumbrances, the deregulation of national economies, and the liberalization of international trade and investment. The second is the re-embedding of markets in broader social institutions and agendas so as to manage or contain emergent systemic tensions. Some of the socio–institutional compensations discussed in the present chapter are in fact strategically driven by anticipated or experienced tensions of reform. In other cases, those compensations may have arisen for quite different reasons, even though they may have been extended and adapted to address those same tensions.

From the standpoint of labor systems, the two seemingly opposed faces of reform can be further specified. The major starting point in the reform-driven transformation of contemporary labor systems lies first in those institutional reforms and economic policies that have fostered, by design or otherwise, more flexible labor markets less encumbered by political constraints, union pressures, collective bargaining, and social protections than was historically the case in many countries. Insofar as such flexibility has demanded reduced social and livelihood protections, major programs and policies of social protection have themselves been drawn into the vortex of market deregulation. Corresponding changes have occurred as well in other phases of labor systems. Processes of social reproduction have been marketized, while the politics of the labor process has been tilted in favor of employers by a diminished role for unions and the gradual displacement of collective employment contracts with individual contracts. These various changes define the deregulatory face of labor reform.

The contrary process of reregulation is more complex and multistranded, and indeed it must be understood from the standpoint of the disparate tensions inhering in labor deregulation itself. Growing official acknowledgment of the social and political limits of reform has been reflected in important changes in the Washington consensus (Islam and Chowdhury 2000, 208–39). The new or "augmented" (Beeson and Islam 2005) Washington consensus

---

2. In their examination of the diffusion of regulatory capitalism in Latin America, Levi-Faur and Jordana note three areas of significant social regulation under reform: pharmaceuticals, environment, and food safety, with no reference to employment or social protections (Levi-Faur and Jordana 2005; see also Majone 1997; Moran 2001).

moves away from the predominantly market-focused agenda of the 1980s to an increased emphasis on institution building and social policy.[3] While the new institutional-regulatory emphasis relates most importantly to finance, corporate governance, intellectual property rights, and competition policy, there is as well a strong social component emphasizing social participation, local governance, expanded education, primary health care, poverty allevia-tion and social safety nets—all areas of putative market failure (Kapstein and Milanovic 2002). That new efforts to more effectively institutionalize and socialize developing-country reform may in some cases have served the eco-nomic interests of international investors has provided a further, if not neces-sarily primary, consideration in fashioning the new Washington consensus.

Reform debates have gained special prominence in the context of market reform in emerging and post-Communist countries where, it is often argued, the institutional foundations for market capitalism must themselves be cre-ated, sometimes de novo, if markets are to function at all (Stiglitz 2000; Dol-lar 2003).[4] There is now a growing consensus among reform advocates and international financial institutions that greater attention must be paid to the socioinstitutional re-embedding and reregulation of markets as a condition for their success and sustainability. And it is this emerging consensus that has transformed the very notion of market reform from an earlier neoliberal emphasis to a more comprehensive view—one that includes the deregulatory emancipation of market forces to be sure, but that includes as well a host of compensatory efforts to institutionally consolidate that liberalization and, at the same time, to balance it against other goals and requirements. At a mini-mum, this would imply a more balanced emphasis on market efficiencies, distributive outcomes, and long-term development. The remainder of this chapter examines this transition as relating especially to developing countries.

The Role of the State under Market Reform: Displacement or Transformation?

A market-fundamentalist view of economic reform understands it as a process of institutional deregulation that augments the role of market forces, largely unimpeded by social, political, or institutional constraints and rigidities, in governing economic life. Rejecting such a neoclassical view, institutional-ist accounts—more prevalent in the disciplines of sociology and political

---

3. Rodrik (2002) offers the initial model of the augmented Washington consensus, one on which Beeson and Islam build.

4. For a dissenting view, see Jeffrey D. Sachs's "Institutions Matter, but Not for Everything" (2003).

science—portray reform quite differently, not as an unleashing of market forces so much as a transition to new modes of socioinstitutional regulation (e.g., WB, *WDR* 2002). Institutionalists thus envision either a partial displacement of the state by nongovernmental regulatory institutions or, alternatively, a transformation (vs. diminution) of the governance role of the state itself. Both displacement and transformation views acknowledge the importance of selective state deregulation but emphasize as well the necessity for, and inevitability of, compensatory reregulation, whether through nonstate institutions or through new forms of state regulation. Neither view envisions markets as supplanting states as a primary basis for economic order.

State Displacement

The state displacement view shares with neoliberal accounts an acceptance of the de-statization of national economies and the privatization of regulatory regimes, as firms along with business organizations, professional associations, and social networks assume increased autonomy in organizing production processes and responding to competitive pressures and market opportunities.[5] An early example of this tradition, Piore and Sabel's seminal monograph, *The Second Industrial Divide* (1984), describes a reemergence of earlier patterns of craft-based production governed by social and business networks among workers, employers, community associations, and in some cases local governments.[6] Similarly, Gary Gereffi's discussion (1994) of global commodity chains emphasizes a growing regulatory role for transnational corporations, whose reach and power increasingly bypass states. A later rendition of this view is that of Manuel Castells (2000 [1996]), who describes the growing importance of informational and economic networks within which nation states play a diminished regulatory role:

> The most direct impact of information networks on social structure concerns power relationships. Historically, power was embedded in

---

5. This view encourages a broader view of "states" than the customary one, seeing them as comprising multiple sets of authoritatively established and coercively sanctioned rules, structures, and action that define *elements in* rather than inclusive *systems of* regulatory regimes. From this perspective, regimes of social and labor regulation are seen as comprising clusters of rules, structures, and social action that include a variety of both state and nonstate actors and structures. Indeed, such a view usefully integrates state- and firm-centric versions of strategic institutionalism. To take an example, the microlevel regulatory regimes linked most closely to the labor process (Burawoy's "factory regimes") embrace rules, norms, and structures that are variously rooted in and influenced by shop-floor relations, family and business networks, local government, and national legislation. The state is thus seen as defining only one subset of regulatory elements in such regimes.

6. Also see Doner and Hershberg (1999) for discussion of the increased importance of local government under economic restructuring.

organizations and institutions, organized around a hierarchy of centres. Networks dissolve centres, they disorganize hierarchy, and make materially impossible the exercise of hierarchical power.... Thus contemporary information networks... bypass the nation-state which, by and large, has stopped being a sovereign entity. (19)

State Displacement and the New Social Economy

A revived tradition of "social" (Everling 1997; Shragge and Fontan 2000), "associative" (Archibughi 2000), and "third-sector" (Gunn 2004) economic studies emphasizes the growing importance of nonprofit social organizations, as states relinquish some of their regulatory functions. This tradition seeks to move beyond earlier understandings of the informal sector as either subsistence activities serving those excluded from the state-regulated formal-sector economy or as economic activities subordinated through subcontract arrangements to formal-sector firms seeking to avoid costly state regulation, undercut or bypass unions, and reduce labor and other production costs. This expanding social economy literature usefully points to a range of new social regulatory structures and agents that operate somewhat independently of both markets and states.

This point of view, anticipated in the conservative early writing of Hernando de Soto (1989), who saw the informal, unregulated economy as the source and seedbed of unbridled capitalist entrepreneurship, has acquired theoretical prominence in the years following the advent of neoliberal reform. In large measure, this new prominence flows from the supplemental and supportive role nonprofit and third-sector social activities play in reform programs themselves. In particular, third-sector organizations may be actively promoted as alternative sites of social reproduction and protection to fill the void left by the rollback of the state, by reduced commitments to social protection by both firms and states, and by the privatization or devolution of social services to nonstate providers. Thus, for example, NGOs, community associations, and nonprofit organizations may assume an increasing social burden in managing the negative social externalities of market reform.[7]

Social Capital Formation

If much of the discussion of state displacement centers on its external causes (namely, the structural pressures of globalization), a growing social capital

---

7. In this sense they fill an important void created by discussions of the informal sector that describe significant portions of national economies by reference to what they lack (state regulation), offering instead a fuller understanding of informal sectors as providing *alternative* regulatory orders.

approach, rooted in the new social economy literature, understands state displacement as flowing in part from the strategies of states themselves. This strategic understanding of state displacement centers on policies that actively seek to socialize, rather than only to privatize, economic governance.

Nan Lin (2001, 24–25) defines social capital as those resources that are embedded in social networks and that may be employed by network participants to achieve economic ends. There is some disagreement among social capital theorists regarding questions of origin and change. Robert Putnam, whose writings have influenced social capital thinking and policy at the World Bank, suggested in his 1993 work on democratic governance in Italy that the associational activities and groups through which social capital is generated do not easily change, an assumption that parallels the related suggestion by many historical institutionalists that national economic institutions are strongly path dependent. On the other hand, Putnam's later writings, as well as World Bank efforts to augment community-based social capital,[8] seem to suggest just the opposite: that strategic innovation in development policy can strongly influence the emergence of social capital and thus its presumed positive outcomes for economic development as well (Grootaert and Bastelaer 2002).

The State Transformation View

The state transformation view greatly qualifies the assertion that states have been displaced under programs of market reform. In some accounts, state deregulation is only partial and selective and is often accompanied by an extension or deepening of other forms of state-organized regulation that address the growing socioeconomic pressures associated with globalization (Weiss 2003). This is a view I embrace in this book. This view, that deregulation is best understood as a change in the nature, rather than the extent, of the state's regulatory role, encourages research on new modes of state regulation as social economies anticipate and respond to the tensions of market reform.

As I suggested earlier, theories of the regulatory state straddle the line between displacement and transformation views of neoliberal states. The state transformation tradition sees politically independent organizations, commissions, boards, and central banks as displacing many of the regulatory functions of states, suggesting a partial privatization of regulatory regimes as business representatives and associations acquire increased voice in these

---

8. See World Bank Social Capital Website: http://worldbank.org/WBI/Resources/Analyzing Social Capital.

quasi-independent regulatory bodies. Conversely, this view also sees a *re-constitution* of the state whereby these independent bodies collectively come to define a more networked, less-hierarchical state whose key functions are devolved to *statelike* bodies. In this sense, regulatory state theory partially rejects a state displacement view in favor of an emphasis on a transformation of the state's economic role—from direct participation (sometimes including ownership) to indirect regulation through depoliticized quasi-governmental agencies.

Critical regulation theory goes further in fleshing out a full transformational view. For regulationists in the 1980s, neoliberalism was an unsustainable project whose endogenous tensions and contradictions could only be resolved by the reinsertion of the state (Gordon 1994a, 301). Writings that reflect the subsequent actual experience of reform during the 1990s have offered a less-speculative, more empirically grounded, account of emergent roles of states under neoliberal reform. These writings suggest that if market reform has diminished or redirected the state's direct economic role, it has at the same time encouraged an enhanced state role in sustaining reform by addressing its institutional and social tensions and dislocations.

Globalization: Displacement or Transformation?

For some observers, I have noted, economic globalization has increasingly undercut the regulatory role of the national state, as transnational networks and flows of trade, finance, communications, labor, and corporate activities have bypassed state overview and control (Gereffi 1994; Castells 2000 [1996]). For others, globalization has been associated less with state displacement than state transformation. Ash Amin (2004), to take one example, adopts a modestly transformative position, arguing:

> Perhaps the key difference in today's circumstance of globalization is that the role of the state in regulation has become less pivotal and that regulation through territorial jurisdiction and control has weakened. This does not necessarily amount to a condition of regulatory disorder, simply a change in the institutional and spatial nature of the order (230).

William Robinson takes a more robust position, arguing that the "national state does not 'wither away' but becomes transformed with respect to its regulatory role and becomes a functional component of a larger [transnational state . . . whose function shifts] . . . from the formulation of national policies to the administration of policies formulated through supranational institutions."

In this way, "national states become incorporated into the (transnational state) as component parts (Robinson 2004, 100–101)."

Similarly, Castells (2000), whose writings on globalization more generally embrace a displacement view, suggests that to the extent states do continue to play a significant role, they are both transformed and rescaled, in this instance both upward and downward:

> The central power-holding institution of human history, the state, is also undergoing a process of dramatic transformation. On the one hand, its sovereignty is called into question by global flows of wealth, communication, and information. On the other hand, its legitimacy is undermined.... However, the state does not disappear. It adapts and transforms itself. On the one hand, it builds partnerships between na-tion-states and shares sovereignty to retain influence... there is a deci-sive shift of power toward multi-national and transnational institutions. On the other hand... most states have engaged in a process of devolu-tion of power, decentralizing responsibilities to nationalities, regions, and local governments, often extending this de-centralization to non-governmental organizations. (14)

Here, I adopt a transformation view of globalization that, while recogniz-ing the growing importance of transnational governance, nonetheless asserts the continuing importance of the agendas and regulatory powers of states at a national level. National states are thus seen as retaining their impor-tance, at least to this moment in history, as key agents in the construction, operationalization, and sanctioning of emergent global economic regulatory regimes, and as offering significant institutional leverage for both dominant elites and oppositional factions and groups (e.g., labor) in their efforts to influence trajectories of development and reform at national and sectoral levels.[9] From the standpoint of development, states have shifted from direct, market-intrusive interventions to more indirect, supply-side interventions in their efforts to leverage national economies, sectors, firms, and workers into higher-value niches in the global economy (for discussion see Weiss 2003), and from an effort to insulate national economies from the influence of global regulatory regimes to increased efforts to influence and exploit op-portunities afforded by those global regimes (see figure 2), an effort that has both reflected and further deepened existing international hierarchies of

---

9. Haworth and Ramsay (1984) note in regard to the tendency of labor to look inward for na-tional protections even as capital looks outward to international opportunities for expansion.

economic power and performance. These strategic state-led efforts to globalize national economies on advantageous terms are discussed by Stephan Haggard and Peter Lange, who describe the ways in which states may seek through a variety of economic policies to influence modes of insertion of national economies into the global economy. Haggard (1995) distinguishes in this regard between "shallow" integration, relying largely on external liberalization of trade and investment, and "deep" integration, involving a range of domestic and international negotiations and interventions to enhance the developmental potentialities of global insertion. Similarly, Lange (1985) emphasizes the importance of state policies in managing processes of adjustment and globalization. For Lange, "on-boundary" state actions seek to negotiate favorable terms of entry of domestic firms into global markets, while "within-boundary" policies are directed toward upgrading domestic-production structures (and, by implication, labor systems) so as to reposition them in international-production networks and markets.

Jessop (2002) usefully extends this notion of externally articulated—or, perhaps better, "open"—developmentalism to the realm of social policy in his discussion of an ongoing, and as yet incomplete, transition among wealthy industrial countries from a "Keynesian full employment state" to a "Schumpeterian competition state." The first of these state forms, associated with "Atlantic Fordism" of the 1950s and 1960s, sought to mediate a variety of institutional tensions at the national level. This included a balancing of market consumption and production; establishing a social pact among management, labor, and the state; maintaining full employment and a secure livelihood for workers and their families; and establishing a set of policies and institutions to stabilize national markets, international trade and finance, and international exchange rates. In this way, state policies and regulatory regimes sought to balance the multiple demands of market efficiencies, social equity, and growth.

Market reform and external liberalization have, according to Jessop, undermined this earlier pattern and, following a period of instability and conflict, encouraged the tentative construction of new institutional forms through which states now seek to foster renewed economic growth within the changed circumstances of market deregulation and global competition. Of particular importance here is Jessop's emphasis on the heightened importance of social policy and social regulation in enhancing national competitiveness in world markets. In this regard, he notes the ways in which states seek to leverage local firms and workers into global markets on advantageous terms by facilitating industrial upgrading, training, vocational and science education, research and development, and other investments in a social and physical infrastructure supportive of entrepreneurship, innovation, and competitiveness. This emphasis on social policy, a major focus here, in part reflects the ascendancy of Third Way social interventionist reforms in the United States under President Bill Clinton and in Britain under Prime Minister Tony Blair (see Peck and Tickell 2002, 380–404).

Market Reform, Economic Structural Change, and Institutional Regulation

In this book I ask how economic reform in Asia has reshaped labor systems, how those changes have been associated with a variety of socioinstitutional tensions, and how and to what extent those tensions have been compensated for or managed through other policies and institutional accommodations that together define an expanded and redirected state role. First are those tensions *within* labor systems, as labor market reforms destabilize labor markets and the labor process while also undermining the social reproduction and protection of labor. Second are tensions that are *external* to labor systems but that imbue those systems with purpose and value. These include the economic impact of reform and its uncertain outcomes for the economic agendas of elites and for the livelihood security of workers. They include as well the destabilizing political outcomes of reform. This book is organized around the ways in which these multiple tensions and imbalances have or have not been addressed by changing social and economic policies and institutions in four Asian countries.

Throughout the discussion, it should be noted that institutional imbalances and tensions are endemic to social systems and processes. They can be managed and contained with varying degrees of success, but their continuance constitutes a major driver of trajectories of reform and of social change more generally. Underlying many of these tensions is the fundamental divide between two critical agendas: the first rooted in the economic paradigms and agendas of dominant policy coalitions, the second in social agendas of livelihood security and social stability. The first of these agendas defined the core program of Washington consensus reform during the 1980s and early 1990s, emphasizing privatization, trade and financial liberalization, a less intrusive and more indirect economic role of the state, and, in cases of debt crisis, economic stabilization and retrenchment. Increased attention to social agendas became most visible during the late 1990s and beyond, as economic changes spawned emergent institutional and social tensions that threatened both economic growth and sociopolitical stability.

Initially, economic tensions elicited reactive institutional and policy accommodations focused especially on the institutional requirements of markets themselves. Private-sector responses to these emergent institutional tensions were quick and substantial, as employers, both individually and collectively, were most directly and immediately exposed to new institutional and labor vulnerabilities. But states were soon drawn in as well as pressures mounted to help resolve continuing tensions facing firms in sectors deemed developmentally important. Such tensions were rooted in new economic circumstances of heightened competition, reduced state protection and promotion, and destabilized labor systems.

But if dysfunctional labor systems and economic pressures were one source of regulatory change, other pressures pushed in different directions. These latter pressures related less to the consolidation of markets and enhancement of economic competitiveness than to a broader and more fundamental rebalancing of economic and social agendas themselves. Here, in response to social and political instability and resistance, the augmentation of social safety nets, employment creation, job safety, pensions, and health insurance came to partially complement, and sometimes to compete with, more narrowly defined economic agendas. Trajectories of national reform, and indeed of the Washington consensus itself, have thus been driven by an intersection of these two sets of tensions: the first between opposed needs of market flexibility and institutional reconsolidation; the second between economic and social imperatives.

Deregulatory Reform and Its Labor Implications

Turning first to the neoliberal deregulatory face of reform, what are its implications and outcomes for labor systems? As noted earlier, there are two avenues through which market reform influences labor outcomes: the first, indirect, through economic structural changes varyingly associated with economic policy reforms not specifically focused on labor; the second, direct, via social and labor policy reforms that explicitly seek to alter regimes of social regulation.

Economic Policy Reforms

Economic restructuring plays an important, if indirect, role in influencing the nature and predominance of particular regimes of social and labor regulation (see figure 2). Indeed, it is impossible to discuss or comprehend trajectories of social-regulatory change without placing those trajectories in the context of reform-driven changes in economic structures. In particular, it is clear that economic restructuring has the effect of moving large numbers of workers from stagnant (sometimes more protected) sectors to expanding (often less protected) sectors. Similarly powerful employment effects have been associated with economic policies closely linked to programs of market-oriented reform, including economic stabilization, the marketization and privatization of state-owned enterprises, and liberalization of external trade and investment. In each case employment structures and practices along with their associated social regulatory orders have been destabilized and reordered in ways that have affected the livelihood of workers, the competitive position of economic sectors, and the developmental prospects of national economies.

In emerging, post-Socialist developing countries, the marketization,[10] increased operational autonomy, and privatization of state-owned enterprises (SOEs) have dramatically reduced state-mandated social programs and benefits for workers, subjected firms to intensified pressures to cut costs and reduce worker compensation, heightened efforts to increase efficiencies and reduce employment levels, and encouraged greater reliance on casual and contract labor. In cases of outright privatization, there has been movement toward integration of operations into regional or global corporate networks and thus consolidation of transnational corporate governance structures and labor policies while pushing previously protected workers into the more uncertain world of market-driven private-sector employment.

External liberalization, a further strand of economic structural reform, generates intensified competitive pressures on local companies through reduced trade protection that was previously enjoyed by domestic and locally operating firms. For some workers, particularly during early labor-intensive stages of industrialization, these pressures may eventuate in work intensification and pay reductions. For other workers, particularly skilled workers in the core operations of firms, those same pressures have led to heightened efforts to bolster training, adaptability, skill diversification, quality, and/or participation in enhanced competitiveness, although even for those workers, increased vulnerability to volatile external markets may push local firms to adopt more flexible production and employment practices and to replace some regular workers with fixed-term contract workers. External liberalization extends as well to greater openness to portfolio and foreign direct investment (FDI), thus presenting both threats (direct competition, acquisitions, increased economic

---

10. By marketization I refer to reduced state subsidization and protection of SOEs against market competition and their consequent increased exposure to market pressures.

volatility) and new opportunities (as suppliers, partners, and investors) for domestic firms and their workers.

Social Regulatory Reform

The second major influence on labor systems, social regulatory reform, seeks more directly to alter regimes of social and labor governance. Paramount among these regulatory changes are labor market deregulation and social-policy reform. The call for flexible deregulated labor markets is succinctly summarized in the World Bank's 2005 *World Development Report* wherein are encouraged a number of regulatory changes including eliminating or reducing the impact of minimum wage setting; drawing a closer link between productivity and worker compensation; easing regulatory mandates on firms in such areas as health and safety, work hours, and paid leave; permitting greater employer discretion in hiring and firing; easing restrictions on the employment of fixed-term contract and temporary workers; and encouraging individual vs. collectively bargained work contracts. These various measures, guided by principles of regulatory privatization and devolution, are justified economically as enhancing enterprise competitiveness and socially as augmenting formal-sector employment, reducing employment segmentation, and enhancing job opportunities for economically vulnerable groups (136–56) by increasing incentives to hire casual or temporary workers, especially at lower skill levels.[11]

This same 2005 report urges a number of market-oriented social-policy reforms as well. These include the decentralization, out-contracting, and partial privatization of education, health, and other social services; reform of unemployment and social welfare programs to increase worker incentives to find employment; increased reliance on contributory social insurance schemes in lieu of government support; a scaling back of "market distorting" consumer subsidies; and reduced government involvement in and support for unions and collective bargaining.

Tensions of Deregulatory Reform

To the extent these economic and social reforms are not accompanied by other compensatory social policies, they tend to create or exacerbate a variety of tensions, both economic and social. Market-oriented reform has

---

11. Efforts in India to deregulate labor markets are defended as promoting increased FDI and more competitive manufactured exports.

sometimes disorganized labor markets and labor systems in ways that threaten to undermine the economic performance of firms and national economies. It is all-too-often assumed that the labor needs of companies and national economies are best met by the tenets of market fundamentalism: flexible labor markets, labor-cost containment, and minimal, narrowly targeted programs of social protection. Such an assumption would seem to set social protection in direct conflict with the economic agendas of firms and governments. In fact, such a view ignores variation in the labor requirements of different kinds of work, labor prerequisites of economic upgrading and development, and differences between corporate and governmental economic agendas.

From the standpoint of the social reproduction of an available, healthy, skilled, and motivated workforce, it may suffice to externalize, individualize, and societalize the reproductive costs and risks to families and communities where casual low-skill labor predominates. But as production requirements demand ever-more-motivated, skilled, and resourceful workers, such externalization begins to take its toll in lagging skills, low worker morale, and inadequate product quality. Similar problems occur in the movement of workers from declining sectors to new, expanding sectors. Inadequate retraining slows job mobility; a lack of social supports for migrating workers increases the risks of geographical mobility; inadequate social protections encourage a retreat to informal-sector activities and only partial commitment to full-time paid employment; an absence of employment and job-information services inhibits labor market responsiveness; and work casualization, increasing job insecurity, and harsh, market-driven employment conditions undercut the sorts of mutual-commitment employment systems demanded in many work situations (see Freeman 1992; ADB *KI* 2005, 26–29, 34–35). These and other institutional frictions compromise the very flexibility assumed to flow from labor market deregulation and encourage new efforts to stabilize, integrate, and lubricate labor markets, thus speeding the transition from 1980's market fundamentalism to policies of reregulation in the late 1990s and first decade of the 2000s (hereafter the '00s).

Corresponding to these economic outcomes are a variety of emergent social and political tensions to which states must also respond, and which centrally define the class politics of reform. Understanding that in reality such reforms are rarely and only unevenly implemented, an ideal typical reform program may eventuate in a host of negative social outcomes: workers and bureaucrats in state enterprises would face the multiple threats posed by privatization and external liberalization; social protection and social policy would become subordinated to the requirements of competitiveness; farmers and manufacturers would face growing global competition; domestic workers would be forced more directly to compete in productivity and pay levels with foreign workers; employment security would give way to labor market uncertainty; and agendas of national development would give way to the imperatives of world-market integration. Finally, the partial deregulation of labor markets, and the heightened employer discretion it encourages, augments employment segmentation, as employers replace standardized labor practices with more differentiated practices keyed to corresponding differences in skill demands, labor markets, and work requirements (Kalleberg 2007, 174).[12]

Reinstitutionalizing and Socializing Labor Systems

The economic and social tensions associated with deregulatory reform have been variably addressed by corresponding efforts to create new institutional frameworks within which markets can more effectively function while at the same time developing new ways of enhancing livelihood security, social cohesion, and political sustainability. This section describes several generic policy responses through which governments have sought to address these often contradictory goals.

Compensating Losers: In seeking to meet the growing threat of social and political instability, states may adopt policies of social compensation for the social externalities, livelihood risks, income inequities, and political tensions that flow from labor market deregulation and economic external liberalization (Weiss 2003).[13] In many cases, such policies of social compensation constitute a partial return to more traditional forms of protection: workplace health and safety laws, expanded social insurance to include informal-sector and marginalized groups, social protections against loss of employment and income, and so forth. But the fact remains that most forms of compensatory social policy are seen at least in part as compromising the reform shift toward market governance by partially reinstating social equity agendas in national policymaking in order to manage the tensions of reform (Freeman 1992; World Bank 2002a).

---

12. The diversification of competitive strategies is extensively discussed by Steven McKay (2006) in his discussion of the electronics industry in the Philippines.

13. See, for example, the work of Linda Weiss (2003) on the continued role of national states, despite globalization, in promoting social protection and national development. Similarly, critical regulationists stress the important role of states in fostering social regimes through which to accommodate class tensions, ensure livelihood security and consumption, encourage social stability, and legitimize existing regimes of production.

Market Incorporation: Parallel to efforts to compensate groups marginalized or excluded from the benefits of formal-sector employment, and in recognition that such compensation only creates new institutional rigidities in labor markets, governments have sought to resolve this policy contradiction more directly by encouraging increased labor market participation, particularly in formal-sector employment. Especially important are efforts to augment active labor market policies through which to enhance information flows between buyers and sellers of labor, encourage or provide necessary retraining, broker and otherwise assist in job placement, and more generally ensure that markets operate flexibly and competitively in response to growing economic instability. Kanishka Jayasuriya (2006) discusses the way in which such policies of labor incorporation redefine social welfare "as involving the enabling of participation within the sphere of the market... so as to enhance inclusion within the market rather than having its earlier emphasis on the redistribution of income" (10), thus encouraging a "shift from social to market citizenship" (19). In some cases, this encouragement has taken somewhat coercive forms, as in workfare approaches to unemployment and social security that shorten the duration of benefits and require active efforts to find new work or to engage in retraining programs as a condition for receipt of benefits. Similarly, market-oriented development of land and natural resources, under which local populations are displaced to make way for logging, dams, urban development, or consolidated commercial agriculture, has the effect of pushing rural populations into paid employment and may be seen as coercive measures of forced labor market participation.[14] In these and other ways, governments have sought to bring a larger portion of the workforce into gainful employment.

As further described by Jayasuriya, a market-citizenship approach views employability and market participation as strongly dependent on individual capabilities (e.g., skills, motivation, personal initiative, effective job seeking), capabilities that may in turn be enhanced through social networks, community-based service organizations, NGOs, and a variety of other not-for-profit organizations. Thus, new programs of market incorporation are often associated with increased state encouragement and funding of private and nonprofit organizations and agencies that provide a variety of social and job-related services and assistance for unemployed workers. Additionally, of course, these organizations provide various types of social assistance, health care, and other compensatory social services as a safety net for unskilled,

---

14. For a more general account of this policy shift, see Nevins and Peluso (2008).

disabled, elderly, or otherwise economically marginalized workers, and for impoverished families more generally, both cushioning the impact of reform and reducing the likelihood of political opposition. As part of its expanded antipoverty agenda, for example, the World Bank has embarked on programs to both include and empower local community groups in actively addressing social problems of health, education, physical infrastructure, and income security.

Encouraging the Entrepreneurial Worker. Given the increased livelihood risks and insecurities associated with labor market deregulation, globalization, and economic reform more generally, and in keeping with the renewed spirit of individualistic entrepreneurial capitalism, it has become increasingly important to encourage a new culture of individual initiative, risk taking, and personal responsibility among workers who can no longer rely on employers and states to protect them from the risks of the marketplace. Jessop provides a useful starting point in addressing this matter. For him, the social strains created by increasing labor market flexibility, a reduced social wage, increasing livelihood insecurity, and the increased need for workers to be adaptable to a variety of jobs among which they migrate, together generate pressures for active labor market policies that create what he terms "enterprising subjects."[15] Because they lack employment security, he argues, workers themselves need to become more flexible, multiskilled, and willing to engage in lifelong learning, upskilling, and continual self-reinvention in order successfully to navigate uncertain and ever-changing labor markets (Jessop 2002, 155–57; Jessop and Sum 2006, 183). The expansion of contingent labor thus invites new policies intended to transform previously stable workers into "self-entrepreneurs" continually seeking ways either to create start-up businesses or to enhance their employability. Where those policies also encourage active engagement with emergent technologies, either through learning, research and development, or innovation, they go beyond the encouragement of market incorporation and participation to developmental augmentation as well, as discussed in chapter 11.

Entrepreneurial employed workers engage in continual self-investment when four conditions are met. First, governments, industries, and firms must provide the training opportunities that help workers develop new skills and upward career trajectories within broad occupational spheres rather than within specific firms. Second, governments must adopt active labor market policies that facilitate movement among jobs. Third, workers must not only

---

15. See Jayasuriya (2006, 10–15) for further discussion of this point.

accept and adapt to the new circumstances of livelihood they face, but they must also embrace new identities defined by personal initiative, adaptability, and flexibility that subordinate organizational, work group, and union attachments to the imperatives of self-responsibility. That organizations and unions have become less and less instrumental for attaining economic security has only hastened this new self-definition. Fourth, they require sufficient livelihood protections, not only to compensate for increased job insecurity and to sustain them during periods of job search but also to encourage them to either invest in new training or to assume the risk of starting small businesses.

Protecting Reform from Political Challenge

Insofar as social and political tensions may threaten to derail reform, governments have sometimes sought to institutionally insulate reform policy from the political process (Harvey 2005, 66). In some cases, governments have embedded reform policies in both legal precedent and statute, as well as in binding international agreements (e.g., IMF loan conditionalities, World Bank structural loan agreements, WTO rules) that would seem to tie the hands of governments. Additionally, regulatory authority has been increasingly exercised by independent "nonpolitical" regulatory bodies such as export-zone authorities, financial supervisory boards, industrial relations councils, and environmental-governance commissions (Majone 1997; Levi-Faur and Jordana 2005). These and other such bodies that exercise legally sanctioned regulatory authority outside the realm of formal politics are not easily influenced by unions, NGOs, and other popular-sector organizations.

In addition, governments have directly and indirectly disempowered trade unions and other popular-sector groups that have often challenged reform policy. Most important in this regard are the devolution of regulatory authority to local levels where the balance of bargaining power typically shifts from labor to employers; reduced security and other protections for workers; withdrawal of support even for "responsible" trade unions and union federations; and a reform-driven shift away from political citizenship and toward various forms of "market citizenship" (Jayasuriya 2006, 15–19). These various institutional changes have collectively disempowered workers' organizations in ways that have further depoliticized and protected reform from public contestation.

In the advanced economies of the Organisation for Economic Co-operation and Development (OECD), these and other institutional measures meant to insulate the new economic order from public dissent and worker contestation have generally, though not always, sufficed to contain dissent.[16] Elsewhere, especially in developing countries, the transition has often been sharper and more divisive, and state authority less secure. In those cases, more coercive economic and political measures have been employed by states and firms (Harvey 2005, 69), as unionization, worker militancy and other forms of popular-sector resistance have been met by managerial and police violence. Attention to institutional measures to contain worker dissent suggests an important inadequacy in the reform literature's emphasis on institutional deregulation, an inadequacy rooted in part in a narrow focus on labor markets and social policy to the exclusion of that "hidden abode of production," the labor process (Jaffee 2001, 10).

Competing Policy Agendas

As noted above, the systemic tensions of market reform revolve around two key issues. The first is that of creating an institutional framework within which labor and other markets function efficiently in enhancing competitiveness, flexibility, and growth. The second pertains to the continuing tension between the requirements of economic accumulation, on the one hand, and sociopolitical efforts to maintain social cohesion and the livelihood security of workers and their families, on the other. If the resolution of the first duality, that between deregulation and institutional coherence, attends largely to "rational" considerations of economic efficiency, resolution of the second pits economic and social agendas against one another. The first of these tensions is resolved with varying degrees of success by institutionally consolidating flexible labor markets. The second invokes new policies that varyingly combine social compensation, market incorporation, depoliticization, and coercion.

Actual reform trajectories are driven by the dynamic tensions created by the interplay of both dualities. That these multiple tensions can never be fully resolved ensures that change and periodic institutional crisis, innovation, and reform characterize all real-world regimes of economic and social regulation. Critical regulationists have sought to identify and characterize a historical succession of these institutional "fixes" (Jessop 2002, 48–51) or social structures of accumulation that are constructed during the interludes between times of crisis to manage, at least for a time, underlying contradictions and tensions. Here, the tensions that characterize older decaying orders

---

16. The 2010 eurozone sovereign debt crisis reignited political conflict relating to fiscal and social policy.

are managed through new arrangements that may come to define a succeeding, more stable, social order.

The institutional fixes these conjunctures bring may, of course, take a variety of forms, depending on the nature of existing institutions that constitute the starting point for change, as well as the economic context and balance of contending political forces within which they are constructed. In many cases, political contention extends to the realm of intrastate competition as well, as different state regulatory agencies and institutions pursue varying policy agendas and reach out for support to disparate political interests and factions. In the context of labor policy, it is thus not surprising to observe sometimes divergent and contradictory agendas and priorities in the regulatory actions of different state agencies in their supervisory or developmental relations with local firms, despite a shared adherence to a single corpus of factory and labor legislation. In this context, market reform has often eventuated in a displacement of those ministries and agencies most closely associated with labor protections, industrial policy, and economic development in favor of other agencies more directed toward priorities of trade and finance. For this reason, the play of politics and thus of regulatory contestation must be recognized even within "states" themselves.

The success of emergent regulatory regimes in managing and containing institutional and social tensions depends on the degree to which they bring together around a coherent institutional order the disparate agendas of workers, firms, and states.[17] Such a convergence of agendas is typically easiest to achieve under conditions of continuing economic growth, economic and industrial upgrading, a degree of state management of the pressures of international competition, and correspondingly strong (regulatory) states. These conditions, which better characterize the political economic context of regulatory policy in the more dynamic East Asian economies than elsewhere in the developing world, suggest the relatively greater possibility for stable institutional fixes in that region than elsewhere.

---

17. See James Lee (2007) on his understanding of "developmentalism" as an *integration* of economic and social agendas.

PART II

Deregulating Asian Labor Systems

CHAPTER 4

Export-Oriented Industrialization and State-Enterprise Reform

Restructuring Employment

The shift in several Asian countries away from import substitution toward a greater emphasis on export-oriented industrialization (EOI) defines a convenient starting point for the study of Asian market reform. This shift occurred initially in Asia's four newly industrializing countries during the 1960s and 1970s, in part in response to new external opportunities created by growing Japanese international subcontracting and direct investment, by expanding world markets, and by increased demand for logistics and supplies on the part of the U.S. military in its prosecution of the Vietnam War. The EOI shift was subsequently replicated in the early and mid-1980s in Indonesia following the collapse of oil prices and in Thailand in response to growing trade deficits, foreign exchange shortfalls, and pressures from international lenders to adopt programs of structural adjustment and economic stabilization (King 2008, 123). In the Philippines, adoption of an EOI strategy was more problematic. President Ferdinand Marcos sought to promote new EOI policies in the early 1970s, but this effort was undermined by lack of supportive policy measures, including a continuance of overvalued exchange rates and other policies driven by demands from powerful agro-elites and from an entrenched domestic bourgeoisie for external-trade protection (Tipton 1998, 317). Later, amid a debt crisis in 1984–5, Marcos was forced to institute painful economic stabilization policies. Following the overthrow of Marcos in 1986, an array of new structural adjustment programs was instituted under presidents Corazon Aquino and Fidel Ramos. These policies provided some impetus to manufacturing exports, particularly in the 1990s, although the developmental and employment gains of that growth were far more limited than elsewhere in the region.

This new strategy, and the dramatic economic transformations and growth with which it was often associated, led many scholars and policymakers to point to East Asia's open export–led growth as offering a new model of outward-oriented market-led industrial development (Belassa 1981), a model that was to define a key element of international development theory and practice over subsequent years. By the end of 2002, the World Bank reported the cumulative creation of some three thousand export-processing zones providing employment for 43 million workers in 116 countries (World Bank 2004, 167).

In retrospect, it became increasingly clear that early Asian EOI strategies involved only partial external liberalization and that the state role in offering incentives to foreign investors, providing export subsidies, licensing state-supported trading companies,[1] providing selective access to cheap credit, regulating inward foreign investment, managing foreign exchange rates, and selectively controlling imports in support of new export industries fell far short of usual standards of market liberalization (see Deyo 1987, 227–47; Amsden 1989; Weiss and Hobson 1995). Such illiberal elements of EOI strategies, most evident in early programs of state-led EOI in the 1970s, were in part a product of the continuing regional influence of the Japanese industrial-policy model.

But having said this, it must be recognized that EOI was also supported by a host of market-oriented policies. Export restrictions and licensing requirements were relaxed. Existing high tariffs on necessary imports of producer goods, raw materials, and product components were reduced, in part under growing pressure from industrial exporting companies reliant on imported materials and components. Previously overvalued exchange rates were corrected.[2] And, in some cases, existing restrictions on foreign direct investment were relaxed in order to encourage imports of capital and technology to support industrial development. Thus, while a broad range of other controls was retained, the new Asian development model provided an example

---

1. The Korean government managed exports through government trading companies affiliated with major chaebols.

2. Indeed, sometimes they were perhaps overcorrected, as in the case of China beginning in 1994–5. Adams (2006, 131) suggests that in 2003 regional currencies were substantially undervalued: by 78% in China, 77% in the Philippines, 71% in Thailand, and 33% in Korea.

(if perhaps only a disingenuous one) to which the World Bank and others could point for some validation of the principles of economic liberalization. And, for this reason, despite the variably important role of East Asian developmental states in guiding, subsidizing, and encouraging export-led development, it is nonetheless clear that the associated expansion of trade and liberalization of imports of manufacturing inputs and capital goods necessary for exporters did constitute a first step toward a broader and more coherent program of market-oriented economic reform. Further, cases of EOI-led industrialization in Southeast Asia and elsewhere during the 1980s and early 1990s, occurring as they did in the new world-historical period of full-blown neoliberalism, have in fact privileged markets more fully than did their neomercantilist predecessors. This difference is seen in the closer association among late EOI-transition countries between external trade liberalization and export promotion, an association that arguably has tended to lock some economies into cost-driven export-market niches to a greater extent than was true of their more statist East Asian predecessors, where activist governments enjoyed greater latitude in engineering industrial-structural transitions to higher-value products and markets in the 1970s and early 1980s.[3] The Philippines, however, presents a stark contrast with that earlier experience of dynamic upgrading. There, a fuller early embrace of market reform was associated with lack of substantial developmental upgrading, as dramatically exemplified by the continuing confinement of the export-oriented electronics and electrical equipment industries to low value-added assembly and testing (McKay 2006, 47).

Export-Oriented Industrialization

The East Asian industrial miracle that has so captured the attention of economists and social scientists has, particularly during recent decades, centered less on rapid industrialization per se than on the (often strategic) insertion of local manufacturing and assembly operations into world markets and production networks.[4] While manufacturing did advance dramatically during the 1970s and 1980s in Korea, it accounted for the same percent of national GDP in 2008 (28%) as it had in 1995 (World Bank 2010). During that same

---

3. Despite WTO rules restricting the use of export subsidies and special import duties, China may continue to rely on these and related practices in support of export-led development. See "U.S. Complains to WTO on China." *USA Today,* April 10, 2007.

4. By world standards Asian manufacturing has grown dramatically. Here the focus shifts to the percentage contribution of manufacturing to national GDP.

thirteen-year period, Chinese manufacturing continued to account for 34 percent of GDP, while that in the Philippines declined slightly from 23 to 22 percent. Only in Thailand did manufacturing increase its contribution to GDP, from 30 to 35 percent.

Rather, the structural imprint of Asian EOI only becomes evident when looking at data on the growth of manufactured exports (table 4.1). In these four countries, the percentage contribution of exports to GDP rose dramatically up until the global recession that briefly, if sharply, disrupted exports across the region.

Export growth was, in turn, strongly driven by manufacturing, which now makes up the lion's share of total exports in all four countries. As exports have grown, the economic role of domestic consumption has correspondingly declined, a matter of growing national and international concern during later years. I return to this problematic economic outcome in chapter 7.

Of course, Asia's industrial miracles could not sustainably rely only on sweat-intensive production for wealthy consumers in affluent countries. Early Asian EOI typically centered on such traditional manufactured exports as textiles, wearing apparel, toys, and footwear. Later, second-stage EOI included such high-tech but still labor-intensive industries as electronics assembly and precision and scientific instruments. During this later stage, capital deepening and, in some cases, skill-intensification, particularly in new industries that were often less export oriented, reflected both developmental state policies and new international opportunities that permitted a transition to higher value-added activities. This transition is reflected in data on temporal trends in the export mix of particular stages of production that cut across industries. In his book about Asian technology development from 1995 to 2001, Adams (2006) finds the percentage changes in export growth rates for selected categories of manufacturing that are shown in table 4.2.

Table 4.1   Growth in Exports and Export Manufacturing

Country	Exports of goods and services[a] Percentage of GDP (%)			Manufacturing exports[b] Percentage of total merchandise exports (%)				
	1990	1995	2009	1985	1990	1995	2000	2008
China	15	23	27	32	50	84	85	93
South Korea	28	29	50	89	90	93	83	89
Philippines	28	36	32	60	73	42	86	83
Thailand	34	42	68	40	62	73	70	74

[a]1990 and 2009 from ADB, *Key Indicators 2010* and 1995 and 2008 from World Bank, *World Development Indicators 2010*.

[b]World Bank, *World Development Report 2010*, except 1995 and 2008, which are from World Bank, *World Development Indicators 2010*.

Table 4.2 Average Annual Percentage of Change in East Asian Manufactured Exports by Stage of Production and Sector, 1995–2001[a]

Country	Mass production	High-tech/ capital goods	High-tech sectors (SITC category)			Low-tech sectors (SITC category)			
			75	76	77	83	84	85	89
China	6.9	15.0	26.5	14.1	17.3	−0.2	16.7	4.2	−0.9
Korea	−2.0	3.9	−4.5	16.7	−2.6	9.8	−3.4	−4.8	−13.4
Thailand	−3.0	5.3	−0.4	−2.1	−2.4	−16.7	−21.1	−0.8	−0.3
Philippines	−0.6	4.5	−8.0	1.6	13.3	−4.7	−12.6	1.0	−0.8

Sources: Adapted from Adams 2006, 127–28.

[a] Standard International Trade Classification (SITC): 75 = office machines; 76 = telecoms; 77 = electrical machinery and parts; 83 = travel goods, handbags; 84 = clothing and accessories; 85 = footwear; 89 = miscellaneous low-tech manufactures.

These data show continued growth in mass production in China, alongside a relative decline of mass production in the other three countries. In Korea, the high-tech telecommunications-equipment category is the fastest growing, while in the Philippines, electronics and electrical machinery has expanded rapidly, even as textiles and wearing apparel have declined (Ofreneo 2009).[5] Labor-intensive clothing, travel goods, and handbags production continues to grow in China, rapidly displacing Thai and Philippine clothing exports.

As economic structures have variably matured, the export mix has moved to more capital-intensive and/or high-technology, higher value-added goods and services. As a percentage of total manufacturing in the Philippines, value-added goods and machinery and transportation equipment have increased from 20 percent in 1995 to 30 percent in 2005 (World Bank 2010). In China, while low-technology, labor-intensive exports still contribute importantly to economic growth, exports of machinery, electronics products, and transportation equipment have all expanded rapidly during recent years,[6] with electronic products and machinery accounting for nearly two-fifths of Chinese merchandise export earnings in 2003 (ESCAP 2004, 47).

In industrially advanced Korea, the more mixed export trends reflect a broad-based shift from manufacturing production to services and other sectors, while manufacturing has itself moved away from direct production, which has been increasingly relocated to China and to lower-cost countries in Southeast Asia. Despite these changes, the Korean economy has remained

5. Electronics accounted for over 60% of total Philippine exports in January 2011. "Electronics Sector Takes a Hit from Costlier Fuel," *Manila Times* (online), March, 11 2011.

6. In 2005 machinery and transportation equipment still contributed only 3% to total value-added manufacturing in China (World Bank 2010).

highly trade dependent, even as it has sought to expand consumer credit in an effort to reduce external trade vulnerabilities in favor of greater reliance on domestic consumption. Korean manufacturing itself has continued to transition into heavy and high-tech industries. In this regard, United Nations Industrial Development Organization (UNIDO) data on trends in industrial production from 1995 to 2006 show dramatic gains in the categories of basic metals; machinery and equipment; office, accounting, and computing machinery; electrical machinery; and transport equipment, including motor vehicles (UNIDO 2009). Particularly dramatic is the increase in the percentage contribution of machinery and transportation equipment to value-added manufacturing: from 40 percent in 1995 to 50 percent in 2005 (World Bank 2010).

The shift to higher value-added exports is similarly dramatic in Thailand, where the greatest precrisis declines were in labor-intensive export industries such as garments and footwear (Athukorala et al. 2000, 12), and where higher-technology exports such as integrated circuits, computers and parts, and motor vehicles and parts now account for a substantial portion of exports. Most dramatic perhaps is development of the auto and truck industry.[7] Thailand is the second-largest pickup truck manufacturer in the world and sought in the early 'oos to expand light-truck exports beyond regional markets to the United States under a proposed Thai-U.S. free-trade agreement that would have reduced high U.S. tariffs on these vehicles.[8]

Philippine exports are heavily concentrated in electronics and primary-commodity processing (Laquian 2005; also see Asian Development Bank 2007). By 2005, electronics equipment (especially semiconductor assembly) alone constituted almost 70 percent of all exports from the Philippines (*Philippine Statistical Yearbook*). The restriction of this and other export-manufacturing sectors to mainly low- and medium-skill production reflects a largely market-driven rather than developmentalist industrial policy (Haggard and Dohner 1994). This difference is seen in a relatively greater reliance in this country than in the others on multinational firms, less effort spent on nurturing local suppliers or on technology development, greater financial incentives to attract foreign investors, and fewer performance requirements for foreign firms (McKay 2006, 55; also see Bello et al. 2006). By consequence, despite very rapid expansion in electronics and other labor-intensive exports during the mid-1990s, Philippine exports are MNC-dominated and strongly

---

7. Doner (2009), however, notes the substantial displacement of the domestic auto parts sector by foreign and transplant production following the financial crisis.

8. "Big Stakes Hang Up U.S.-Thai Trade Pact," *Wall Street Journal*, January 30, 2006.

concentrated in the lower-value rungs of only a few industries. As well, a more general stagnation in manufacturing is reflected in an across-the-board decline in the index of industrial production for almost all categories of industry from 2000 to 2006, with the exception of two categories, basic metals and fabricated metal products (UNIDO 2009). During this same period, there was an overall decline in the index of industrial production from 100 in 2000 to 86 in 2006.

State-Enterprise Reform

State-enterprise reform is a second strand of economic restructuring that has transformed Asian employment. In Thailand and the Philippines, SOE privatization began in the early 1980s and accelerated in the 1990s under the terms and conditionalities attached to international structural-adjustment loans. In the Philippines, the government was pressed to reverse its 1970's nationalization program under which the state-enterprise sector had grown rapidly (Haggard and Dohner 1994). Later, beginning especially during the Ramos presidency (1992–98), a number of infrastructure and service sectors, including water, power, sewage systems, and shipyards were either sold off or contracted out to private business groups,[9] in some cases partnered with international companies (Laquian 2005; Bello et al. 2006, chap. 3). Most critical from the standpoint of social policy were new initiatives to privatize or defund health services,[10] education, and pension funds (Bello et al. 2006).

But it was China's turn to "market socialism" beginning in the late 1970s and accelerating during the 1980s and 1990s that offers the best-documented and most extensively studied case of the social impact of SOE reform in the Asian region. Initially, reform centered on exposing state enterprises to increased market pressures, on enhancing their operational autonomy and flexibility (extending to employment practices and policy), and on creating new incentives for improved productivity and efficiency (Taylor 2002). Under a related policy of decentralization, state enterprises were given the right to retain a greater share of profits, SOE managerial discretion was expanded, and government funding was partially replaced by market-based bank lending.

It was only in the mid-1990s that outright privatization began to supplant SOE managerial reforms in China. In 1995–6, many small SOEs were sold off to private buyers under a strategy of "grasping the large, letting go of the

---

9. "State Stake in Subic Shipyard for Sale," *Manila Times* (online), January 8, 2011.

10. "GOCC Subsidies Cut by Nearly Half in Aquino's First Month," *Manila Times* (online), August 23, 2010.

small" (Zhua Da Fang Xiao), resulting in the elimination of over 10 million jobs. Between 1994 and 2003, over three thousand Chinese state-owned enterprises were closed or declared bankrupt, while 80 percent of county-level SOEs and 60 percent of municipal SOEs were privatized. After 2002 many other SOEs were transformed into companies with shareholders, thus paving the way for possible later privatization under the direction of the State-Owned Asset Supervision and Administration Commission. In general, larger national-level SOEs that have been profitable and that operate in strategically important sectors have been retained by the state.[11] This selectivity in the privatization process is borne out by data for the period 1999 to 2004 that show a dramatic decline in the total number of state-run companies (from 61,301 to 31,750), a substantial reduction in the number of unprofitable enterprises, and significant increases in overall profitability within the now-smaller SOE sector.[12]

Changing Structures of Employment

Associated with these dramatic reform-driven changes in economic structures have been related changes in the industrial distribution of national workforces.

In all cases, employment in agriculture has declined, largely in favor of the rapidly growing services sector. Only in Thailand has the percentage of industrial employees continued to grow over the entire period. In the Philippines, industrial employment has been stagnant over the past three decades, while that in Korea is high but in noticeable decline, reflecting the gradual movement of labor-intensive industrial production to China and other low-wage countries and the corresponding shift of employment from light to heavy industries and to modern service sectors. But let us look more specifically at manufacturing, the focus of this book, in each of the four countries.

China

China most dramatically exemplifies the pattern of light first-stage EOI, with large numbers of low-skilled workers, many of whom are migrants from rural areas, flooding into coastal export-processing centers to take up jobs in the rapidly growing factories and small workshops producing shoes, clothing,

11. "State-Owned Firms' Profits Soar Tenfold," *South China Morning Post* (online edition), March 25, 2005.

12. "China Seeks to Cut State-Run Firms," *Wall Street Journal*, April 13, 2006.

and toys for world markets (Meng 2002). Initially, in 1980, four "special economic zones" were established along the coast in areas adjacent to Hong Kong and Taiwan. As these zones grew and flourished, more zones were established, at first along the coast but increasingly in inland provinces as well (World Bank 2004, 167), employing over 30 million workers by 2002.[13] In late 2004, it was estimated that 114 million migrants, initially seasonal but increasingly geographically settled, worked in cities, many in export zones.[14] While urban export zones produce a large percentage of all manufactured exports, nearly one-third of those exports are still produced by the town and village enterprises (TVEs) that flourished in smaller towns following agricultural liberalization in the 1980s.

But what of trends since 1985? Table 4.3 shows trends in manufacturing employment in these four countries over a twenty-five-year period.[15]

The decline in Chinese manufacturing employment between 1990 and 2000, despite increasing manufacturing output and exports, reflects in part the massive layoffs associated with SOE reform during that period. The Asia Development Bank estimates those layoffs as being more than 36 million between 1995 and 2002, eventuating in a 15 percent decline in manufacturing employment during that period (ADB 2005 [based on ILO 2004]).[16] That change contrasts with substantial growth in service-sector jobs, which have grown at a rate four times that of industrial jobs since 1973.[17]

Another explanation for the longer-term decline or stagnation in Chinese manufacturing employment relates to productivity gains, and points to the displacement of inefficient, employment-bloated SOEs as well as large numbers of labor-intensive TVEs by lean, larger-scale private-sector firms, reflected in growing manufacturing output and exports alongside declining total manufacturing employment. This argument is supported by World Bank estimates that Chinese labor productivity in manufacturing improved

---

13. The relative scale of Chinese export manufacturing is suggested by the fact that Chinese export zones employ nearly three-quarters of all such zone workers in the entire world (World Bank 2004, 168 [table 8.1]).

14. "In Chinese Factory, Rhythms of Trade Replace Rural Life," *Wall Street Journal,* December 31, 2004.

15. A word of caution: in view of important differences in the scope and methodologies of employment surveys across these four countries, these data should be seen as suggesting national *trends* but not actual *cross-national differences* in the percentage contribution of manufacturing employment to total employment.

16. It is further estimated that private-sector employment grew by 20% during this period, versus only 9% for the entire economy.

17. "Economic Focus," *Economist,* January 27, 2007.

by an average of 23 percent per year from 2002 to 2006.[18] ESCAP data, as well, show markedly faster productivity growth in China from 2000 to 2005 (11%) than elsewhere in Asia, or in the world as a whole (ESCAP 2008).[19]

A third explanation for declining manufacturing employment relates less to efficiency gains than to a possible *informalization* of employment under China's early phase EOI. If, given a formal-sector bias in employment data collection, we assume "paid manufacturing employment" is a rough proxy for registered (formal-sector) employment, stagnation in manufacturing employment may in small part only mirror the increase in unregistered employment in small private-sector firms that often operate outside the purview of the state. Partial support for this explanation comes from Asian Development Bank data showing formal-sector job growth from 1995 to 2002 of 17.5 million, as against 75 million new jobs in the informal sector during those years (ADB 2005).

Korea

If China presents a case of transitional EOI-led development still strongly dependent on light, labor-intensive export manufacturing, Korea presents the very different case of an industrially more mature, if still export-dependent, economy. Table 4.3 shows early growth in the relative share of manufacturing employment, followed by a gradual decline beginning in the 1990s as industry shifted into more capital-intensive activities, as labor-intensive production migrated to countries with cheaper labor, and as the modern service sector grew in relative importance. It is important to note that this employment decline was not associated with a decline in the economic role of manufacturing more generally, which remained at 28–29 percent of GDP through the 1990s and up to 2006. This role, however, has increasingly centered on manufacturing services, R & D, financial services, and logistics, rather than on production itself (Yoo-Sun Kim 2007).

Thailand

Contrary to trends in the other countries, Thailand's manufacturing workforce as a percentage of total employment grew substantially during the

---

18. Andrew Batson, "Chinese Inflation: A Complex Picture," *Wall Street Journal,* November 14, 2007.

19. ESCAP reports Chinese productivity growth during this period at 11% versus 4% in Korea, 2.5% in the Philippines, 4.3% in Thailand, and 3.2% worldwide (ESCAP 2008).

Table 4.3   Manufacturing Employment (Percentage of Total)[a]

Country	1985	1990	2000	2002/3	2007/8
China[b] (a)	15 (1987)	13	11	11	—
(b)	—	—	—	27	29
Korea	23	27	20	—	17
Thailand	9	10	15 (2002)	—	14
Philippines	10	10	10	—	9

[a] ILO, LABORSTA, http://laborsta.ilo.org.

[b] (a) 1987–2002, using International Standard Industrial Classification (ISIC) Revision 2; (b) 2003–8, using ISIC Revision 3.

1990s, a trend only briefly interrupted by the financial crisis of 1997–98. This expansion in manufacturing employment reflects not only substantial growth in export-led manufacturing and more sluggish growth in the service sector (particularly finance, severely hit by the financial crisis), but also the high labor intensity of much Thai manufacturing, at least through the mid-1990s, when growing shortages of unskilled labor began to undercut this country's cheap-labor export strategy and to encourage restructuring and a transition to automotive and other capital and skill-intensive industries (Athukorala 2000, 39).[20]

Philippines

Unlike China, where rapid EOI expansion alongside privatization has been associated with a gradual decline in the percentage of workers in manufacturing despite continued increases in the volume of manufacturing production, and unlike Korea, where a more dramatic percentage decline in manufacturing employment was associated with a gradual transition out of standard production manufacturing activities, stagnant manufacturing employment in the Philippines is rooted in what is sometimes seen as a partially failed EOI strategy (Bello et al. 2006). Here, growth in two labor-intensive sectors, textiles and clothing, during the 1980s and early 1990s, and electronics, since the mid-1990s, has not been accompanied by growth in most other manufacturing sectors.[21] That dramatic growth in electronics employment did not

---

20. Japanese auto assemblers and auto parts industries alone employed 122,000 workers in Thailand in 2004–5 (ANN).

21. Hal Hill estimates that labor-intensive manufacturing employment increased from 48% of total manufacturing employment in 1975 to 57% in 1988 and 59% in 1997. In 1997 food processing, electronics, and garments together accounted for more than 46% of all manufacturing employment (Hill 2003, 229).

propel overall growth in manufacturing employment is in part explained by the concomitant decline in the garment industry: from almost a million workers in the early 1990s to around 300,000 in 2006 (Ofreneo 2009, 544).

In part this stagnation in manufacturing employment stems from an absence of strong domestic multiplier effects among industries, an absence linked to extensive reliance on foreign companies for investment, imported parts, R & D services, and marketing arrangements, and in part it is rooted in the institutional isolation of much export production within export-processing zones, industrial parks, and high-tech enclaves (Laquian 2005, 109). Lacking, above all, are linkages to a growing domestic supplier base that might have built on and generalized the growth of the few externally oriented sectors that dominate Philippine exports. In the case of garment production, re-export legislation encourages garment producers to import fabrics and other inputs from overseas suppliers without paying duty so long as finished garments are then exported to foreign markets (Ofreneo 2009). Lack of substantial employment creation in manufacturing has in turn contributed to rates of unemployment that are high by regional standards, at over 10 percent during the otherwise booming 1990s (Herrin and Pernia 2003, 229, 293).[22] Absent a coherent industrial strategy, these developmental impediments have not been addressed as they have been in the other three countries.

Consequences of First-Stage EOI

The labor impact of EOI, of course, goes far beyond the redistribution of employment across industrial sectors. More important here are the changing employment practices with which those distributional changes are associated. The export zones established during early periods of light labor-intensive export manufacturing were strongly cost driven. Cost pressures have increased under the intensified competition generated by continuing globalization. In this regard, China-based exporters, especially those in which Taiwanese, Hong Kong, and South Korean firms are invested, have sometimes tried to push pay and benefits below even market-clearing levels, in part through reliance on physical intimidation, labor bonding, and a variety of other coercive measures, in many cases in contravention of Chinese labor law (Chan 2001).

First-stage export-processing zones typically permit or encourage relatively flexible labor markets with less stringent employer mandates than

---

22. Estimated at over 19% if underemployed are included (ADB 2010).

apply to other formal-sector firms or to state enterprises, precisely to attract domestic, and especially international, investors seeking investment sites for low-cost production. Thailand's newly proposed "special economic zones," for example, are exempt from much industrial regulation, including less-restricted access to alien labor (itself in part a response to increasing wage pressures),[23] while firms operating in China's export-oriented economic zones tend to offer more short-term work contracts and to enjoy less strict work-hour regulation than do SOEs or collectively owned firms (Chen and Hou 2008). Aihwa Ong notes in this regard that the special economic zones along the east coast were created precisely to allow markets, rather than social or political considerations, to drive economic activity, and to exempt the large numbers of migrant workers who seek work in the zones from many of the labor laws and protections that are enjoyed by workers with urban residency (Ong 2006, 104–6). In China's even-less-regulated informal-export zones, such as those adjacent to but outside the government-established Shenzhen Industrial Zone in Guangdong, employment is even less regulated than in the statutory zones themselves.

Growth in export zones may thus have the effect of shifting large numbers of workers, particularly young women during early EOI, into employment sectors that lack the locally embedded social and governmental regulations and protections found outside those zones. The initial outcome is thus to casualize a substantial portion of industrial-zone labor while at the same time intensifying despotic labor controls over workers and unions, controls reinforced by local and zone authorities who typically share in the benefits of rapid growth through both tax revenues and joint ventures with private and foreign investors.

Second-Stage EOI and Industrial Upgrading: Implications for Workers

To this point the discussion has emphasized the employment outcomes of early labor-intensive EOI. But what of strategies and structural transitions to higher-value high-tech exports, heavy and chemical industries, and modern service activities? The earlier data on industrially advanced Korea suggested stagnation in manufacturing employment, as workers either moved into higher-value activities that are ancillary to manufacturing but not included in manufacturing employment per se or, alternatively found work outside

---

23. "Economic Zone Bill 'Risk to Sovereignty,'" *Bangkok Post* (online), May 16, 2005.

manufacturing altogether, especially in modern services. This shift has its own employment consequences, as workers move into the quite different labor systems associated with those more-demanding activities.

Confining attention to manufacturing itself, we can see variation in the extent of employment movement out of first-stage EOI sectors into higher technology- and capital-intensive sectors in the four countries (table 4.4).

China shows relative stagnation in employment in traditional labor-intensive exports as well as in a sharper decline in heavy industry alongside rapid growth in high-tech labor-intensive exports (e.g., electronics and electrical machinery

Table 4.4 Industrial Distribution of Manufacturing Workers by Selected ISIC Categories (Percentage of Total Manufacturing)[a]

Country and year	Traditional light EOI[b]	High-tech light EOI[c]	Heavy/chemical industries[d]
China[e]			
1990	16.9	7.0	45.6
2000	20.6	10.8	36.1
2008	18.3	16.5	27.5
Korea[f]			
1995	22.4	12.2	27.0
2000	20.7	14.5	27.1
2006	15.1	21.0	34.0
2008	15.0	20.5	32.7
Thailand			
1989	36.6	6.8	8.6
1996	24.9	12.5	10.7
2000	29.1 (2001)	15.4	11.9
2003	19.7	18.3	14.8 (2001)
Philippines[g]			
1985	27.5	6.9	8.9
1990	28.5	7.3	7.5
1996	26.2	17.0	11.3
—	—	—	—
2001	25.6	12.3	12.5
2008	21.3	16.8	11.0

[a] Paid manufacturing employment only.

[b] "Traditional" refers to textiles, wearing apparel, leather products, leather footwear, and plastic products. EOI = export oriented industries.

[c] "High-tech" refers to industries with high R & D content. Light labor–intensive EOI industries include electrical machinery, electronics, professional and scientific instruments.

[d] Basic and industrial chemicals, petroleum refining, basic metals (including iron and steel), nonelectrical and general purpose machinery, vehicles and transport equipment.

[e] *China Labor Statistics Yearbook 2009.* The Chinese data should be interpreted with caution. 1990 includes state-owned enterprises only. 2000 and 2008 include both private and state enterprises with annual sales greater than 5 million yuan.

[f] UNIDO, *International Yearbook of Industrial Statistics,* various years; and Korean Ministry of Labor, *Yearbook of Labor Statistics 2008.*

[g] Until 1991, establishments with 20 or more employees. For 1992–98, establishments with 10 or more employees. From 1999, establishments with 20 or more employees. 1985–1996 from UNIDO International Yearbook of Industrial Statistics. 2001–2008 from ILO, LABORSTA, http://laborsta.ilo.org.

and appliances) (Chiu and Frenkel 2000, 19). Reflecting a gradual decline in employment in both rural and SOE heavy-industry sectors, China's employment has incrementally shifted from heavy industries into the high-tech industrial sectors led by companies headquartered in the United States, Japan, and Europe. Korea shows a similar decline in traditional exports alongside continuing growth in both high-tech and heavy industries,[24] the former led by relatively high wage, high value-added products and the latter reflecting Korea's huge international successes in auto manufacturing, steelmaking, shipbuilding, and aircraft-parts manufacture.

Augmenting the Value of Labor

Industrial upgrading into higher-value activities, an important aspect of development, is closely related to an increasing value of labor itself. In part, this may be seen in the contrast between the value added by workers in industrially advanced Korea, on the one hand, and that in the more industrially stagnant Philippines, on the other. The value added and average wage or salary per employee in selected manufacturing industries in these two countries is shown in table 4.5.

This table invites several observations. First, the Korean data in particular show dramatic increases in both value added and average pay levels as the industrial mix moves into more capital- or technology-intensive industrial categories. Second, even within particular industrial categories, Korea's significant technological (and presumably human capital) lead over the Philippines is reflected in dramatic *intra*-industry differences between these two countries, differences that from the standpoint of employers signifies the greater economic "value" of Korean employees than of their Philippine counterparts. This difference in the economic value of workers is associated with greater efforts by Korean employers to retain and motivate their employees.

Upgrading and Occupational Change

Have differences in industrial upgrading and employment restructuring been reflected in changes in the *occupational* distribution of workers in manufacturing? Has there been a corresponding increase in the percentage of workers in technical and skilled jobs? Unfortunately, available ILO statistics are of

---

24. In the case of high tech, emphasis is on high-wage, skilled, and technical activities rather than the simple assembly operations that tend to predominate in the other three countries.

Table 4.5   Value Added and Average Pay Per Employee: Selected Manufacturing Industries

Industry	Korea (2006)		Philippines (2005)	
	Value added[a]	Average pay[b]	Value added[a]	Average pay[b]
Textiles	58.5	20,000	4.2	2,000
Furniture	71.4	22,000	4.1	1,800
Machinery	97.0	26,900	—	—
Office and computing machinery	134.1	27,400	11.9	2,700
TV and radio receivers	104.7	33,500	10.7	2,000
Basic chemicals	247.4	41,400	13.7	2,900
Motor vehicles	251.0	54,900	—	—
Iron/steel	274.2	38,600	13.6	2,600

Source: UNIDO 2009.

[a] In early 2011 U.S. thousand dollars.
[b] In early 2011 U.S. dollars.

only marginal use in answering this question.[25] Most countries have, until recently, utilized a 1968 version of the International Standard Classification of Occupations, which offered a very crude indicator of occupational status, failing in particular to distinguish clearly among professional, technical, craft, skilled, and assembly workers. It was only with the introduction of the 1988 ISCO that these finer, and for our purposes very important, distinctions were made. But most regional countries did not adopt the 1988 protocol for some years. We do, however, have ILO 1988 ISCO data for Korea beginning in 1994. While much of Korea's industrial restructuring had begun before 1994, data for subsequent years clearly show the continuing imprint of industrial upgrading for the skill levels of manufacturing workers. Between 1994 and 2007, professional and technical employment increased from 8 to 15 percent of total manufacturing employment, while production workers (disregarding the 2000 figures that reflect the many manufacturing layoffs associated with the late 1990's financial crisis) declined modestly, from 33 to 30 percent of the total, reflecting in part the relocation of standard production to China and elsewhere in the region. Other data based an enterprise surveys, and covering a longer time period, highlight this change more dramatically. Between 1985 and 2006, the ratio of professional and technical to production workers in Korean manufacturing firms more than doubled, increasing from 100:409 to 100:194.[26] By contrast, the corresponding ratio for the

---

25. Based in turn on the national labor force and enterprise surveys conducted by ILO member countries.

26. Data compiled by Kwang-kun Lee, from ILO data, based on Korea industrial census surveys, provide further confirmation of this trend for the critical transitional years 1980–1993, during which

more stagnant Philippine manufacturing sector remained largely unchanged during the 1990s, at roughly 1:30 to 1:35 (table 4.6).[27]

The increase in the ratio of Korean technical workers to production workers has had important consequences for employment practices, as firms seek to retain their technical and skilled workers and to insulate them from the harsher employment practices associated with low-skilled work. Industrial upgrading may thus encourage both progressive labor practices and a macroregulatory shift to policies that encourage more positive, commitment-engendering labor strategies on the part of firms. Conversely, of course, other changes associated with globalization and labor-market reform have tended to discourage precisely those practices, a matter to which I return below.

State-Enterprise Reform and Its Employment Outcomes

As suggested earlier, state-enterprise reform goes well beyond a simple question of ownership. More generally, such reform may be understood as a form of labor deregulation, as direct employment regulation on the part of the state gives way to more autonomous regulation on the part of marketized SOEs, of authorities in semiautonomous economic zones, and, in cases of outright privatization, of private-sector managers.

As also noted, in the context of privatization, mergers, bankruptcy, and liquidation, state-enterprise employment in China fell dramatically during the late 1990s. By 1995 employment in publicly owned enterprises had declined to only 11 percent of total employment, and thereafter it declined even further to 8 percent in 1998.[28] Between 1994 and 2002, total SOE employment declined from 148 million to 105 million (ILO 2004; ADB 2004). During this same period, SOE manufacturing employment declined from 54 million to 29 million. The large majority of those losses occurred among small and medium-sized SOEs. By contrast, private-sector employment increased rapidly, to over 55 million workers in private and individual enterprises in 2004 (Chen and Hou 2008). Between 1990 and 2002, private-sector manufacturing employment increased from roughly 5 to 26 percent of total manufacturing employment (*China Statistical Yearbook*). This dramatic transition, associated with employment growth in export-processing zones,

---

the ratio of professional and technical workers to production workers and laborers in manufacturing increased from 1:119 to 1:22.

27. Bureau of Labor and Employment Statistics, DOLE, *2006 Philippine Industry Yearbook of Labor Statistics*. Also DOLE, *Yearbook of Labor Statistics*, annual.

28. ILO, Labor Statistics online, http://laborsta.ilo.org/cgi-bin/brokerv8.exe.

Table 4.6 Percentage of Korean Manufacturing Workers in Selected Occupations: Total and by Sex

Year	Professionals			Associate-professionals/ technicians			Craft and skilled trades workers			Operators/ assemblers			Unskilled laborers		
	Total	M	F	Total	M	F	Total	M	F	Total	M	F	Total	M	F
1994	2	2	1	6	7	3	31	31	29	33	34	32	9	4	17
2000	3	4	2	8	11	2	31	29	35	26	31	18	13	6	25
2007	5	6	4	10	12	4	21	21	21	30	35	21	13	6	29

Source: ILO, LABORSTA, http://laborsta.ilo.org.

has eventuated in a relative shrinkage of employment in "protected" labor sectors in favor of expansion of private economic sectors and locations where labor protections are more minimal.

In non-Socialist Asian countries, privatization has been less significant and less consequential for employment. In those countries, SOE employment, and public-sector employment more generally, made up a far smaller portion of total employment at the outset of reform. For the Philippines, ILO data show that publicly owned enterprises accounted for 5 percent of total employment in 1985 and 6 percent in 1999, with total public-sector employment remaining constant at roughly 8 percent from 1985 through 2006. In Korea, state-enterprise employment increased from 258,391 in 1986 to 299,161 in 1990, thereafter peaking at 330,866 in 1995 and subsequently declining to 286,211 in 2002 (Korean Ministry of Finance). Corresponding ILO data for Thailand show public-sector employment at 6 percent in 1985 and edging slightly upward to between 8 and 9 percent from 2000 to 2006. In this instance, declines in state employment in enterprises under the ministries of transport, interior, and industry were offset by employment growth in enterprises under the ministries of finance and public health.

In these two countries, the primary target of reform was the strongly unionized public-utilities sector. Under IMF loan conditionalities agreed to during the financial crisis, both governments pledged to accelerate privatization and government divestiture in this sector. But, despite concerted efforts to carry through with these pledges, there was little real progress. In the case of the Philippines, of course, most public utilities were already in private hands. There, government employment dropped from 26 to 21 percent of total sectoral employment from 2001 to 2005. In the Thai case, government employment as a percentage of total utilities employment barely declined at all: from 94 percent in 1994 to 93 percent in 2004. In both cases the explanation for lack of utilities reform is mainly to be found in strong political opposition mounted by public-sector unions, a topic to which I return in later chapters.

EOI and the Feminization of the Industrial Labor Force?

Teri Caraway (2006) has documented a regionwide association between first-stage Asian EOI and increasing percentages of females among manufacturing-production workers. Her analysis suggests that this feminization of the manufacturing workforce is linked to high levels of labor intensity and competitive market pressures found among expanding export industries such as textiles and garments, plastic products, sports shoes, and electronics (see also World Bank, *World Development Indicators,* 2001). In the context of her Indonesian fieldwork, Caraway shows that this workforce transition may have flowed as much from the feminization of existing, previously male-dominated industries as from the emergence of new labor-intensive export industries. A 1999 United Nations report finds a similar pattern of early feminization followed by defeminization as advancing industries in middle-income countries become increasingly skilled and capital intensive.[29]

Female manufacturing employment trends in the four countries are shown in table 4.7. Consistent with Caraway's discussion, these data show a modest increase in the female percentage of manufacturing workers during the 1980s and early 1990s, a time of expanding light-manufacturing exports, followed by a slight percentage decline in the first decade of the 2000s. During the earlier period, large numbers of rural women workers were drawn into rapidly growing export-processing zones,[30] a trend reflected in an increase in the percentage of all females working in industry from 13.7 percent in 1980 to 16.8 percent in 1990 alongside a corresponding decline in the percentage of all males working in industrial jobs: from 17.2 percent in 1980 to 13.5 percent in 1990 (ADB 2003, 97). Many of these industrially employed women found work in the small- and medium-sized firms set up by overseas Chinese to produce garments, toys, and other light-manufacturing goods for export. Given their primary focus on low-cost production, these employers relied heavily on young migrant workers willing to accept low wages, poor working conditions, harsh work discipline, and insecure employment (Chiu and Frenkel 2000, 23). The large numbers of women flooding into export manufacturing, along with ongoing reductions in more male-intensive SOE manufacturing,[31] contributed to the earlier noted feminization of the industrial workforce during the 1980s and early 1990s.

In Korea, female employment in manufacturing peaked during the late 1980s, following which the percentage of male workers rose as heavy and chemical industries begin to supplant early first-stage export manufacturing (Sundaram 2009). This decline in the female intensity of Korean

29. Employment and Displacement Effects of Globalization," in *The 1999 World Survey on the Role of Women in Development: Globalization, Gender, and Work* (New York: United Nations, Division for the Advancement of Women). Cited in Sundaram (2009).

30. Ngai (1999) notes the common reference to these workers as "dagongmei," or unmarried temporary female workers, and the common experience among these workers in SMEs of nonpayment or delayed payment of due wages. Cited in Lin 2010.

31. ILO data for the mid-1990s show male employment roughly 73% greater than female employment in publicly owned enterprises. ILO, Labor Statistics online, http://laborsta.ilo.org/cgi-bin/brokerv8.exe.

Table 4.7   Females as a Percentage of Total Manufacturing Employment[a]

Year	China	South Korea	Philippines	Thailand[b]
1960	—	27	—	38
1980	—	39	—	42
1985	40	39	49	45
1990	44	43	46	50
1995	45	36	—	50
2000	43	36	—	49
2002	43	36	46	53
2008	42	32	45	54
2009	—	—	—	53

Sources: ILO, *Yearbook of Labour Statistics.* Philippines after 2002 from *2006 Philippine Statistical Yearbook.* China, from *China Labor Statistical Yearbook.*

[a] Figures for China refer to percentages of paid employees in urban factories only. For other countries, figures refer to shares of total manufacturing employment based on national surveys. China: figures after 1997 exclude laid-off workers still on enterprise rolls. Korea 1960 and various for the 1980s, and Thailand to 1993, from Jomo Kwame Sundaram (2009). Korea from 1990: *Yearbook of Labor Statistics.*

[b] Thai data from 2001 not comparable with earlier data due to a change in statistical protocol.

manufacturing is further confirmed by ILO data showing an increase in the percentage of all employed females working in industry, from 23.8 percent in 1980 to 30.2 percent in 1990, followed by a sharp decline to only 19.2 percent in 2001 (ADB 2003).

Quite different are the Philippine and Thai cases. There, a continuing emphasis on light-manufacturing exports and a more modest increase in skill-intensive and heavy industry have been accompanied by a continuance of high levels of female employment in manufacturing and indeed a modest *increase* in the percentage of all employed females who are working in industry. In Philippine export zones, in particular, females still make up nearly 80 percent of all workers (*Asian Labour Update,* April–June 2009).

As important as percentage changes in the female share of overall manufacturing employment are, corresponding changes among manufacturing *production* workers themselves are more telling, for it is there that EOI growth had its greatest impact. The trends in female percentage shares of skilled and assembly and production workers can be seen in table 4.8.

While pre-1995 data for the Philippines and Thailand fail to distinguish craft and skilled workers from assembly workers, several trends and contrasts may be seen. Korea in particular shows little decline in the female share of operators and assemblers, but a sharp decline in the percentage of female workers in craft occupations and the skilled trades. Thus, to the extent the (proportionately) shrinking manufacturing sector has experienced an upgrading into more skilled occupations, women have apparently failed to

Table 4.8 Females As a Percentage of All Workers in Selected Production-Related Occupations[a]

Year	Korea		Philippines		Thailand	
	Craft/Skilled Trades	Operatives/ Assemblers	Craft	Operatives	Craft	Operatives
1995	24	14	21		33	
2000	23	13	19		34	
2001	22	13	28	8	35	31
2002	20	12	27	8	35	31
2003	18	12	26	9	34	31
2004	17	14	25	8	33	31
2006	15	13	—	—	—	—
2007	15	12	24	10	33	31
2008	15	13	21	11	31	31
2009	—	—	—	—	31	28

Sources: Korea: *Korea Statistical Yearbook* and *Korea Yearbook of Labor Statistics.* Philippines: *Philippine Statistical Yearbook.* Thailand 2008–9 from Thailand Labor Force Survey 2008 and 2009 (April–June round).

[a] Defined here as all workers classified as "craft and related trades workers" and "plant and machine operators and assemblers." While these data include both manufacturing and nonmanufacturing sectors, these two occupational categories are most closely associated with manufacturing employment. Other occupational categories such as "technicians and associate professionals," and "elementary occupations," do include many other manufacturing/industrial employees, but they include too many nonindustrial occupations to be useful here in establishing employment trends in manufacturing. 1995–2004 calculated from ILO, *Yearbook of Labor Statistics.* Later years from ILO, LABORSTA, http://laborsta.ilo.org.

share in the fruits of that transition. That pattern is replicated in the Philippines. A possible explanation for the Philippine case relates to the decline in female-intensive light industries such as wearing apparel, where females readily move into the more skilled jobs, and modest growth in heavy industries, where males typically perform skilled work. The striking finding of the high percentage of female skilled and craft workers in Thailand invites further research.

CHAPTER 5

External Liberalization
of Trade and Investment

Asia's post-1980's policy shift to market-oriented reform may generally be characterized as gradualist and selective. In this regard, Asia marks something of a departure from other regions, inasmuch as relatively more robust economic growth, a lower external debt burden, more adequate foreign reserve holdings, and relatively strong states—particularly in the more dynamic regional economies—have meant that external reform pressures were less intense than in other developing-world regions.[1] In 2008, just prior to the world economic slowdown, public and publicly guaranteed debt as a percentage of GDP stood at 4 percent in China, 13.8 percent in Korea, 16 percent in Thailand, and 35 percent in the Philippines.[2] These percentages, excepting that of the Philippines, contrast with the generally higher levels of sovereign external debt in many other developing countries. In the case of China, large positive trade balances have contributed to massive and politically consequential foreign reserve holdings in excess of $2 trillion in 2009 (ADB *KI* 2010, 134), equivalent to nearly 22 months' coverage of imports (World Bank *WDI* 2010).[3] Conversely, rapid growth, expanded employment

---

1. With the exception of the crisis years of 1997 to 1999.

2. These figures were calculated from World Bank, *Global Development Finance,* 2010 and World Bank, *World Development Report,* 2010.

3. By contrast, foreign reserves held by the Philippines are equivalent to only 5.1 months' imports.

opportunities, and reduced poverty in many of these countries has meant that Asian market-reform programs were less militantly contested by labor and other popular-sector groups than in other developing regions. In this context, dominant elites have generally enjoyed greater independence from both international creditors and domestic political groups in national policymaking.

Trade Liberalization

In all four countries, and across the region more generally, average import tariffs, especially on manufactured imports, were substantially reduced during the 1990s. In 2005, mean manufacturing tariffs stood at 5.0 percent in Korea, 5.9 percent in Thailand, and 4.6 percent in the Philippines, while those in China were 5.5 percent in 2009. These rates contrast dramatically with far higher earlier tariffs of 40 percent (1992) in China; 19 percent (1988) in Korea; 38 percent (1991) in Thailand; and 28 percent (1989) in the Philippines (World Bank, *WDI* 2011).

In Thailand and the Philippines these reductions were based on agreements negotiated within the ASEAN Free Trade Agreement and the General Agreement on Tariffs and Trade (GATT)/WTO. In the Philippines, substantial economic liberalization was initiated under the pressures of debt restructuring and economic stagnation in the early 1980s, with average tariffs dropping from 43 percent in 1980 to 28 percent in 1985 (Sicat and Abdula 2003, 140–41). Under the post-Marcos presidencies of Aquino and Ramos, import liberalization continued (Bello et al. 2006), while export taxes were reduced as well, despite strong opposition from a variety of previously protected producer groups in agriculture and domestically oriented industries.

The role of foreign trade has grown correspondingly. Between 1995 and 2008, trade in goods as a percentage of GDP increased from 39 to 57 percent in China, from 49 to 83 percent in Korea, and from 76 to 129 percent in Thailand (ADB *KI* 2010). In the Philippines, this percentage stood at 65 percent in 2008 (WB, *WDI* 2010).

Financial Deregulation of External Capital Flows

Financial markets were also deregulated and opened to foreign participation during the 1990s. In Thailand, government controls over foreign exchange were reduced starting in 1992, and the following year regulations and restrictions on deposits of foreign funds in local banks were eased (Doner 2009, 118). This led to a huge, and ultimately destabilizing, influx of financial capital during subsequent years. The Philippines, strongly dependent on inflows of foreign investment, continued a program of financial liberalization, including passage in 1991 of the Foreign Investments Act, which allows foreign equity in domestic enterprises to exceed an earlier maximum of 40 percent, permits foreign banks to own up to 60 percent of the voting stock of local banks, and opens the Philippine stock exchange to foreign investors. This act, adopted in part to attract increased international and Japanese investment, was followed by other financial-liberalization measures, including lifting foreign exchange restrictions, permitting unlimited repatriation of profits, a further opening of insurance and banking sectors to foreign investors, and retention of high interest rates to attract foreign investment. In response to these measures, foreign-portfolio investment increased markedly between 1993 and 1997 (Bello et al. 2006, 102), while foreign direct investment (FDI) showed a nearly fourfold increase from $1.3 billion in 1992 to $5.1 billion in 1994.[4] In South Korea, financial-sector reforms during the 1980s, including privatization of banks, were followed in the early 1990s by further relaxation of international capital controls that some later blamed for the severity of that country's financial crisis.

Finally, the major role of foreign direct investment in these economies should be noted. The liberalization of incoming FDI has been an essential component of EOI development, as seen most dramatically in the flood of Taiwanese and Hong Kong manufacturing capital into Chinese export-processing zones following enactment in 1986 of new legislation that greatly simplified approval procedures for foreign investors. After 1992 the earlier pattern of joint venture direct-manufacturing investments with local governments gave way to an increased role of wholly owned foreign investments (Chiu and Frenkel 2000, 5–6, 9–10).[5] Of China's 200 biggest exporters in 2009, 153 were firms with a foreign stake.[6] Applebaum (2009) notes as well the easing of restrictions on investments by foreign retailers following entry into the World Trade Organization. And in the Philippines, Kuruvilla et al. note that foreign equity in Philippine manufacturing rose to 65 percent of the total in the late 1990s (2000, 12).

Between 1990 and 1999, FDI as a percentage of gross capital formation increased from 2.8 to 10.5 percent in China, from 0.8 to 8.5 percent in Korea, and from 6.9 to 23.8 percent in Thailand. Only in the Philippines did those external flows decline as a percentage of gross domestic investment,

---

4. The foregoing account of Philippine economic liberalization is based on Laquian (2005).

5. Also see Andrew Browne, "China Drew Over $60 Billion in Foreign Investment in 2005," *Wall Street Journal,* weekend edition January 14–15, 2006.

6. "The Next China," *Economist,* July 31, 2010, 48.

from 5 percent in 1990 to 4 percent in 1999 (WB, *WDI* 2001). In the case of Thailand, data from 1995 to 2009 show a more than doubling of FDI flows (WB, *WDI* 2011) as well as a greater overall reliance in 2008 on foreign direct investment as a percentage of total GDP in China (3.4% of 2008 GDP) and Thailand (3.6%) than in Korea (0.25%) or the Philippines (0.8%). Relatedly, there was a relatively greater reliance on foreign portfolio investments in the Philippines (1.7% of 2008 GDP) and Thailand (3.6%) than in Korea or China (WB *WDI* 2010).

The developmental role of FDI continues to be recognized across the region. The Korean government established six free economic zones in the '00s precisely to attract international investment. And both Thai auto exports and Philippine electronics exports are heavily dependent on FDI. A regionwide shift to more capital- and technology-intensive manufacturing and exports has only deepened this dependence on FDI.

Of course, the external liberalization of trade and investment was everywhere linked to broader and more general deregulatory change. Under President Kim Young Sam (1993–98), Korea announced an open embrace of globalization. Kim's successor, Kim Dae Jung (1998–2003), sought to loosen the previously close ties between government and business, in part to rein in the excessive power of the chaebols, in part in response to the new thinking of increasing numbers of Western-educated technocrats who were advancing into senior government posts, and in part in response to heightened international pressures for external liberalization. As part of this gradual deregulation, Korea's Economic Planning Board, a key development planning agency, was subordinated to the Ministry of Finance in 1993 and subsequently dismantled (Palat 2007, 183). This change, it may be noted, was paralleled some years later by a corresponding reduction in the planning role of Thailand's National Economic and Social Development Board under Prime Minister Thaksin Shinawatra (Doner 2009, 123).

Labor Outcomes of External Liberalization

Growing external economic engagement has influenced Asian labor systems through the increased competitive pressures to which firms are exposed. Depending on the market or technology niche in which a firm competes, those pressures may encourage greater attention to production costs, operational flexibility, improved quality, product development, or a host of other performance dimensions. In an important sense domestic-market deregulation has opened new discretionary space for corporate managers to determine their own competitive strategies, while international economic integration has created both constraints and opportunities for firms seeking to find profitable niches in global production networks.

Competitive strategies in turn shape the labor policies and practices of firms. In cases of standardized mass production (e.g., inexpensive clothing, plastic toys, rubber shoes) firms are pushed to hold wages down and to casualize or subcontract work. Conversely, where firms compete in markets demanding higher-quality production (e.g., computer components, auto parts) greater attention is directed to worker training, skill retention, job commitment, and self-responsibility. Where technologies and the product mix are relatively stable, as in shipbuilding and auto assembly, firms encourage organizational loyalty through internal labor markets, employment security, and other commitment-building incentives. Where technologies and products are subject to rapid and continuing change, as in information technology and solar or biotechnology, firms rely more extensively on fixed duration, yet highly paid, technical and professional workers.

Further, labor market deregulation and the declining importance of union-based collective bargaining encourage more *differentiated* labor practices even within firms (Kalleberg 2007, 174), as managers seek to address the varying competitive requirements associated with particular operations or phases of production employing different categories of workers. For this reason, consideration of the impact of reform must take into account the sectoral diversity of labor outcomes as well as temporal change, as industries and national economies continue to move beyond labor-intensive low-skill manufacturing.

While an account of social outcomes of external financial liberalization is beyond the scope of this book, the obvious importance of this dimension of market reform urges a brief consideration. Of particular importance is the enhanced role of highly mobile equity (vs. direct foreign investment) and of short-term international loans, and the increased financial and economic instability that change has arguably brought to the region (see Sundaram 1998). Most dramatic in this regard are the cases of Korea and Thailand, where deregulatory financial reforms implemented during the early and mid-1990s were followed by severe crises, heightened unemployment, and political conflict. Increased financially driven volatility in domestic economies has brought with it an attendant destabilization of employment, as rapid movements of capital into and out of domestic markets and among alternative domestic sites and sectors continually destabilizes lending, investment, and production (Green 2003, 58).

Of particular importance are two types of labor market instability, the first structural and the second macrocyclical. Structural instability refers to the continuing fluidity of labor markets, a consequence both of the continued movement of workers among jobs and of efforts by firms to insulate themselves from increased market and financial volatility by seeking greater labor flexibility in order to respond to short-term economic fluctuations. Macrocyclical volatility, by contrast, refers to those economywide fluctuations of investment and production that are driven by cumulative global economic influences and that generate booms and crashes in national economies, as occurred during 1997–99.

Both types of volatility bring hardship to workers. But if structural volatility tends to elicit individual job strategies that are variably supported by active labor market policies, cyclical volatility encourages macroregulatory change because of the increased visibility and politicization of reform brought by crisis. It is in this context that we examine trajectories of Asian reform, especially in postcrisis years.

Changing Situations of Labor

Discussion of the employment consequences of structural reform and change offers a basis for a more systematic effort to describe patterns of change in Asian labor systems over the past three decades. That effort is assisted by a provisional schematic characterization of the major situations of employment and their associated labor systems in the manufacturing sectors of these countries (Table 5.1).

Early stage EOI was generally associated with a general decline in the numerical importance of family-based production, as family members relocated to seek factory employment.[7] Of course, this well-recognized general pattern finds many exceptions. In some instances, family systems have been sustained and even reinvigorated as large companies have established supply chains reaching down to family-based workshops in such labor-intensive industries as shoes, toys, sports equipment, and garments. An excellent illustration of this is to be found in the fishnet industry of northeast Thailand, where large companies outsourced production to households in rural villages during the 1990s, ensuring the continuance and even reinforcement of family-based labor systems. In many instances small firms have themselves played an important role in export manufacturing, particularly in labor-intensive low-technology production, as for example in China beginning in the late 1980s. In the latter situation, family-based labor controls may sometimes give way to abusive supervision and market

---

7. Between 1993 and 2006 unpaid family work in Korea declined from 11 to 6% of total employment (Kim Yoo-Sun 2007).

Table 5.1   Major Employment Situations and Associated Labor Systems

Situations of employment	Characteristics of associated labor systems			
	Labor reproduction	Labor protection	Labor markets	Labor process
SME/family	Family-based or funded education/ training	Family or community safety net	Family status-based allocation and advancement	Patriarchal, personal, despotic
Casual, light EOI production	Little education, informal training	Minimum coverage	Contingent/ casual/ migratory	Market despotic
Contractual, light EOI production	Formal secondary education, vocational/ technical training	Legal contractual	Fixed duration, qualification based	Contractual, bureaucratic, impersonal
Temporary, "dispatched" work	Minimal, self-financed training	Minimum coverage as offered by temporary placement agency	Short-term, contingent, contractual	Market despotic, contractual
Technical contract employment	Formal higher education, public technical certification	Legal protection, individual contractual	Contingent, professional/ technical	Legal contractual and market calculative
"Regular" factory work	High school/ technical internal training	Job security (unions), social security, company benefits	Internal	Mutual commitment and legal, contractual
SOE employment	Intrafirm education/ training	State benefits, social security	Internal	Normative patrimonial

despotism as cost-driven overseas Chinese export firms assume an ever-more-important economic role (Chiu and Frenkel 2000, 32).

Early export-oriented industrialization led as well to the rapid expansion of casualized factory employment, most commonly associated with textile, toy, and wearing apparel industries. Many of these new industrial recruits were young, relatively "unskilled,"[8] female workers from rural areas (ADB *Outlook* 2010; Chiu and Frenkel 2000, 148 [on Korea], 134–35 [on China]).[9] Other, more often male, workers were attracted to construction and heavy manual labor, particularly in urban export centers. For many of these migrant workers movement into the "new economy" entailed a shift from economic activities socially embedded in relations of kinship and community, where

---

8. Whether such workers are unskilled or not is problematic, given their often extensive seamstress skills learned during childhood at home.

9. In both cases, the ADB report notes the important role of females and migrant workers in providing the numerical flexibility sought by these firms among their low-skilled workers.

social protections, if only informal, were taken for granted, to new situations of employment where those protections are largely absent. This did not necessarily imply a total elimination of those protections so much as their differentiation and delinking from the labor process and their relocation to rural communities that were increasingly transformed from places of production into sites of social reproduction and protection for migratory workers.

Third, the transition to higher technology but still routinized factory production, best exemplified by foreign-invested electronics assembly work, saw a transition from casual to semiskilled contractual employment, from discretionary to qualifications-based recruitment, and from despotic to bureaucratic labor controls.

Fourth, state-enterprise reform and privatization policies have reduced state-enterprise and public-sector employment, pushing workers into less-protected and more-precarious situations of labor. This transition has been most dramatic, and most disruptive, in China and other post-Socialist emerging economies.

Fifth, increasing labor costs and new development strategies have pushed companies to transition into higher value-added niches in global markets. In lieu of casualized market-despotic labor arrangements, companies have moved to more consensual regimes in order to secure fuller worker participation in new programs of industrial upgrading. Expansion in the ranks of technically trained workers is suggested by the surprising observation that Samsung Electronics, previously a mass producer of standardized consumer electronics equipment, now employs fully two-thirds of its workers in non-production-line activities. More than half of these non-production workers are in research and development.[10] The developmental labor regimes constructed for these workers has tended to enlarge the scope of both regular and contract employment among skilled and technical workers in large formal-sector firms.

It is clear that stable or "regular" employment and protected regular factory work never achieved the degree of institutional dominance in developing Asia that they attained in North America, Western Europe, or Japan. Only in Korea did stable factory work assume a dominant role in some industrial sectors. To the extent a stable primary workforce did emerge during the period of import substituting industrialization and later periods of development, it has tended to decline, as firms have turned, on the one hand, to contract and outsourced work (to increase flexibility in the employment of

---

10. "How to Improve the Workforce." *Joong Ang Daily,* December 17, 2003.

skilled and technical labor) and, on the other, to deskilled casualized work (to cut costs and increase the flexible use of lower-skilled labor). Stable primary employment has here, as elsewhere, been vulnerable to the abandonment of internal labor markets and to increased cost pressures that have pushed companies to rely more often on contingent labor. The financial crisis of the late 1990s had the effect of speeding this transition, as large numbers of regular workers faced layoffs (Kang 2001, 99).

Sixth, as stable primary employment has proven ever-more problematic, fixed-duration contract employment for technically trained workers has grown rapidly, as companies have sought to enhance both functional and numerical flexibility in skilled and technical areas. More and more knowledge-based work is being contracted out (to suppliers) or in (through contract hiring, sometimes of foreign technical workers) in order to meet fluctuating market demand, develop new products or processes, complete time-delimited projects, and generally address the need for innovation-intensive and quality-based demand without transforming skilled labor into a fixed cost. Specialist supplier services play a particularly important role as well, as firms increasingly contract with outside suppliers and referral companies to provide high-level consultancy, technical and financial services, plant maintenance, and other professional and managerial support services.

CHAPTER 6

The Deregulatory Face of Labor Reform

In chapters 4 and 5 I argued that economic reform and restructuring have powerfully, if indirectly, influenced Asian labor through their consequences for the redistribution of workers across different economic sectors, types of work, and associated labor systems. This chapter addresses the second, more direct, reform influence on labor systems: that of social-regulatory reform and changing labor regimes. During the 1990s, China, Korea, Thailand, and the Philippines to varying degrees and in different ways pursued market-conforming policies of labor market deregulation, institutional devolution to local and private sectors, and market-oriented social-policy reform. I focus here on the deregulatory face of labor reform, especially during the years leading up to and during the regional financial crisis of the late 1990s. In later chapters I look at the reregulatory face of reform that variably functioned, with greater or lesser success, to counterbalance or compensate for the institutional deficits, social instabilities, and political threats fostered by this deregulation and dramatically exposed and politicized by the crisis. Reregulatory policies and changes certainly accompanied earlier years of reform but became particularly visible during the '00s.[1]

---

1. This phase of reform, sometimes referred to as "second generation" reform, received increasing emphasis in the mid-1990s, following a primary focus on economic restructuring and adjustment

Labor Market Deregulation?

In chapter 1 I identified several important formal and substantive dimensions of regulatory regimes in terms of which Asian labor regimes might usefully be characterized. Based on the subsequent discussion of economic reform in chapter 3, I suggest that neoliberal reform, or at least a stylized version of reform, would include a reduced scope and depth of state regulation,[2] decentralization of regulatory authority to local levels, and an increased orientation to market conformity and efficiency with a correspondingly reduced emphasis on social equity or long-term national development. If these changes define essential elements of market deregulation, how usefully do they describe actual trajectories of market reform in China, Korea, Thailand, and the Philippines? I begin with the question of labor market deregulation.

China

Prior to the market reforms of the 1980s, Chinese labor markets scarcely existed at all. Strict residency rules (the *houkou* system) largely confined workers to local residence, both by denying them protection and social services outside their home districts and by discouraging their employment in other places. Urban jobs were generally allocated by local officials of the Ministry of Labor. State-owned enterprises, wherein workers were generally guaranteed lifetime jobs, employed over three-quarters of the urban workforce (PRC, *CSY,* 1996 and 2004). Work units (*danwei*) were given little latitude in the selection of employees—workers generally stayed with the same work unit for many years, and job mobility was low. Of particular importance here, both collective-farming units and state enterprises offered a range of important social services including housing, health care, education, pensions, and other livelihood supports that guaranteed broad, if only shallow, livelihood security (see Whyte and Parish 1984; Parish 1985; Lü and Perry 1997, 9–12).

Post-1978 reform brought dramatic and continuing changes to this system. Under the household responsibility system, introduced in the early 1980s (Parish 1985), rural families were able to diversify income sources and to establish nonagricultural enterprises, thus encouraging an employment shift from agriculture to rural services and local industry. This change eventuated not only in rapid growth in markets for privately produced agricultural

---

during the 1980s. In the Asian context, the late 1990's financial crisis led to new IMF efforts to speed labor market deregulation in Korea and elsewhere in East and Southeast Asia.

2. These would suggest a process of informalization.

products but also in a proliferation of TVEs, small- to medium-sized firms producing simple commodities for domestic markets. These collectively owned enterprises were supported by local governments and managed by party cadres and government officials (Arrighi 2009). As well, the greater economic freedom afforded rural families encouraged rural-urban migration, although lack of secure title to land alongside lack of legal access to urban services, health facilities, and education continued to encourage migratory workers to return home on a seasonal basis.

Rural reform was paralleled by labor market deregulation within the SOE sector itself. Under 1986 legislation, newly hired SOE workers were employed under fixed-duration employment contracts (Chen 2003, 112; World Bank *WDI* 2005, 123), a departure from earlier practice and one that fostered increased labor flexibility while at the same time retaining some job security for older workers. In cases of outright enterprise sale to private investors, even workers with many years of service found themselves working on a temporary basis or under short-term contracts.[3] By 1990, it is estimated that 18 percent of SOE workers were fixed-term contract workers (Naughton 1995), a percentage that continued to rise following enactment of 1994 legislation that mandated extension of fixed-term labor contracts to all workers other than those SOE workers who had more than ten years' seniority (Chen and Hou 2008). From 1992, SOE managers were given further discretionary rights in setting prices and wages, and in hiring and firing. Under these and other legislative changes, earlier mandated worker benefits including schooling, housing, medical protection, and other expensive welfare programs were to be phased out in order to enhance the operational competitiveness and employment flexibility of firms (Taylor 2002). Finally, in the context of China's entry into the WTO, local governments were permitted to relax private-sector labor codes in order to enhance operating flexibility (ADB *KI* 2005, 62). Given the magnitude of state-enterprise employment in China, these various changes were reflected in a substantial increase in the ranks of contingent labor in urban areas, as suggested by the finding by Chou and Hou (2008) that only 23.2 percent of formal-sector workers were "regular" workers with long-term job security.

A final indication that Chinese labor markets underwent continuing deregulation are data showing a marked decline, stretching over nearly

---

3. Chen and Hou (2008) estimate that temporary workers make up a significantly larger proportion (roughly 50%) of workers in private firms than in either foreign-invested firms or state enterprises, which suggests that the substantial reduction in SOE employment tended to increase temporary employment.

two decades, in the percent of manufacturing workers in paid employment (vs. own-account work and unpaid family labor),[4] from 60 percent in the early 1990s to less than 30 percent in 2005, when self-employed workers accounted for over two-thirds of all manufacturing workers. This decline in paid employment, while only a partial and uncertain proxy for informalization, suggests at a minimum a shrinking pool of workers for whom formal protections are a real possibility. In this regard, Chen and Hou (2008) note a gradual increase in Chinese informal-sector work, estimating that between 1996 and 2001 the ratio of informal to formal-sector workers increased from 1:4 to 1:2 in response to growing numbers of migrant workers and of workers laid off by state enterprises. This indirect indication of growing informalization is also supported by Amin's (2002) research suggesting that the retrenchment of SOE (formal-sector) workers combined with an easing of restrictions on rural-urban migration has significantly increased the scope of informal-sector employment.

The devolution of regulatory controls to municipal and local levels (Zhu 2003) and to the governing boards of expanding export-processing zones should be noted as part of China's integration into international markets. This devolution of responsibility, part of a larger policy of local reform experimentation, eventuated in substantial local autonomy in the management of labor markets (Chiu and Frenkel 2000, 31) and in setting the minimum wage. Under 2004 minimum wage legislation, provincial and municipal governments are empowered to adjust national wage guidelines to local economic conditions. This legislation has had some effect in raising the pay for less-skilled workers, although, again, lack of enforcement and a corresponding tendency to pay below the legal minimum has in practice compromised this intended outcome. It should also be noted that China's minimum wage rates are among the lowest in the world to start with. In any case, this devolution to local levels has typically disadvantaged workers, who now increasingly confront municipal officials whose interests are often closely aligned with those of local and foreign employers.

It must be recognized that Chinese labor legislation continues to offer a broad range of labor protections, including, inter alia, employment contracts, the option for workers with at least ten years' seniority to shift to non–fixed-term, regular contracts, restriction of probationary employment status to six months, restrictions on dismissals including severance payments and prior

4. A World Bank (*WDI* 2009) report notes the high level of flexibility of China's labor market. See Aaron Back and Brian Spegele, "World Bank: Wages Can Rise in China," *Wall Street Journal*, June 19–20, 2010.

notice, limitations on working hours, and occupational and safety rules.[5] But, while these legislative protections are in principle quite progressive, their substantive impact is reduced by a growing body of legal exemptions for a variety of reasons relating to economic contingencies, competitive pressures, and the like. This is in addition to widespread gaps in local enforcement. Thus, while formal legislative protections remain substantial, de facto protections have become ever weaker, thus enhancing the actual flexibility of employment even among formal-sector workers.

But before concluding that labor market reform has had the effect of fundamentally deregulating Chinese labor markets, several cautionary observations are in order. First, labor market deregulation has been only partial. Rural workers may now legally travel to urban industrial areas for work, eventuating in the presence by the late '00s of an estimated 200 million migrant workers in cities.[6] Nonetheless, such migration remains tightly controlled, inasmuch as workers must obtain government-issued temporary-residence permits to live and work in urban zones, and must return to their home districts upon loss of employment. Until the mid-'00s (see chapter 9), migration had been further restricted by rules denying migrants access to a variety of social services and benefits enjoyed by permanent local residents, harassment by local police in cases of labor disturbances, and a variety of management abuses that are encouraged by these same restrictions.

Second, SOE labor market reform has, in conformity with a more general policy of gradualism, been incrementally introduced (Taylor 2002). As noted above, the labor-contract system does not change terms of employment for workers hired before 1992, and numerous other legal provisions have softened the bite of the market for workers who had been laid off, including continuance of pay without work, the seconding of released workers to other firms, and other social safety net policies.

And third, of course, is the observation, so often neglected in state-centric accounts of labor market "deregulation," that state agencies and regulatory regimes are but one element in functioning regulatory orders. As important are a host of societal organizations, networks, and regulatory structures that continue to function even under the most dirigist governmental regimes. In this regard, Chen and Hou (2008) cite the findings of a worker survey taken midway through the '00s showing the continued, if somewhat diminished, importance of worker networks of friendship, kinship, and home locality in

---

5. For a useful review, see World Bank (2006) and Gaelle and Scarpetta (2004). Also see a formal codification of these protections in China's Labor Contract Law, which took effect January 1, 2008.

6. "Beijing's Migrant Workers: School's Out," *Economist*, September 3, 2011.

organizing job search and mutual assistance, even amid otherwise disorderly labor markets (see also Lee 1998). Dorothy Solinger (1999, 270) notes in this regard the multiple ways in which these networks may provide to migrants a degree of protection, mutual assistance, and collective defense of particular crafts or trades against competition from outside groups.

Korea

Through the 1980s, South Korean labor markets were circumscribed by legal restrictions on the rights of companies with more than five employees to fire workers without establishing just cause, thus legally buttressing a long-standing tradition of lifetime employment in large firms. In addition, the Korean government, in part to compensate politically restive workers for the privations of repressive labor policies, instituted labor regulations to protect wages and working conditions. While in practice largely confined to the ranks of regular workers in large firms, these various provisions placed Korea among the top OECD countries in terms of the strictness of employment protection (Kim, Bae, and Lee 2000; Yang and Moon 2005). Given this historical background, it is not surprising that efforts in the late 1990s to deregulate Korean labor markets became so politically charged.

At the same time, under repressive military-based rule from the early 1970s to the late 1980s, Korea's "productivist" labor regimes sought to bolster exports and economic growth in part through strict controls over workers and unions. Such restrictions, while directed primarily at the labor process, had the indirect effect of containing labor costs and thus distorting labor markets in support of export promotion. Under labor market deregulation, direct state intervention in the labor process gave way to fuller reliance on the less-visible but equally effective discipline of the market.

In December 1996, the Kim Young Sam government passed legislation easing requirements for layoffs for regular employers and making it easier to replace union with nonunion workers.[7] The new legislation, embodied in the revised Labor Standards Act of 1997, weakened a long-standing tradition of job security among formal-sector workers by permitting employers to dismiss workers for "economic" reasons, such as the need to reduce costs and enhance competitiveness (Kang et al. 2001, 106).[8] In addition, the new

7. In the face of protracted labor opposition, this legislation was delayed in implementation.

8. These labor market changes are often attributed to IMF pressures during the economic crisis of the late 1990s. In fact, earlier enabling legislation began in 1989, and the new layoff rules were introduced in 1996, *before* the crisis and IMF involvement.

legislation (subsequently rescinded and revised in response to protracted labor opposition) permitted more flexible work hours and freer use of temporary workers while also legalizing the "leasing out" of employees to other firms. Beginning in 1998, the Dispatched Workers Act opened the way for a proliferation of manpower-placement firms to hire out temporary workers for periods of up to two years in twenty-six occupations that required special skills and experience (Yang and Moon 2005, 81). That same year, restrictions were eased on fixed-term (vs. permanent) employment, while firms were granted increased power to engage in collective dismissals for "managerial reasons"—although such dismissals continued to require government approval. Subsequent judicial rulings reduced employment protections in cases of mergers and acquisitions. In this regard, Yang and Moon (2005, 78) note a 1996–2000 decline in the ranks of regular workers, both overall and in manufacturing more specifically, alongside increased reliance on temporary and daily workers, following which the percentage of non-regular workers remained relatively stable.[9] Other research shows an increase in the percentage of temporary workers in the overall economy: from 7.4 percent in 1980 to 22 percent in 2006, thus in part accounting for the finding that a majority of Korean workers (55 to 56 percent) were engaged in non-regular employment during the 2001–2007 period (Kim 2007). In the context of high levels of open unemployment during the financial crisis, these various deregulatory measures were initially defended as increasing employment by reducing impediments to labor mobility (Kang et al. 2001, 106). In part, too, increased labor market flexibility was linked to official efforts to shift Korea's economy more decisively toward knowledge-based industries, to accommodate increased market instability, and to attract foreign direct investment.

As in China, the new legislation did not entirely deregulate labor markets. A range of other provisions continued to protect regular formal-sector workers, including provision that layoffs and dismissals could only be made for "justifiable reasons," a required sixty-day notice of termination, limits on the duration of fixed-term employment contracts, provision of severance pay, and the like (ADB, *KI* 2005), in part because of the influence of trade unions (ADB *Outlook 2004 Update,* ADB *KI* 2005, 77). Indeed, the World Bank continues to rank Korea well above the other three countries in its "rigidity of employment."[10] But since many worker protections in Korea have been restricted to regular long-term workers and in the past did

---

9. See Republic of Korea: *The Economically Active Population Survey,* annual.

10. As measured by difficulty of hiring, rigidity of hours, and difficulty of firing (World Bank *WDI* 2010). For discussion and critique, see Caraway (2009).

not extend to irregular and part-time workers or to workers in very small firms,[11] they have tended to encourage many firms to replace regular with non-regular workers, thus effectively undercutting the bargaining power of regular workers. In the context of increasing reliance on skilled and technical labor in Korea's advanced industries, the choice was less often to casualize labor than to find new ways to combine flexibility with high levels of worker skill, commitment, and initiative. In part, this was accomplished in traditional ways, by offering skilled core-function workers good pay, job security, and advancement opportunities within internal labor markets, which effectively reregulated labor markets by partially embedding them in organizational and career hierarchies. Here, labor flexibility was achieved less by numerical flexibility in external labor markets than by functional flexibilities deriving from continuous multiskill training and continued adjustments in work organization and technology. But if this high-road labor strategy has been one means of combining flexibility with high-value labor, another increasingly common strategy is that of hiring skilled and technical labor under generous but fixed-duration individual contracts. This second approach extends employment contingency to the growing ranks of skilled and technical workers.

A final, though important, consideration relates to the growing numbers of low-skill immigrant workers, among whom casual labor is often the rule. Most such workers are employed in small manufacturing firms, construction, and fishing enterprises that cannot afford to pay the going rates for Korean workers. These workers, estimated at 330,000 in the early years of the first decade of the 2000s, cannot legally be hired as regular employees. Rather, at least in formal sector firms, they must remain "trainees" on three-year contracts and are largely precluded from the protections and benefits accruing either to regular workers or to skilled contract workers (U.S. Department of Labor 2003a).

Korea, of course, stands out as one of the "miracle" economies of the region. What of the other economies, where economic upgrading has been more problematic and where irregular, casual, and short-term contractual labor has played a noticeably greater role?

Thailand

The regulation of Thai labor markets takes a variety of forms, of which three are most relevant here. First, public-sector employment in the civil services

---

11. Of fewer than five workers, thus excluding roughly one-third of all Korean workers (Lim, Kim, and Kim 2003).

and in state-owned enterprises is both formally regulated by rules governing pay grades, employment security, health and retirement programs, and other protective measures, and more informally by vertical networks of personal loyalty and clientelism through which career advancement is often secured. Second, and in the wake of widening student and worker militancy during the early 1970s, new legislation at that time established a tripartite Central Wage Committee to set minimum wages,[12] worker compensation, and the beginnings of a national social insurance program that was to be expanded in later years. Third, Thailand stands out for its long-standing reliance on severance pay to reduce market risk for workers. Indeed, severance requirements were increased from six months' to ten months' pay (Caraway 2009, 161).

While in principle these protections offer a fairly comprehensive social safety net, they are restricted to nonagricultural formal-sector workers (Brown 2003, 359) and fail to cover major portions of the workforce including a huge informal sector of small firms, agricultural laborers, home-based workers, and the like. Further, increased competitive pressures have pushed Thai employers to hire larger numbers of contingent workers in order to enhance flexibility, reduce costs, evade labor-law provisions, and sometimes to forestall unionization or to weaken existing unions (Lawler and Suttawet 2000; Brown 2003, 100). For example, AutoAlliance Thailand, a large automotive assembly joint venture between Ford and Mazda, employed 3,400 workers in 2010, of whom 1,200 were contract workers. The extensive use of contract labor enabled this company to maintain production despite an unresolved dispute with the union representing regular workers.[13] More generally, a 2008 business survey found greatly increased use of temporary and seasonal labor among forty-nine leading companies surveyed.[14]

As important, very weak and inadequate enforcement of existing legislation has imparted more flexibility to this system than one might infer from formal statistics and legislative provisions (Caraway 2009).[15] Pay flexibility

---

12. For more recent developments, see "Protests Likely after Unequal Wage Hikes," *Nation* (online), December 13, 2001.

13. "Thailand: AutoAlliance Resumes Single Shift Ops." *AutomotiveWorld*, http://www.automotiveworld.com/news. January 18, 2010.

14. "Outsourcing Popular Trend in Thailand—Survey Finds Use of Temps Increasing." *Bangkok Post Business* October 30, 2008.

15. I spent a day with a government labor inspections officer visiting factories in Khonkaen, a city in Thailand's northeast, during 1994. Virtually all the factories were in violation of some health, safety, pay, or worker benefits provisions of labor legislation in effect that year. None of these violations, however, resulted in immediate government action. While filing the day's reports at her office later that day, the labor inspector explained to me that to take action against these firms would have compromised their profitability.

has always been substantial, given union weaknesses in collective bargaining, and given very low (and thus often substantively irrelevant) minimum wage rates. That private-sector labor markets have become quite wage-flexible is suggested by substantial private-sector pay reductions (alongside layoffs) averaging 20 to 40 percent during the late-1990's financial crisis (Athukorala 2000, 44; Birdsall and Haggard 2002). Indeed, wage flexibility was further enhanced under 1998 legislation that devolved tripartite wage setting from national to provincial and local bodies (Siengthai 2008). And, finally, as in China, legislative coverage is quite limited. Not only are workers in the huge informal sector (including home-based workers) excluded, but the Labor Protection Act of 1998 specifically excludes the very large numbers of agricultural workers.

To the limited extent that Thai workers are in fact covered by employment protections, this legislation has had the predictable consequence of encouraging private-sector employers to restrict the number of workers legally qualifying as eligible permanent staff and to rotate many other workers through extended periods of temporary, casual, and probationary employment, effectively bypassing existing regulatory requirements while also indirectly increasing casualized employment. Such efforts to avoid expensive legislative mandates eventuates in marked labor market dualism, reflected in substantial differences in the terms of employment and job security of permanent large-firm employees, on the one hand, and other workers (including those in small subcontract firms), on the other. Of course, this dualism would likely have been even more pronounced had existing labor legislation been more vigorously enforced during this period.

The Thai reform experience until the early to mid-00's might best be described as one of expanding formal protections for a small segment of the workforce, especially public-sector workers, while engendering huge gaps in effective private-sector coverage, even among workers nominally covered by social insurance and other protective labor legislation. In this context, labor market deregulation resides less in legislative reform than in non-enforcement and in the informal practices of employers (especially in small- and medium-sized firms) as they confront growing market pressures under economic deregulation, trade liberalization, and intensified competition.

The Philippines

Like South Korea, the Philippines presents a case of deregulation of major employment sectors that had enjoyed substantial protections during earlier years. But beyond this superficial parallel the resemblance quickly breaks down. In Korea, protective labor legislation only embraced workers in large firms and the public sector. By contrast, that in the Philippines embraced (if only officially) a more inclusive workforce. Early Korean labor legislation was at once protective and repressive, providing job security for regular male workers in large companies while at the same time forcefully containing labor militancy and independent unionism. Until the 1972 declaration of martial law enacted by President Marcos, Philippine labor legislation was both protective and progressive. And, even under martial law, the 1974 Labor Code provided strong employment protections for workers, regulating employment contracts, the minimum wage, limitations on temporary employment, advanced notice of termination, statutory protections from arbitrary dismissal, and so forth.[16]

While the Philippine Labor Code also provided guidelines for collective bargaining and tripartite deliberations, those guidelines were largely ignored until passage of a new constitution in 1987.[17] In 1989 more generous minimum wage legislation was enacted to promote both economic growth and worker welfare.[18] But in fact the tremendous flexibility this legislation gives to wage setting through regional tripartite boards, openness to appeals from industries and employers, a multiplicity of minimum wage objectives and determinants, special exceptions to take local economic circumstances into account, and widespread lack of enforcement greatly compromises the nominally progressive goal of minimum wage legislation.

The experience of labor deregulation in the Philippines must be understood in the unique political context of early labor mobilization, followed by autocratic repression and then a new politicization associated with the popular mid-1980's overthrow of the Marcos regime. In this politically charged context, labor deregulation has only partially taken the form of the de jure legislative rescinding of earlier protections. Under 1989 revisions to the 1974 Labor Code, restrictions on subcontracting were eased, and job security was reduced under new rules allowing layoffs in cases of technological displacement, economic redundancy, retrenchment to permit economic losses, and plant closings, but with the important safeguard that those layoffs require prior official approval.[19] These deregulatory measures were further extended under Department of Labor and Employment guidelines issued in

---

16. See Caraway (2009) for discussion of the Philippine pattern of "protective repression," a pattern applicable to predemocracy Korea as well.

17. This discussion draws heavily on the ADB *KI* 2005: Part I in special edition on labor markets.

18. The Republic Act no. 6727.

19. Both collective and individual dismissals still require government approval (ADB KI 2005, 56).

the context of the 2008–10 world recession that further increased employer discretion in hiring and firing.[20] Reflective of these changes are data reported by the ADB showing increases in the percentage of "non-regular" Philippine workers from approximately 21 percent of the total workforce in 1991 to 28 percent in 1997, thereafter continuing to increase to 30.6 percent in 1998, and to 32 percent in 2004 (ADB, *KI* 2005).

But equally consequential has been de facto labor market deregulation. Sibal et al. (2009) find a continuing trend, beginning in the 1990s, toward increased hiring under fixed-duration labor contracts (doubling between 1991 and 1997 and continuing into the early '00s). This trend has been accompanied by a continuing decline in inflation-adjusted real minimum wage rates and by selective but widespread nonenforcement (vs. formal rescinding) of existing labor legislation (McKay 2006, 15–16; Kelly 2001),[21] thus both permitting and encouraging high rates of noncompliance by firms (ADB, *KI* 2005, 58–59).[22] Further de facto deregulation was achieved through the covert reclassification and misclassification of large numbers of workers as non-regular, contractual, and temporary, thus permitting employers to evade existing worker protections that apply only to regular workers (McKay 2006, 60) by shifting reclassified workers into nonprotected employment categories (Quintos 2003).

If these changes have eventuated in de facto deregulation at the national level, they have also been associated with a new regulatory augmentation at local levels. Most important were a devolution (as in China) of economic and labor regulation to local levels of government and a quasi-privatization of labor regulation to new governing bodies in export-processing zones and strategic industrial centers. Both changes were justified as enhancing the adaptability of firms and making labor markets more flexible and responsive to local circumstances. Several legislative changes highlight this regulatory, scalar shift. In 1990 minimum wage determination was shifted from the National Wages Council to regional tripartite wage and productivity boards, even as the government tended not to enforce existing minimum wages.[23] Export-processing zones in particular were progressively freed from direct

---

20. "Guidelines on the Adoption of Flexible Work Arrangements," DOLE, Departmental Advisory No. 2 Series of 2009 allowing establishments to implement policies such as compressed workweek, shortening of work hours, job rotation, broken-time schedules, and flex-holiday schedules. *Asian Labour Update*, April–June 2009, 11.

21. Also see Kelly on the pervasive problem of nonenforcement in the Philippines despite comprehensive protective national labor legislation.

22. The ADB estimates that roughly one-half of all firms were in noncompliance with major provisions of labor law during the 1990s.

23. Jane Hutchison (2006, 52) estimates that lax government minimum wage enforcement results in below minimum wages for some 60% of the workforce.

central controls and were increasingly privatized or governed by semiautonomous regulatory boards, especially the Philippine Economic Zone Authority
(PEZA). PEZA has assumed a particularly prominent role in matters of labor
recruitment, worker housing, management of labor relations, and labor control in local communities (McKay 2006, 60).

Finally, what of the implications of the Philippines' labor export strategy?
Under what terms of employment do those workers operate? Hutchison
(2006) notes that in 2003, 3.85 million Filipinos (roughly 10% of total employment) were working temporarily on overseas fixed-term contracts. A
substantial portion of other overseas workers are in fact employed on an
irregular or illegal basis, in many cases in informal sectors in construction,
entertainment, domestic service, and manufacturing sweat shops. Inclusion of
those informal workers brings the estimated number of overseas workers far
higher than official data would indicate (Scott 2009). In some instances, as in
the entertainment industry, these workers may participate in illegal bonded
labor. Data presented by Hutchison (2006, 46), based on Philippine Overseas
Employment Administration figures for 2003, suggest the presence of large
numbers of temporary workers in the Middle East and in East and Southeast
Asia, and of "irregular" workers heavily concentrated in Asia and the United
States. This implies that labor-export policies, part of a larger export-
development strategy, may have the indirect outcome of enlarging informal-
employment sectors that do not appear in official Philippine data. Conversely,
of course, it must be recalled that substantial numbers of expatriate Filipinos
are employed in professional or semiprofessional positions in information
technology, health care, computer programming, and other fields.[24] These
highly educated overseas workers, estimated at over 13 percent of all tertiary
graduates in 2008 (World Bank, *WDI* 2010), represent a substantial transfer
of the value of investments in social reproduction to foreign sites of production, only partly compensated by remittances of earnings back to the Philippines. The major difference between these college-educated "contingent"
workers and more casualized, less-educated Filipino workers is that they are
typically employed under more generous, secure contracts.

Deregulation and the Question of Informalization

With important exceptions, it is clear that labor market deregulation has played
a generally important role in encouraging ever-more-shallow protections

---

24. See "OFW remittances growing above forecast," *Manila Times* (online), April 17, 2010.

among previously protected formal-sector workers[25] and in devolving regulatory authority to local levels. This deregulatory shift has taken de jure
forms through legislative reform. In other instances it has been achieved
more informally through lax or selective enforcement, most dramatically in
the Philippines (Caraway 2009), where this less-visible form of deregulation
has the great advantage of avoiding political challenge.

But at this point an important distinction must be made between two understandings of "informalization": the first based on sectoral *location* in informal or formal employment sectors, and the second on the changing *degree* of
informalization along the major regulatory dimensions discussed in chapter 1.[26]
The first approach seeks to identify informal employment by reference to
particular places, sectors, or situations of work, such as the employment status of workers as irregular, own-account, or unpaid family workers. Such an
approach fails to address the central goal of labor market deregulation: the
partial and often gradual attenuation of state regulation of terms of employment within labor sectors traditionally deemed *formal,* and including even
long-term full-time paid employees. Stated differently, sectoral approaches
cannot adequately account for the more complex multidimensional changes
that define processes of deregulatory *informalization.* Labor market deregulation, after all, is not directed at workers in already unregulated sectors. Nor
does it seek to move formal-sector workers into informal sectors. Rather,
its primary goal is to informalize already protected formal-sector employment, one of whose outcomes is, following Portes (1994), "the elimination
of the very distinction between informal and formal sectors" (432). It is
there, after all, that the problem of "rigidity" most clearly resides. Indeed,
longitudinal-employment studies in these countries offer little support, with
the exception only of China, for the supposition that labor market reform
has been associated with an expansion in conventionally identified informal
sectors. To the contrary, national data on Korean manufacturing employment show very little change in the percentages of (informal) own-account
or family-based workers since the mid-1980s (ROK: *YLS* various years),[27]
while showing modest declines in those percentages for workers in all

---

25. For discussion of alternative understandings of informalization, see Portes et al. 1989.

26. This discussion parallels but goes beyond an ILO reconceptualization of informality that
distinguishes between informal enterprises and informal employment, recognizing that informal employment may occur outside the informal sector (ILO *Statistical Update on Employment in the Informal
Economy* 2011). I go further here in rejecting such binary distinctions in favor of an understanding
that informalization may occur even within formal employment itself.

27. The extent of own-account and family-based unpaid labor is often taken as an indicator of
the scope of the informal sector.

sectors including manufacturing (Kim 2007). Between 2000 and 2008, the percentage of total Korean employment accounted for by own-account and family workers declined from 30 percent to 25 percent (ILO 2011, http://www.laborsta.ilo.org).

Thailand too shows clear declines in those percentages during the same time period.[28] ILO data show a decline in the percent of unpaid and own-account Thai workers between 1990 and 2008: from 67 to 52 percent for males, and from 74 to 56 percent for females, with only 42 percent of all Thai workers now in situations of informal employment (ILO 2011, http://www.laborsta.ilo.org).[29] Only in China do official government statistics suggest increasing numbers of own-account manufacturing workers, totaling nearly 70 percent in 2006, alongside a dramatic decline in the percentage of "paid employees" during the 1990s and the '00s (PRC, CSY 2010).

In Korea, Thailand, and the Philippines, women increasingly moved from own-account and unpaid family labor into paid employment in manufacturing during early phases of EOI growth. ILO data suggest that this transition tends to occur first among unpaid family workers, presumably young unmarried women, and somewhat later among own-account workers, more often older women whose family and existing employment opportunities present a greater deterrent to their entering paid factory employment until pay levels begin to rise. This two-stage transition is seen in five-to-six-year lags between declines in the percentages of female family workers and subsequent declines in the percentage of female own-account workers in Korea (mid-1970s vs. late 1970s and early 1980s) and in Thailand (mid-1980s vs. 1990s).[30]

More informative for the study of regulatory informalization is reference to profiles of deregulatory change along the four key dimensions of regulatory form: scope, depth, level, and enforcement. This chapter thus highlights the importance of reduced regulatory depth, increased localization (especially in China and the Philippines), and deepening gaps in enforcement (Thailand, the Philippines) as suggesting increasing levels of informalization despite declines in the size of conventionally defined informal sectors.

Contingency and Informalization

A second major reform goal, that of increased employment flexibility, has been an even more prominent aspect of labor market reform. But does

---

28. ILO, Bulletin of Labor Statistics, various years.

29. Siengthai (2008, 318) suggests that much of this decline was accounted for by reduced numbers of family workers.

30. Calculated from labor status data in ILO YLS, various years.

increased labor market flexibility, and a corresponding increase in employment contingency, imply an increase in informality as contended by some critics of labor market reform? In answering this question, it is first necessary to recognize that informality and employment contingency relate to quite different aspects of regulatory regimes: the first to the four primary dimensions of form, and the second to the three dimensions of substantive orientation. More specifically, labor market flexibility and contingency refer not to the scope, depth, scale, or degree of enforcement of labor regimes so much as to their substantive and intended outcomes, as the emphasis on distributive outcomes and developmentalism yields to a greater emphasis on market efficiencies and integration into world markets. The growth of contingent employment thus says little about the extent of informalization.

Further, contingency itself varies considerably in its associated degree of formal regulation. On the one hand are the large numbers of temporary and casual workers who play so important a role in enhancing the numerical flexibility of firms in cost-driven markets. On the other hand are the smaller but growing numbers of contract workers, particularly skilled and technical workers, among whom flexibility is combined with skill and industrial upgrading. Casual and temporary workers inhabit less-regulated zones of labor markets, while fixed-duration contract workers enjoy more substantial, contractual (formal) protections. This distinction is often institutionalized in national regulatory regimes. The survey of Chinese firms reported by Chen and Hou (2008), for example, notes the way in which SOE labor contracts reinforce employment segmentation through the link between type of work and length of contract—ranging from fifteen to sixteen months for migrant and temporary workers to twenty-nine months for technical workers and thirty-two months for professionals.

Social-Policy Reform: Deregulation?

But what of social policies relating to the social reproduction and protection of labor? How closely has the Asian experience modeled the precepts of market-oriented reform in this area? As changing employment structures, on the one hand, and de jure and de facto labor market deregulation, on the other, have cumulatively shifted market risk to workers and their families, the ILO and other international agencies have typically encouraged the instituting and expansion of employment-based social insurance, including unemployment insurance, jointly funded by employers and employees. This ascendant "market friendly" approach to social protection, most fully developed in Korea, is discussed in chapter 9.

But what of other elements of social policy, including primary health care, basic education, and social services, that are less closely linked to employment status than to citizen entitlement? Here, the imprint of market reform has been mixed.[31] Market principles have found their way into new modes of administering and funding a variety of health and social services, including out-contracting; user-pay financing that shifts access and eligibility from citizen entitlement to ability to pay; and the decentralization, privatization, and marketization of social and health services (J. Lee 2007). In China many government services and facilities have been transformed into commercial services. Even as government-sponsored basic health care is expanding (chapter 9), China has encouraged growth in private supplementary health insurance, now even including participation by foreign insurers.[32] By 1998, housing, once almost entirely publicly owned and managed, had given way to sale to tenants. New housing is now almost always sold on the open market (Guan 2000, 123). Similarly, subsidies and services previously offered by municipal governments have largely disappeared, and price controls on basic commodities have been sharply reduced (So 2009, 52). When the old health-care system associated with communes and work units was progressively dismantled during the 1980s, it was not substantially replaced by a new system of public provision, giving way instead to a largely pay-for-service system, as government-owned hospitals were forced to become largely self-funded (Brown, de Brauw, and Du 2009, 198; Blomqvist and Qian 2008). In the 1980s, roughly 40 percent of all health-care expenditures came from private sources, an amount that subsequently rose to 59 percent in 1999 and to 64 percent in 2004, much of which was out-of-pocket rather than insurance based.[33] Official government figures show out-of-pocket private health outlays at 20 percent of total health expenditures in 1978, 36 percent in 1990, and 59 percent in 2000, subsequently dropping sharply to 40 percent in 2008 as new public health programs were rolled out (see below) (PRC *CSY* 2010).

This dramatic transition parallels that in Thailand, where private health expenditures as a percentage of total health expenditures rose from 36 percent in 1991–93 to 69 percent in 1998 (WB *WDI* 2001). And in the Philippines, government health organizations have faced sharp funding cuts as the

---

31. Unlike labor market reform, social-policy change has, during the first decade of the 2000s, sought less to deregulate than to reregulate employment, often to compensate for or address the tensions of deregulatory reform. Here I address the deregulatory moment of social-policy reform, reserving for later consideration the more important reregulatory policy.

32. "Health Insurers' China Puzzle," *Wall Street Journal,* January 13, 2011.

33. "In China, Preventative Medicine Pits Doctor against the System," *Wall Street Journal,* January, 16, 2007.

state role has transitioned from direct provision to coordination of services through PhilHealth.[34]

Educational Reforms

In the Asian context, educational reform has taken a variety of forms. On the one hand, the Asian Development Bank notes a regional trend toward privatization and deregulation of secondary vocational education.[35] On the other hand, the ADB also notes more varied trends relating to educational privatization more generally, including an increasing predominance of public education at the secondary level alongside increasing private enrollments at the tertiary level.[36] This general trend is reflected in the experience of the four countries included here. Private enrollment as a percentage of total secondary enrollments in Korea stayed in the low-to-mid 40 percent range during the late 1980s and 1990s (ADB *KI* 2003). Neither Thailand nor the Philippines show increased private enrollment at the secondary level. Indeed, Thai private secondary enrollments have remained relatively low, in the 10 to 15 percent range since the early 1980s (KOT *SY* various years), while those in the Philippines have markedly declined, from 47 percent in 1980 to 36 percent in 1990, 23 percent in 2000, and 19 percent in 2008–9 (ROP, *YLS* 2008). In the case of China, private secondary enrollments are negligible (ADB *KI* 2003, 26).

These data would thus confirm the more general ADB finding of a lack of increased private participation in regional secondary education. But does this suggest a more general conclusion that education has been largely untouched by the broader embrace of markets? Probably not. First, these findings on enrollment trends fail to take into account the growing role of private funding in secondary education. In Korea, it is true that government educational outlays are among the highest among OECD countries.[37] But even more dramatic is the increasing role of private tutoring and after-school instruction. Here, nongovernmental expenditure on education, including private tutoring, is very substantial and has grown rapidly over the past two decades. Ramesh (2004, 163) notes that despite a 1980 ban on private tutoring at the secondary school level, the ratio of students in private tutoring tripled

---

34. See Philippine Health Insurance Corporation website at http://philhealth.gov.ph.

35. But note growing disagreement as to the developmental outcomes of this emphasis (ADB *KI* 2003, 27).

36. At the primary level, private enrollments make up a very small percentage of total enrollments in all four countries.

37. Accounting for roughly 7.1% of GDP. January 7, 2004.

between 1980 and 2000 while private expenditure for tutoring increased by a multiple of 22! Ramesh (163) further cites OECD findings that "Korea is unmatched in the extent to which it relies on private provision and financing of education." In part, this growth of private financing is driven by competition for university and technical college admission. In addition, the public/private educational divide has become ever more porous, as regional public institutions have increasingly relied on special fees, private tutoring, and student purchase of books and supplies to meet their own financial requirements.[38] Further, from the standpoint of government policy, educational reformers beginning in 1985 recommended increased autonomy for school administrators and local authorities as well as greater government support for private schools (Ramesh 2004, 163). And at the tertiary level, growing reliance on student tuition at public universities is evidenced by sharp tuition increases of nearly 83 percent between 2001 and 2010.[39] Three of Korea's most prestigious universities, Ehwa Women's University, Yonsei University, and Korea University, are all private.

In China, primary and middle school education was once provided by rural collective organizations (Guan 2000). As China has increasingly relied on tuition-based and private school instruction, tuition costs have increased beyond the means of many working-class families,[40] thus exacerbating a class-stratified educational system.[41]

At primary and secondary levels, children of migrant workers in urban industrial zones rarely qualify for public school admission since they lack local residency status. Instead, they often are forced to enroll in rudimentary private schools. Roughly seventy such schools operate in Shenzhen alongside a number of other schools established by local NGOs or other civil society organizations.[42] Indeed, given that only 2.5 million of a total Shenzhen population of more than 14 million can claim legal local residency, this city's educational disparities have become quite alarming, pushing China increasingly to encourage NGOs and a variety of other registered "social groups" to provide educational and other social services to temporary residents of

---

38. There has been a trend toward privatization of education in Malaysia and Indonesia as well. Also see Ramesh (2003, 2004).

39. Kwangkun Lee, doctoral candidate at Binghamton University, personal communication, 2011.

40. In China, inadequate resourcing for public education has led to rapid growth in family expenditures for private education (and tutoring), and even to new opportunities for foreign investors to enter this sector. "China Goes for Private Lessons," *Wall Street Journal*, January 6, 2004.

41. Ibid.

42. "A Work in Progress," *Economist*, March 19–25, 2001, 12–14.

Beijing, Shanghai, Shenzhen, and other urban centers (Hsu forthcoming).[43] At the tertiary level, while virtually all Chinese universities are public, student fees make up a substantial portion of university revenues, as do the private businesses those universities sometimes establish to produce additional revenues (ADB *KI* 2003, 35).

Similarly, regional public universities in Thailand and elsewhere have been pushed to become more financially and operationally independent of government, with the ultimate goal of financial autonomy or full privatization.[44] Further, there is increasing interest in establishing private for-profit universities. Nation Multimedia group, for example, is creating regional universities on the model of the for-profit Kaplan College chain in the United States.[45] And of the four countries included here, the Philippines has most fully embraced the core principles of devolution and privatization in education. By the early 2000s, private tertiary enrollments were nearly half of total enrolments (ROP, *SY* 2005, 73). And roughly 80 percent of all students enrolled in technical and vocational education courses are in privately run organizations funded and utilized by major corporations to generate needed worker skills (McKay 2006, 73).

Deregulating the Labor Process?

A labor-systems perspective directs attention not only to labor markets and social protections, the predominant focus of mainstream accounts, but to the labor process as well, and to the relationship between the labor process and other phases of labor transformation. Of particular importance in the context of reform, labor market deregulation has frequently brought social dislocations and political opposition. Insofar as these emergent social tensions have spawned disruptions in the labor process, it is there that states and employers have sought to manage social tensions through efforts to contain oppositional unionism and labor militancy. In this sense, tensions in one phase of the labor system may evoke compensatory responses in another.

The earlier transition to export-oriented industrialization most dramatically illustrates such a scenario, as governments mounted organized efforts to reduce labor costs, only to face mounting worker militancy. But if early

---

43. "Taming Leviathan," *Economist,* March 19–25, 2011, 3–4. It must be noted that government policy toward these NGOs has vacillated, from support to repression, depending on the changing political climate. Notable here is the sudden closure of large numbers of migrants' schools in Beijing in 2011. "Beijing's Migrant Workers: School's Out," *Economist,* September 3, 2011, 40.

44. "Autonomy Plan on Back Burner," *Nation* (online), February 11, 2007.

45. "NMG Introduces Nation University," *Bangkok Post* (online), February 22, 2011.

EOI sometimes encouraged repressive labor regimes, a second pattern of state regulatory disengagement from the labor process more clearly reflects the imprint of market reform in which private or local agents and structures partially displace state regulatory agents. This latter pattern is most evident in the state-enterprise sector. Here, the close linkage of the production politics within SOEs with larger political and clientelist relations that are themselves intermeshed with state politics ensured an interpenetration of employment, politics, and the state. That interpenetration took a variety of forms. In China, party officials made up a line of authority and official oversight that paralleled and often subordinated management-labor lines of authority. In Thailand, and to a degree also in the Philippines, workers in state enterprises linked to different ministries and political factions often become caught up in bureaucratic turf wars and in the larger politics of privatization. In this situation politicians and bureaucrats cultivated the clientelist loyalties of employees and public-sector unions through wage and benefit increases; union accommodations and protections; and efforts to thwart, delay, or negotiate the terms of privatization in ways favorable to employees. In such a context, deregulation implied an increased institutional separation of enterprise from state through the granting of greater managerial discretion and autonomy, whether through a reduction in the oversight powers of government, the granting of greater managerial autonomy in personnel and production decision, or the outright privatization of state enterprises themselves. This more general delinking of state and enterprise applies as well, although less dramatically, to private-sector firms, where labor-management relations were less closely managed by government, an outcome further reinforced under transitions to democratic reform.

This general disengagement of the state from the labor process has been encouraged by other structural consequences of labor market deregulation. Of particular importance are the growth of contingent employment, SOE privatization, increased international competition, and growing employment vulnerability—trends that have cumulatively reduced the organizational capacity of workers and unions to challenge firms and governments. This structural demobilization of labor has had the effect of reducing the *need* for state intervention in labor relations or for repressive state regulation.

In this context may be noted the implications of ILO efforts to encourage international ratification of ILO conventions relating to the freedom of association, collective bargaining, and the right to strike, as well as a host of more specific conventions supporting worker rights, elimination of child labor, improving conditions of work, supporting freedom from discrimination, and the like. If ratified, it would seem, these conventions should foster new freedoms for workers and organizational opportunities for unions, in part redressing the power imbalance between workers and employers. Recognizing the uncertainties in determining whether these ratifications have been effectively implemented, they are nonetheless informative in signaling official intentions.

The continuing legacy of progressive Philippine labor legislation is seen in both a greater number of ratifications in that country than in the others (twenty-one as early as 1980 and thirty-three by 2010) (ADB, *KI* 2005, 40; ADB, *Core Labor Standards Handbook* [http://www.ilo.org/ilolex, accessed Sept 21, 2011]). Thailand has ratified the fewest conventions (fourteen by 2010), while Korea has ratified twenty-four, and China (officially) twenty-two. These data suggest that the Philippines, more than the other countries, has sought to provide at least formal legislative protections to workers and unions, although enforcement gaps seriously undermine those protections.

To the extent ILO ratifications, along with political reforms in some cases, have eventuated in less-restrictive labor regimes, the resulting deregulation of the labor process might seem to work to the advantage of workers and unions as they exploit their new independence of state controls in confronting employers. But, in fact, the outcome for labor has been more problematic. First, as noted earlier, economic structural changes associated with reform have tended to undermine the organizational strength of trade unions. Second, acceptance of the right of workers to associate freely and to form unions has often only *diminished* the power of unions by encouraging organizational fragmentation and plural unionism among competing groups of workers (Caraway 2009), as has happened in Thailand. I return to this possibility in later chapters.

The disempowerment of organized labor in part explains the earlier finding of increasingly shallow social protections among formal sector workers whose position has thus been compromised by labor market deregulation (especially in Korea and the Philippines), the structural outcomes of economic reform, SOE marketization and privatization, selective or weak enforcement of labor legislation, labor-movement fragmentation and weakness, growing international competition, regulatory localization, and increased labor market instability. In many cases, of course, these reform outcomes have been countered or balanced by the continued functioning of existing protections (e.g., Philippine social programs, Korean livelihood protections and health programs) that had responded to earlier political pressures or that were instituted in tandem with deregulatory reforms (e.g., contractualization in China and Korea). In chapter 9 I discuss ways in which some of these existing protections have been expanded, adapted, and supplemented in more recent years.

PART III

The Tensions
of Reform

CHAPTER 7

Compromising Economic and Social Agendas

> [T]he change from regulated to self-regulating markets at the end of the eighteenth century represented a complete transformation in the structure of society.... such an institutional pattern could not have functioned unless society was somehow subordinated to its requirements.... A market economy must comprise all elements of industry, including labor.... But labor (is) no other than the human beings themselves of which every society consists.... To include them in the market mechanism means to subordinate the substance of society itself to the laws of the market.
>
> —Karl Polanyi 2001 [1944], 74–75

Economic restructuring and reform have brought mixed outcomes from the standpoints of both economic and social agendas. In seeking to understand ongoing reform-policy trajectories, it is necessary to identify the tensions and instabilities associated with reform policies, tensions that have importantly influenced the policies and institutional strategies of ruling groups across the region. These tensions may or may not be directly evidenced in the actual flow of events and trajectories of reform. Rather, they are seen as only latent or tendential, instead of necessary, outcomes of deregulatory policies, contingent in their outward manifestation on the extent which, and the success with which, they have been accommodated and addressed in particular countries and economic sectors. I begin with the most prominent element in most programs of labor reform: the deregulation of labor markets.

Transforming and Disorganizing Labor Markets

If the partial freeing of formal-sector labor markets from the regulatory oversight of states is typically justified as enhancing the flexibility of labor allocation among competing uses, its institutional tensions may become apparent in the context of rapid economic change alongside a slow or difficult integration of workers previously displaced from stagnant economic sectors into newly emerging or rapidly growing sectors. These tensions may be rooted in the displacement of long-established informal-employment networks; the loss of informal social supports and safety nets to cushion employment change; heightened transitional risks for workers; and new patterns of structural unemployment and employment segmentation. These institutional frictions and social imbalances, relating to the economic agendas of businesses and governmental elites and to the livelihood needs of workers, have the effect of impeding, rather than facilitating, the transition to flexible labor markets, both because they fail to efficiently move workers from declining to growing sectors and because they provoke opposition and social instability.

In the context of development and reform in Asia, six tensions have proven especially difficult in this regard: first, the sometimes problematic movement of workers out of declining sectors (e.g., agriculture and state enterprises) in order to make them available for reemployment in rapidly growing manufacturing sectors; second, the training and adaptation of these now mobile workers for new, more demanding types of employment; third, provision for a degree of predictability and security of livelihood in the context of the transition; fourth, mechanisms to ensure the efficient movement of workers into new employment; fifth, institutional support structures and safety nets for workers and their families settling in new manufacturing centers; and sixth, the reestablishment of stable labor-management relations in now-more-fluid labor markets.[1]

Of course, these various institutional tensions vary in importance across different sectors and labor systems. The need for regulated stable employment, for example, is less important in the construction trades and in early stage export processing than in other sectors that require continuous workforce development and worker participation, just as the need for institutional support structures is less pressing for incoming single migrant workers than for workers accompanied by families and looking for more permanent work and stable residency. Inasmuch as some of these requirements, relating especially to stable employment relations and the creation of social support structures for relocated workers, affect the labor process and of the social reproduction of labor, their discussion continues into subsequent sections dealing more specifically with those other phases of labor systems.

---

1. Here we refer primarily to the securing and definition of the employment relation between worker and employer in external labor markets. This external face of employment is to be distinguished from the labor process itself.

China provides the most dramatic illustration of the institutional dislocations and instabilities economic reform may impart to labor markets. Since
the late 1980s, Chinese populations have faced increasingly difficult times
in economically stagnant rural areas.[2] Rural stagnation has been paralleled
by burgeoning new employment opportunities in coastal economic zones
along with rapidly growing service, financial, and heavy industries in major
cities, but in the context of institutional rigidities that render economic and
geographical relocation risky and difficult. Some of those rigidities relate
to educational inequalities that render rural populations uncompetitive for
many higher-paying urban jobs. Others relate to lack of secure property
rights in rural land that makes long-term migration risky, along with *houkou*
residency requirements that curtail migrant access to and claims on legal protections, education, health, and social services in urban areas. By consequence
of these impediments to stable urban employment, China's "floating mass"
of itinerant workers seeks primarily short-term employment on a casual basis
in urban centers, often migrating back and forth seasonally depending on
the labor requirements of farms and family businesses back home (Solinger
1999).[3] The absence of urban support structures is, in turn, partly explained
by the rapidity and scale of migration,[4] and partly by the reluctance or inability of urban authorities and resident populations to assume the financial,
institutional, and social burdens of accommodating large numbers of new
residents.[5] One obvious consequence of this labor market rigidity is to further widen existing disparities between urban and rural incomes.[6]

Other institutional difficulties arise in regard to the dislocation of the
large numbers of Chinese workers laid off from state-owned enterprises. By
comparison with urban immigrants, these former SOE workers are afforded
at least rudimentary social protections inasmuch as they often hold urban
residency status and thus qualify for a number of social services while they
seek new work. In addition, their former SOE employers usually provide

2. A problem that will likely become worse as WTO-required reductions in agricultural sub
sidies, along with increased liberalized agricultural trade regimes, place even greater pressure on
Chinese farmers.

3. "For Migrants, Chinese Factory Offers a New Life," *Wall Street Journal,* December, 31, 2004.

4. Estimated at 200 million rural migrant workers at the end of the '00s. "Beijing's Migrant
Workers: School's Out," *Economist* September 3, 2011.

5. A high-ranking Chinese official suggested to me in a personal interview that there is a growing desire among urban workers and within trade unions to place greater restrictions on worker
migration into urban centers.

6. One estimate for 2002 posited an average monthly family income of 2,366 yuan in rural areas
as opposed to 7,000 yuan in urban areas. "China: Migrant Workers," *South China Morning Post,* May 8,
2003. "Rising Inequality in China," *Hindu Business Line,* January 3, 2006 (www.thehindubusiness
line.com/2006/01/03).

some continuing benefits to retrenched workers. Since many of these workers are seeking skilled jobs that are more stable than those sought by rural
migrants, a more pressing problem for them is their lack of qualification for
reemployment. By consequence, many wind up in petty service sectors trying to supplement meager SOE severance and retirement benefits.[7] Discontent and protest among these former SOE workers, along with the frustration
and disillusionment of migrant workers, creates a source of social and political
instability that the national leadership has been forced to address.

If a contradiction arises in simultaneous pressures to speed the movement
of migrant and other workers into expanding economic centers and also to
manage and at the same time to slow that movement in order to permit a
more controlled urban assimilation, other institutional dilemmas arise relating to job information and matching, recruitment, retraining, and the regulation and stabilization of employment. These further institutional problems
reflect the more general disorganization of labor markets stemming from a
disruption both of earlier systems of state-organized labor allocation and of
the informal social networks in which employment systems were embedded.[8]

The institutional failures of Chinese labor markets go far in explaining
seemingly contradictory patterns and trends: labor "surpluses" alongside employer reliance on coercive measures to prevent workers from quitting; very
rapid growth in labor-intensive employment sectors alongside continuing
high rates of unemployment and underemployment; a growing imbalance
between the need for and availability of technical skills; and institutional
and political efforts both to facilitate rural–urban migration and to manage
or even impede it. These and other contradictions, and the floating mass of
workers caught up in them, are symptomatic of institutionally disorganized
labor markets.

As Polanyi observed, in the short term the dislocations associated with
efforts to commodify labor typically call forth informal societal modes of
reregulation (Polanyi 2001 [1944]). In Chinese coastal cities, to take one
example, increased crowding into petty services sometimes leads workers to
form gangs in order to protect their particular occupations or trades from
competing groups. Of greater importance are new, locale- and kinship-based
recruitment networks that have flourished under reform and informalization,

---

7. "China's Entrepreneurs Cash In on Odd Jobs." *BBC News,* January 2, 2004 (http://news.bbc.
co.uk/go/pr/fr/-/2/hi/business).

8. Solinger (1997) notes a continuance of reliance on informal social networks, in lieu of impersonal labor markets, for job search and recruitment in Chinese industry. It is suggested here that
the current scale and volatility of the movement of rural workers to and from urban factories has
increasingly disrupted those informal networks, thus speeding the transition to market allocation.

which have mediated and channeled labor flows through personal references, information sharing, and social-support systems, while also enhancing
employment stability through social and kinship intermediation and support. Illustrative of the functioning of these networks is the frequently noted
tendency for young migrant women to search together for jobs and to work
for the same employers (Lee 1998).[9] For their part, employers often utilize
these informal networks to their own advantage in recruiting and managing
workers (Lee 1998). Inasmuch as the very rapidity and scale of migration has
stressed and taxed these evolving social networks, they have been paralleled
by the growth of largely impersonal and noninstitutionalized labor markets
that have failed to play these necessary stabilizing roles of managing the
sectoral and geographical mobility of workers. More generally, the Chinese
case illustrates the destabilizing consequence of socially disembedding labor
markets without quickly re-embedding them in new regimes of institutional
regulation and social protection.

Thailand shares with China a long-standing reliance on seasonal migration
from poor rural areas to meet the needs for low-skill labor in industrial and
commercial centers. But, unlike China, where this migration has spawned a
disruptive, unbalanced, and socially destabilizing mass migration of workers,
Thailand continues to have kinship and community networks that embed
and organize the migration. This greater continuity derives from a long-
established pattern of accommodation and reciprocity linking the relatively
poor but stable regional economies of the North and Northeast, where the
seasonal agricultural cycle encourages and permits outward migratory flows,
with Bangkok and other urban centers.

If China provides the most dramatic case of labor market disorganization,
social instability, and high rates of frictional unemployment,[10] South Korea
presents a somewhat different case—one of structural unemployment rooted
in a loss of low-skill manufacturing jobs caused by the relocation of standard-
production manufacturing to China and elsewhere, on-going trade liberalization, and a sectoral shift from manufacturing to modern services. Loss of a
manufacturing base is rooted as well in continued dependence on Japanese and
other foreign companies for higher-value goods and services that, if produced
domestically, might compensate for at least some of this job loss through a creation of higher-skilled and technical employment, thus addressing the serious
problem of high levels of unemployment among college graduates.[11]

---

9. "For Migrants, Chinese Factory Offers a New Life," *Wall Street Journal,* December 31, 2004.
10. Which is to say, labor market inflexibility.
11. "Policy Fails to Curb Soaring Youth Unemployment," *Chosun Ilbo,* May 20, 2003.

The Philippines, by contrast, highlights a somewhat different set of employment tensions rooted in a convergence of reform and economic stagnation. Given a historically long trajectory of market reform in this model debtor nation, the social tensions of reform have cast a long shadow over three decades of Philippine development. If in the other three countries rapid growth and poverty reduction have partly compensated and muted the tensions of reform, the Philippines more nearly resembles Latin American nations that have experienced cyclical economic stagnation, debt-driven economic stabilization, relatively high levels of unemployment,[12] and social discontent. It is in this context that successive governments have relied on labor exports as an economic and social safety valve during hard times. It can be argued that early economic reform, especially in the areas of external trade and finance, largely precluded the sorts of state-led developmental upgrading more evident in other Asian countries that eventuated in the growth of higher-level jobs for technical and college graduates. Rather, the types of efficiencies realized under reform have tended to lock this economy into a static trajectory of market-led global integration. In this context, the country's significant investment in higher education has only eventuated in cumulative pressures on domestic labor markets, a continuing outflow of human capital, and political instability.

Undermining Social Reproduction and Protection

From the standpoint of economic competitiveness and growth, a critical function of labor systems is to assure the continuing replenishment of human capital, relating especially to education and training, primary health care, housing, and the adequacy of pay and benefits to sustain the ongoing livelihood of workers and their families. In earlier discussion I suggested some ways in which economic reform has compromised this essential function, as social-policy reform increasingly disadvantaged the working population and poor families in gaining access to primary health care and education. New competitive pressures posed by external liberalization and economic restructuring have only aggravated this problem. Intensified cost pressures have led employers to limit training expenditures to a restricted pool of long-term skilled workers in core production activities, at the expense of lesser-skilled workers whose potential economic contribution is thus wasted. And the push for increased labor market flexibility, along with an attendant

---

12. Jorge Sibal et al. (2008, 285) estimate unemployment at around 10% and underemployment at around 20% during the 1990s and early '00s.

reliance on contingent (both skilled and unskilled) labor, has discouraged employer investments in skills, which are lost when workers change jobs. Here, as in education and primary health care, families and communities are forced to assume an increasing share of the costs of social reproduction, just as intensified cost pressures have forced employers to hold down wage and benefit costs for all but their most valuable workers. Insofar as women often assume the major burden of social reproduction, the typically greater impact of casualization and cost cutting on women than on men further exacerbates this problem.[13] Siengthai (2008, 316) notes in this regard that the late-1990's crisis in Thailand eventuated in a disproportionate movement of females from formal-sector employment to family and own-account work, especially in rural and agricultural activities. More generally, in the context of increasing labor market flexibility, women workers have been disproportionately affected by the economic crises across the region.[14]

Given the critical importance of job earnings for the replenishment of labor and the sustaining of family livelihood, it might be expected that heightened competition in cost-sensitive export sectors might tend to push pay levels below minimal subsistence requirements. Indeed, some workers in China's expanding export zones, in both construction and manufacturing, are actually denied pay for months at a time (Lee 2007), a problem that has been exacerbated by company failures and bankruptcies during the most recent world recession. By consequence, low-skill workers in these export sectors may be forced to rely on supplemental family support, and often exhibit high turnover rates and early withdrawal from industrial labor after only a few years' employment.

Similarly, in the export zones of industrial Guangdong, legislation on permissible work hours stipulates a maximum of forty hours work per week plus a maximum of thirty-six additional hours per month at overtime rates.[15] But this same legislation is then compromised by lack of enforcement and by legislative loopholes, such as an appended legal provision allowing additional hours if they are deemed "economically necessary." Because of the resultant work intensification, many workers (sometimes working as much as sixty-five hours per week) effectively burn out after two or three years and quit. This outcome forces employers into a constant search for replacements.

---

13. World Bank (cited in Islam and Chowdhury 2000, 173); ADB 2010, 148. Also see "Improving Gender Parity to Fight Poverty," *Bangkok Post,* April 13, 2010.

14. "Improving Gender Parity to Fight Poverty," *Bangkok Post,* April 13, 2010; "The Battles of Filipino Women Workers," *Asian Labour Update,* April–June 2009: 10.

15. Interview with Stephen Frost, then at Hong Kong City University, November 20, 2003.

While high labor turnover rates are not entirely unwelcome, being both a source and a consequence of labor market flexibility, they do impose their own costs relating to recruitment, training, and work discipline.

Reliance on migratory labor for low-skill casual work provides an important structural foundation for the externalization of market risk and of the costs of social reproduction and protection more generally to families and rural communities. In China, the beginnings of this externalization or "societalization" of social reproduction are to be found in the increased reliance of TVEs on short-distance migratory workers after 1984 legislation allowed farmers to work in nearby towns. These workers relied less heavily on their new work units than on family and community for basic support and services (Arrighi 2009, 41). In the urban industrial centers of both China and Thailand, labor is called forth on demand from what are essentially labor reserves in which rural families and communities substantially assume the burdens of labor force reproduction, maintenance, and protection (Lee 1998).[16] Lack of access to urban social services among Chinese migrant workers only reinforces this pattern (Zhao 1999, 767).[17] As noted earlier, Chinese employers may rely heavily on locality-based social networks and rural families, not only for recruitment of the many young female workers needed for export processing and assembly but also to absorb the costs of preparing and motivating these workers to make themselves available for employment and to reabsorb and support them when their labor is no longer needed.[18] It may be noted that even in industrially advanced Korea, agriculture temporarily absorbed large numbers of workers during the late 1990's crisis (Kang et al. 2001, 99).

These cost-driven migratory labor systems often link dynamic industrial centers with families and communities in impoverished rural areas. Where rural development programs fail to address problems of rural poverty or more directly undermine rural livelihoods, as in the case of land seizures from Chinese farmers or the widespread polluting of rivers and land across much of Asia, the increased financial burdens associated with education, primary health care, and housing may prove overwhelming. And, under these circumstances, many rural families and communities are unable to sustain workers and their dependents during economic downturns and heightened unemployment. This problem became dramatically evident during the first year of

---

16. For a similar argument on Indonesia, see Diane Wolf (1992) on the importance of family support for the livelihood of their "factory daughters" in urban factories of Indonesia.

17. Also see Denise Hare (1999, 45) on "push" versus "pull" factors in Chinese migration flows.

18. Lee (1998) discusses the importance of such networks for young "maiden workers" in China's export-processing zones.

Thailand's financial crisis in the late 1990s, when employers and government agencies encouraged Bangkok's laid-off workers to return to their home communities in the rural northern and northeastern regions of the country. It quickly became apparent that these communities could no longer reabsorb returning family members and that the social problems of urban unemployment were simply being transferred to rural villages.[19] Similarly, Guan (2000) notes the diminished capacity of rural areas of China to provide effective social safety nets, previously organized within worker collectives, for migrant workers returning home from cities. While these rather extreme manifestations of labor-system failure pertain to only the more disadvantaged segments of the workforce, they do exact a developmental toll.

Closely related to these tensions of social reproduction are other problems of social protection, including economic support during times of unemployment due to old age, disability, illness, or retrenchment. I have noted that home villages provide an essential, if sometimes inadequate, social safety net for many migrant workers. As discussed earlier, the attenuation of traditional social-support networks and locality-based mutual assistance and the structural dislocations of labor market deregulation, privatization, nonenforcement of labor laws, external trade liberalization, and a number of other factors associated directly or indirectly with reform have effectively compromised livelihood protections for large segments of the workforce. Of particular importance is social-policy reform, which tends to shift the rules of access and eligibility from citizen entitlement to ability to pay. These changes, along with reduced subsidies for essential goods and services, enhance market-based opportunities for some while undercutting citizen-based provision for others.

China's experience with state-enterprise reform offers a good illustration of the impact of reform on social reproduction and protection. A central purpose of this reform has been to force state enterprises to rely less on state subsidies and more on profitability to sustain themselves. This change has been paralleled by legislation freeing state enterprises from many of their social mandates relating to community services, social welfare, the generation of employment, and the social well-being of their workers. This has meant that long-standing requirements that state enterprises provide for the health care,

---

19. While it is difficult to disentangle the effects of reform and crisis, the reforms had been underway for twenty years in countries such as Thailand and China, and haltingly in South Korea itself. As noted earlier, what the late-1990's financial crisis did was to exacerbate, more starkly reveal, and thus politicize many of the social and institutional vulnerabilities and fault lines consequent on the reforms.

education, housing, and other social needs of workers and their families have been transferred to local and municipal governments. Given the reluctance or fiscal inability of local governments to assume these new roles, social services and supports have languished, or, alternately, become unbearably expensive, as local hospitals, schools, and other public agencies have imposed fees, taxes, tuition assessments, and other required payments on users, thus pushing the costs of those services beyond the means of many poor families.

Diminished livelihood protection bears its own economic costs, such as the diminution of short-term income support that enables unemployed workers to remain in the workforce while looking for other work or entering retraining programs. In this context, social insurance protection from short-term loss of income may be an essential requirement of labor market deregulation itself, insofar as it socially and politically buffers the social dislocations of labor market flexibility and job instability. But, despite the important economic role of livelihood protection, the incentives for corrective policies and action in this area are weak. First, by contrast with the more obvious benefits to employers of proactive social-reproduction policies, those of social protection are more indirect, less visible, and longer term. The pressure to expand social protections is further diminished by two partly erroneous but widespread assumptions: first, that social protections are generally incompatible with labor market flexibility and, second, that social protections reduce wage dependency and thus undermine labor discipline. Thus, those economic pressures that often elicit positive policy responses to deficits of social reproduction are typically less effective in encouraging enhanced social protections. And for this reason, labor politics, rather than economic considerations, must typically drive new policies of social protection.

It should of course be recalled that these negative consequences of reform and deregulation apply unevenly across the labor force. In the context of deregulation, dualistic outcomes are more common, as employers seek to protect (and retain) their skilled core workers from direct labor market competition while they shift the burden of retaining these costly workers to casual, temporary, and subcontract workers in noncore activities.[20]

The consequence of increasing dualism is apparent in South Korea, where continuing problems of unemployment are accompanied by increasing bonuses offered permanent workers in major companies. In this context, the growth of a cumulatively disadvantaged underclass threatens long-term social

---

20. Dualism is consistent with the assertion of a growing skill premium in the wage outcomes of workers in countries undergoing trade liberalization (World Bank 2002; also see McMichael 2008, 191).

stability. And, for this reason, fear of the emergence of a permanent underclass has entered national development debates in Korea and elsewhere in the
region (Kang et al. 2001, 107).

Linking Employment Protections with Social Reproduction: Disincentives to Training

Korea's "Toyotaized" stable primary employment sectors provided an institutional foundation for the developmental upgrading of the heavy-industry
sectors in which they are predominantly found. In particular, these mutual-
commitment employment systems, rooted in job security, seniority-based
pay, and internal labor markets, created incentives for both workers and employers to invest in continuous worker training and upgrading. As noted by
Castells (2000 [1996]) in his discussion of Toyotaism:

> The full participation of workers in the innovation process, so that they
> do not keep their tacit knowledge solely for their own benefit... re-
> quires stability of the labor force in the company because only then
> does it become rational for the individual to transfer his/her knowl-
> edge to the company, and for the company to diffuse explicit knowl-
> edge among its workers. (171–72)

This linkage in Korean firms between job security and training investments worked to the benefit of both firms and national development, while
the need for workforce stability carried over as well into the upper tiers of
supply chains. From the standpoint of skill upgrading, Korea's regular workers
are enmeshed in institutional structures and commitments that support and
sustain ongoing training programs and career ladders in firms. Until the late
1990s, these arrangements were reinforced by employment laws that protected
workers from easy dismissal and by social-insurance programs that mandated
a variety of protections and benefits tied to a person's employment status, all
of which discouraged labor turnover.

But it is clear that Korea's stable primary labor systems have in fact become
more and more circumscribed in the face of organizational deverticalization, growing economic turbulence, market segmentation, new technologies
favoring small dynamic firms, and the growth of contingent and contract
employment across all skill groups, including professionals. Of particular interest here is the expansion of contingent labor among skilled and technical workers, and the consequences of increasing contingency on training.
Increasingly prevalent fixed-duration contracts among skilled and technical

workers, along with the growth of "non-regular" work (whether formal or not) for many others, has so foreshortened the time horizon for returns to training and so increased the risk that trained workers may be poached by other firms that an important institutional foundation of Korea's industrial training system is now threatened.[21]

As increasing labor market fluidity and a corresponding growth in contingent and contract employment reduce training incentives for employers, social reproduction is potentially compromised. Where a steady pool of replacement workers can be had for the asking, as in China at least until the mid-'00s, a failure in social reproduction may not pose a direct threat to growth, although it does impede longer-term developmental upgrading as seen in increasing shortages of skilled and trained workers, a situation viewed with alarm by many companies.[22] In other cases, as in industrially advanced South Korea with its greater need for technically trained workers, training deficits have become more and more problematic.[23]

Institutional Tensions in the Labor Process

Structural change and labor reform have variably disembedded the labor process, both organizationally and socially, with important social and economic consequences. As increasingly fluid labor markets have in some instances overwhelmed and marginalized kinship, friendship, and clientelist networks that may either challenge or, in more stable environments, embed and buttress managerial authority, so too have they increasingly undermined firm-level labor processes. For employers, the effective options have been to resort to the blunt disciplining power of pay regimes and threats of dismissal within casual labor markets or, alternately, to try to create mutual-commitment labor relations based on long-term mutual benefits. For most lower-skilled work, the

---

21. An example of this problem is to be found in the experience of Toyota's Thailand assembly plant, where strong reliance on contingent labor discourages plant-level training; 2003 personal interview with plant managers during factory visit.

22. "China Faces Skills Crisis among Senior Skilled Workers," *People's Daily,* December 20, 2003. Also "Companies in China Struggle to Train, Retain Qualified Managers," *Wall Street Journal,* December 30, 2003. The *Economist,* October 21, 2006, 51, reported huge Chinese labor shortages for skilled workers and corresponding growth in the skilled–low-skilled wage gap. Also see, "Factories Struggle to Keep Skilled Workers" (*South China Morning Post,* February 14, 2007), where it was reported that in the Pearl River Delta more than three vacancies exist for every available skilled technician or worker with specialized skills.

23. Conversely, continued reliance on low- and semi-skilled labor for low-cost production has generated little pressure for substantial government commitment to training (see Kuruvilla et al. 2000, 27–28).

labor process increasingly resembles Burawoy's market despotism, in which labor discipline resides primarily in the whip of external labor markets.

As I noted earlier in the context of labor market deregulation, firms may be less motivated to informalize work through subcontracting to other firms than to casualize labor within the firm itself. In this context, deregulation has initially differentiated labor markets from the labor process by disrupting established social networks, only to bring them back together as managers have sought to employ external labor markets, and the material sanctions they provide, as a basis for worker discipline within firms. Alternately, where higher levels of skill and work involvement are required, deregulation may have one of two other outcomes. First, employers may create internal labor markets that institutionally segregate the labor process from external labor markets while encouraging and rewarding workforce stability and long-term organizational commitment. Second, and increasingly, companies may seek to combine flexibility with normative commitment through fixed-term contracts secured through professional and managerial networks of mutual referral and information sharing. These three labor-process strategies correspond respectively to casual, stable, and contract employment.

The gradual marketization of employment relations tends generally to undermine labor control and industrial discipline in a number of ways. In human capital–intensive developmental labor systems employers seek to capitalize on the knowledge, tacit skills, and inventiveness of skilled (and relatively costly) labor through incentives designed to elicit full involvement and commitment rather than only sullen compliance.[24] To the extent reform-driven competitive pressures undermine the costly mutual-commitment employment practices that sustain such involvement, including some combination of job security and benefits, accommodation of personal and family needs, investment in training and career building, and delegation of operational decision making, a principle foundation of responsible autonomy and competitive developmental upgrading is lost.[25] A 2003 study in South Korean found that 65 percent of companies surveyed were concerned about the significant

---

24. I draw a crude but useful distinction here between "cost driven" labor systems in routine, standardized, labor-intensive (vs. skill-intensive) production and "developmental" labor systems requiring constant upgrading of skills, motivation, and employee involvement in critical core economic activities within and across firms.

25. An alternative type of developmental labor system is associated with career structures organized less by stable organizational affiliation (with high levels of interorganizational movement) than by individual career advancement strategies characterized by high levels of interorganizational movement but enduring embeddedness in networks of social and professional relations (e.g., IT software programmers and upwardly mobile academics).

morale and labor tensions following corporate downsizing.[26] By extension, such cost pressures undermine as well the motivation and capacity of large firms to promote and assist suppliers and thus to invest in quality-focused supply chains so essential for industrial upgrading.

A similar challenge to managerial authority occurs in the state-enterprise sector, where the pressures of privatization and marketization undermine normative controls rooted in paternalism and employment security. Under heightened competitive pressures, state enterprises are forced to abrogate many of their traditional employment obligations through reduced job benefits and gradual replacement of protected regular-status workers with contract workers and subcontractors.

Workers who migrate to the expanding export-processing zones face a corresponding transition from family or personal controls previously experienced within small firms or on farms to an impersonal disciplinary power in larger factories.[27] Export factory workers are often enmeshed in a fine division of labor, along with the tedium such a division often creates, that goes beyond the wildest imagination of time and motion engineers in U.S. factories of the 1920s. One report counted two hundred work stations required for the manufacture of an athletic shoe in a single large factory![28] Here the outcome is less one of workplace labor protest than of disruptive rates of absenteeism, job turnover, low morale, and individual indiscipline, along with associated difficulties in recruiting and training new workers on a continuing basis. Indeed, the growing difficulties experienced by employers in filling job vacancies in the coastal export zones may derive as much from work tedium and discipline as it does from pay differentials vis-à-vis other regions and sectors.

In smaller, more poorly resourced domestic firms both family workers and paid employees may operate in a more intensely personal system of controls that variously draw on relations of patriarchy, personal despotism, paternalism, and reciprocity to sustain family labor in order to maintain production during unprofitable periods when wages cannot be paid and more generally to encourage discipline and hard work, if not skill and initiative. Where these smaller firms act as suppliers of goods or services to larger client firms,

---

26. "Report Warns of Layoffs: Long-Term Pain," *Joong Ang Daily,* October 30, 2003.

27. See my discussion of the market-disciplined "hyperproletariat" among first-stage export-processing workers (Deyo 1989, 189–96). For historical discussions of the disruptive influence of established normative commitments in new employment situations during early industrialization, see Wilbert Moore 1965; David Montgomery (1979) and Herbert Gutman (1977).

28. "In Chinese Factory, Rhythms of Trade Replace Rural Life," *Wall Street Journal,* December 31, 2004.

intensified reform-driven competitive pressures may be transferred down supply chains to doubly impact them. In this situation, local firms are forced to rely more and more on social networks and family obligations to sustain operations during chronically difficult times. But since the replenishment of such relations of mutuality depends on periodic financial recapitalization during more profitable periods, trade liberalization may have the effect of generating such unrelenting competitive pressures (particularly among lower-tier informal-sector suppliers) as to preclude this necessary occasional resuscitation. Doner's (2009) discussion of the devastating impact of the financial crisis on Thailand's domestic auto suppliers demonstrates just such an outcome. To the extent a chronic exploitation of social obligation exhausts domestic labor systems, both families and local firms experience stress and sometimes failure.

Under reform, these varied situations of production share two fundamental institutional dilemmas: the first rooted in normative conflict between different forms of labor control associated with different types of jointly functioning labor systems; the second flowing from the transition from older to newer forms of control. Both state-owned and private-sector firms respond to new competitive pressures in part by increasing their numbers of lower-skilled casual workers and skilled and technical contract workers. The market-governed employment practices experienced by these growing numbers of contingent workers presents a stark and unacceptable contrast to the employment conditions enjoyed by those technical, skilled, and supervisory workers who enjoy regular employment status within the same firm. As problematic is the situation in which equally skilled and comparably tasked workers, in many cases working side by side, have vastly different terms of employment depending on whether they are in-house workers or employees of supplier or outplacement firms.[29] Here, segmented and unequal work situations generate resentments and conflicts that may undermine production processes.

The second, but closely related, instance of normative conflict is apparent in cases of SOE reform and privatization. Here, protest is not simply a consequence of threats to job security and benefits. As important is the erosion of existing and expected patterns of mutual obligation, as among Chinese state workers who had enjoyed work protections and extensive (if shallow) benefits during earlier decades. Labor deregulation, whether structural or policy-based, encourages a systemic transformation from a more socially

---

29. As described, for example, by Siengthai (2008, 341) for Thai factory workers.

regulated labor system to one more fully exposed to market competition. Insofar as social regulation, especially as it affords security and conformity to established norms of discipline and mutual obligation, gives way to the relatively anomic governance of markets, expedience, power, and exploitation may displace mutuality in labor recruitment and in the sphere of production. Chinese state enterprises, with their earlier commitment to providing a broad range of educational, health, housing, and other benefits for workers and their families, now confront growing worker opposition to the progressive dismantling of these earlier mandated social supports (C. K. Lee 2007). Similarly, employment practices in large South Korean firms encouraged group and team loyalties along with long-term organizational loyalties, qualities sharply at odds with the market culture now embodied in individual-performance incentives, merit-based job progression, and increased employment contingency. In this context, labor resistance is strongly rooted in the institutional decay of established values and expectations.

A final outcome of deregulation and reform is a progressive undermining of associative modes of labor control, especially through government-sponsored or controlled union federations. In part this outcome flows from the structural demobilization and bypassing of unions and collective bargaining in favor of individually negotiated work contracts. South Korean union densities have declined dramatically. And in China, the decline of the SOE sector alongside rapid growth in private-sector and foreign-enterprise employment has been associated with a gradual attenuation of state influence, which was formerly channeled through the quasi-official All China Federation of Trade Unions (ACFTU).[30] Despite a legal requirement that all firms employing one hundred or more workers must establish a union, many firms in this country have failed to comply.[31] Of course, here as elsewhere, sectoral differences and dualistic employment practices make a difference. Honda, for example, has established a union to help stabilize labor-management relations in their new Guangzhou auto-assembly plant. That top-level managers occupy key leadership posts in this union transforms it into an effective means through which to encourage participative rather than confrontational employment relations. In other cases, particularly in lower-skilled labor-intensive sectors, company unions fail to play even this somewhat passive role, degenerating

---

30. "Official Union Recognition Strategies in China: A Case Study of the Crisis Facing the ACFTU (All China Federation of Trade Unions)."

31. "Accidents Plague China's Workplaces," *Wall Street Journal,* July 29, 2010.

instead into non-functioning or entirely management-dominated agencies of downward control.[32]

Similarly, Korea's government-linked Federation of Korean Trade Unions (FKTU) has been partially displaced by the more militant Korean Confederation of Trade Unions (KCTU), whose independence from government control contributes to an undermining, rather than a buttressing, of workforce discipline. Here, a principle destabilizing role was played by the 1987 presidential Declaration of Democratization and its follow-on endorsement of freedom of association and autonomy in collective bargaining on the part of trade unions (Kang et al. 2001, 104). This endorsement had the effect both of undermining employer control and of enhancing the independence of workers' organizations, with the result that both union militancy and labor costs escalated during subsequent years.

From Exports to Consumption-Led Growth?

Asia's first-stage export drive, along with a host of complementary policies relating to currency exchange rates, external-trade liberalization, FDI incentives, productivist social policies, and repressive labor regimes, encouraged competition based strongly on cost containment. The relative emphasis on international, rather than domestic, markets further contributed to the instituting of low-wage economies across the region.

Low-wage competition both reflected and reinforced a number of the economic tensions of reform. First, of course, is the negative impact of low-wage policies and cost-driven competitive strategies on the social reproduction of labor, as discussed earlier. Second is the way in which competitive cost pressures discourage developmental investments in R & D, in worker skills, and in worker protections and benefits that may be necessary to elicit the organizational or professional commitments necessary for industrial upgrading, thus creating the possibility of a developmental low-wage trap.[33]

As important are the consequences for economic stability. All four countries exhibit high levels of external-market dependence, especially dependence on the major export markets of the United States, Europe, and Japan. Lacking adequate domestic demand to buffer periodic declines in exports, this dependency creates a heightened vulnerability to world-market fluc-

---

32. "When Chinese Workers Unite, the Bosses Often Run the Union," *New York Times,* December 29, 2003.

33. For further discussion, see "R & D Spending Needed to Escape the Middle-Income Trap," *Bangkok Post* (online), August 19, 2010.

tuations, increasing investment risks and undermining long-term economic planning (Palat 2010). The ADB notes in this regard the negative impact of weak domestic demand on growth in these countries and the corresponding need to strengthen domestic markets (ADB *Outlook* 2001, 137, 144, 219).[34]

It is true that the earlier experiences of developmental intervention in Korea, Taiwan, and Singapore suggest ways in which states may engineer transitions from the self-reinforcing deficits of low-wage competition. But such transitions become increasingly difficult as external liberalization and domestic deregulatory reforms weaken the capacity of states to intervene in markets. China, of course, provides an important exception here, as its multilevel state has retained key levers of control through a still-dynamic public-enterprise sector.

It cannot be denied that the dynamic Asian economies have produced rapidly growing middle classes able to purchase increasing numbers of cars, homes, appliances, and other goods that depend heavily on domestic demand. A 2006 study showed, for example, that 23 percent of registered residents in China's Pearl River Delta were at that time officially classified as middle class, based on a growth rate of roughly 11 percent per year since 1986.[35] But even in these fast-growing economies, a very large proportion of the workforce remains locked in low-wage employment, thus precluding the emergence of the broad-based mass-consumption required for more self-reliant development (see Jessop and Sum 2006, 195–96). The Pearl River Delta figures, further, do not include the many migrant workers who lack local residency status but who make up a large proportion of workers there. More important, the well-documented long-term increase in income inequality in China implies a continuing drag on consumer spending,[36] as large numbers of persons remain locked in poverty.[37] Other research shows that the aggregative household share of national disposable income has been in gradual decline since 1995.[38] The World Bank (WB *WDI* 2010) reports in this regard a decline in the contribution of household final consumption to China's GDP from 42 percent in

---

34. This same report notes as well the importance of foreign remittances and government consumption in the Philippines and of fiscal stimulus programs in all four countries in countering the effects of global recession and declining exports during 2009.

35. "23 pc of Delta People Now in Middle Class," *South China Morning Post,* January 10, 2007. This percentage, however, excludes nonresident migrants.

36. See discussion in "Rising Inequality in China," *Hindu Business Line* (online), January 3, 2006.

37. An early study by Mark Selden (1985, 212) of changing levels of rural economic inequality found mixed evidence of a modest decline in income inequality during the initial years of post-1978 reform. This was a result of increased opportunities for nonagricultural employment, but it cautioned that those data failed to take into account that the offsetting attenuation of rural education, health care, and welfare benefits likely increased inequalities in effective levels of living.

38. Bai Chog'en and Qian Zhenjie, China Labor Market Information Center, cited in "Striking Workers in China Win Wave of Raises, New Clout," *Wall Street Journal,* June 9, 2010.

1995 to 34 percent in 2008. In Korea and Thailand, private consumption has played a somewhat more significant role, but it has not increased during this period—remaining in the 50 to 56 percent range in both countries. Only the Philippines, with its somewhat less successful export performance, has relied more extensively (74–77%) on private consumption (WB, *WDI* 2010).

That dependency on narrow middle-class markets may sometimes create new vulnerabilities is suggested not only by the employment outcomes of the 2008–10 crisis in China (ADB *Outlook* 2010, 134) and elsewhere in the region, but as well by high rates of credit card debt among South Korean consumers (147), where the middle class has been in decline both as a percent of households and in relative income levels over recent years,[39] and where reduced consumer spending is seen as having greatly reduced the numbers of new business start-ups.[40] Even in China, middle-class demand for such expensive durable goods as automobiles is in part dependent on rapid expansion of consumer credit.

In recognition of this problem, the Korean government has since the late 1990s sought to increase reliance on domestic markets through expansion of consumer finance.[41] During those same years, several Southeast Asian governments have sought to increase reliance on domestic markets amid uncertain export markets.[42] In the context of the recent global recession, a growing awareness of the need to partially insulate national economies from global export markets led to renewed calls for greater reliance on domestic consumption to sustain development. Indeed, national leaders in the Philippines have attributed the relatively lesser impact of the recession there to that country's relatively greater economic reliance on domestic consumption.

In any case, the longer-term and more general problem remains: that of overreliance on export markets,[43] which further reinforces downward pressure on wages in many sectors by severing the link between production and consumption while simultaneously increasing cost competition for local firms and thus deepening existing economic disparities and muting pressures for industrial upgrading at home. Whether this problem will prove to be an enduring one is at this point uncertain. There are indications of upward wage pressures in China and elsewhere that suggest the countervailing pressure of labor market forces that may already be driving new development strategies.

---

39. "40 Percent of Households Mired in Technical Default," *Korea Times*, November 6, 2003.

40. "Number of Startup Firms Declines Sharply," *Chosun Ilbo*, December 18, 2003.

41. Private consumption is estimated to account for roughly 15% of overall economic growth in 2004. See "Korea Sees Slight Recovery in Consumption," *Wall Street Journal*, March 23, 2005.

42. "Southeast Asia Hits Soft Patch," *Wall Street Journal*, June 7, 2005.

43. Roughly two-thirds of the South Korean economy is export based.

CHAPTER 8

Political Tensions of Reform

Labor Opposition and Public Disorder

> [T]he principle of social protection, aiming at the conservation of man and nature...rel[ied] on the varying support of those most immediately affected by the deleterious action of the market...primarily, but not exclusively, the working and the landed classes.... laboring people to a smaller or greater extent, became representatives of the common human interests that had become homeless.
>
> —Karl Polanyi 2001 [1944], 138–39

> Both in the US and in the UK, the conservative obsession with rolling back the welfare state was met with fierce social and political resistance, as well as with the realities of historical inertia and the basic needs of society.
>
> —Manuel Castells 2000 [1996], 139

Associated with the various institutional and economic tensions of reform are political pressures that must be addressed and that are sometimes primary drivers of the social protections and compensations that have been increasingly prominent in national reform policies and in the augmented Washington consensus more generally. Much of the literature on the politics of Asian economic reform has attended to interelite factional conflicts, as various business groups, government agencies, and elite coalitions have pursued one or another pathway of reform that they see as consistent with their material interests and collective goals. Insofar as this book is focused more specifically on the social regulation of labor systems, the relevant political divide rotates—from horizontal divisions among elite factions to vertical divisions more closely linked to social class and material circumstance. Put differently, if issues of economic structural reform sharply divide factions of capital, those divisions are less sharp in matters of social and labor policy in which employers and state managers tend to converge in seeking to contain labor costs, increase productivity, achieve flexible labor markets, and secure labor peace. For this reason, to the extent changing regimes of social and labor regulation embrace a politics of reform, those politics tend to highlight social class over contending elite factions. This discussion of the labor politics of reform emphasizes regulatory contestation on the part of groups of workers who variably share the circumstances of particular labor systems, and who seek collectively, and sometimes in concert with other groups,[1] to influence policies affecting the adequacy and security of their economic livelihood.

Before discussing the nature and role of labor politics in regulatory change, it is useful to recall the foundational, structurally determined conflicts that drive labor opposition. Such opposition, it will be recalled, may be understood by reference to the differing agendas of workers, employers, and states in the endless cycles of construction and reconstruction of labor systems and national regulatory regimes. From the standpoint of workers, critical considerations relate to access to jobs, conditions of work, and the adequacy and security of livelihood. From the standpoint of employers what is important is access to qualified, disciplined labor within terms of exchange compatible with competitiveness, efficiency, and profitability. State agencies may emphasize yet other goals, such as national economic growth and political stability or legitimacy, that are only loosely associated with firm-level competitiveness and profitability and that focus on longer-term structural changes rather than short-term competitive efficiencies. Each phase of the labor system may thus be understood in quite different ways. What is social reproduction from the standpoint of capital becomes economic livelihood for workers; labor market allocation becomes, for workers, the struggle to find adequate work and for employers the need for flexible access to qualified labor; and the labor process itself becomes the experience of deprivation or self-realization for workers, the essential site of production and valorization for employers, and a potential site of political challenge to states. The often-conflicting agendas of livelihood and accumulation intersect politically in the social construction of labor systems, becoming a critical focus and domain of class conflict, as dominant elites seek to institutionalize and adapt labor systems to the requirements of economic expansion and profitability while workers seek to mold those same labor systems to requirements of livelihood adequacy and security. This institutional conflict varies in nature and intensity across sectors, national economies, and time. Rapid economic growth, periods of unchallenged domination by capital, political repression,

---

1. As in "populist" movements or regimes.

and other conjunctural factors may mute this conflict or, alternately, define situations that offer shared benefits of cooperation. But during periods of economic decline or rapid and uneven structural transformation, conflict tends to sharpen, while the domains within which such conflict occurs (national politics, sectoral negotiations, shop-floor bargaining, community-based confrontation, and the like) vary widely depending on structural and political circumstances. The domains of contestation are associated in turn with somewhat distinct forms of labor politics and social regulation (Kotz 1994).

As well, it is important to distinguish between micro level labor contestation within the labor process, and the broader labor politics that, intentionally or not, more directly influences national regulatory regimes. Within the labor process, the various situations of employment (as seen in table 5.1) are associated with correspondingly different forms of worker response and resistance. Thus, stable primary workers rely more heavily on labor organizations, collective contracts, work disruptions, collegial solidarities, and personal relations with superiors to improve their work situation; on formal and informal negotiations with employers to enhance pay and benefits along with new training opportunities; and in some instances on internal labor markets for individual career advancement. Skilled contract workers rely to a relatively greater extent on labor market bargaining power, the rights and protections afforded by individual employment contracts, job-linked social insurance, and state regulatory agencies to enforce legally established contracts and protective-labor standards. Casual, informal, and less-skilled contingent workers varyingly contest their work conditions through sullen compliance, appeals to personal relations with superiors, job change, and disorganized resistance, while relying on NGOs and social movements for social protections and compensations through government social policy. In this sense these more economically vulnerable workers rely more heavily than do stable and contract workers on the regulatory protections of the state. By contrast, family workers rely on the mutuality and obligations of kinship, while non-family related workers in small firms appeal, with varying success, to the personal responsibilities of their employers and patrons, and to the normative standards of the local social networks in which smaller firms are often enmeshed.

In this book I attend less to the micro-politics of the enterprise-level labor process than to the broader patterns of labor politics that varyingly influence national regimes of social and labor regulation. Discussion in the previous chapter identified a number of institutional tensions relating to the economic strategies of firms and governments. But that same discussion noted as well the sometimes negative implications of those tensions from the standpoint of workers' agendas of livelihood security, equity, conditions of work, and participation in economic decision making. Of particular importance were the problematic outcomes flowing from the uneven externalization of market risk and costs of social reproduction from firms and governments to families, communities, and private-sector providers; retrenchment of the social wage and a corresponding shift from the principal of citizen entitlement to that of market access to essential goods and services; the marketization and privatization of public enterprise; the informalization of employment, and the growing contingency and insecurity of employment in more flexible, globalized labor markets. I now turn to the ways workers have sought politically to address these difficulties.

Labor Resistance: Six Modalities of Labor Struggle

In the context of developing Asian countries, workers have sought to influence labor regimes and social policy through several means:[2] (1) trade union activism; (2) social-movement unionism; (3) labor-oriented NGOs; (4) broad popular-sector social movements; (5) engagement with labor-friendly political parties; and (6) the generalized threat of social disorder.[3]

Union-based labor politics revolve around the terms of employment and the production process; social-movement politics address these same labor issues but insert them into more general issues of collective consumption and the social wage; and labor-oriented NGO-led politics focus on broader livelihood concerns of both employed and unemployed workers. Non–union-mediated social-movement politics center more exclusively on the social wage and social policy. And in some cases, workers have found an additional institutional vehicle in labor-oriented political parties that extend and amplify the power of the other modalities.[4] The final type, the "politics of social disorder," is defined less by a coherent agenda than by the aggregative pressure of public disturbance and an absence of coherent organizational forms through which to address livelihood demands. Each form of labor politics has

---

2. As argued by Dae-Oup Chang (2009), a more radical understanding of labor politics would attend as well to more direct forms of political engagement that fundamentally challenge capitalist institutions rather than seeking to work within those institutions. This book addresses the more conventional question of how labor works within established capitalist institutions, especially by influencing state regulatory regimes and policies.

3. These alternatives refer to collective and noninstitutionalized political mobilizations. Chapter 9 addresses individual institutionalized action, especially that fostered by the elaboration of employment contractualization and legal recourse.

4. One example is the KCTU-linked Korean Democratic Labor Party, established in 2000. This party attracted significant electoral support in 2004, but subsequently languished.

both influenced and been shaped by economic and political reform, and each may usefully be illustrated by reference to the political jurisdictions, economic sectors, and labor systems in which it has assumed a prominent role.[5]

Unions and the Politics of Production

Has trade unionism, following conventional thinking, played only a marginal role in Asian national-development strategies and reform policies? Historically, such a conclusion cannot be supported. Many accounts of the 1949 Communist victory in China emphasize the importance of leftist union militancy in major cities in support of the revolutionary cause. In both Malaysia and the Philippines, labor militancy during the 1930s encouraged the transition from primary-export to import-substituting industrialization. In Indonesia, the Philippines, and Malaysia labor played a significant role in post–World War II independence movements and in the dismantling of colonialism. During the 1950s, Philippine labor militancy played a critical role in the enactment of progressive labor legislation. In Singapore, labor mobilization nearly succeeded in creating a leftist government in the late 1950s and early 1960s, and even after the defeat of radical unionism helped shape the social agenda of the People's Action Party government that came to power under Prime Minister Lee Kwan Yew and quickly adopted the disarming slogan "Socialism That Works" (Nair 1976). After emancipation from Dutch colonial rule in Indonesia, the labor movement was a core political base for the prolabor Sukarno regime.

In Thailand, immediately following the Japanese defeat in World War II, a radicalized labor movement was instrumental in supporting a new, leftist government headed by Prime Minister Pridi Banomyong (1944–47). And, in the context of the unraveling of military rule during the early 1970s, organized labor, supported by students and university academics, mounted a series of rolling strikes that eventuated in passage of the 1975 Labor Relations Act. This act established or consolidated new rights to unionize, to bargain collectively, and to strike; provided for tripartite labor representation in national policymaking; and enacted new livelihood protections, including a minimum wage and workers' compensation (Brown 2004, chap. 5). That these new rights and protections were subsequently abrogated in the wake of

---

5. The remainder of the discussion is confined to China, South Korea, the Philippines, and Thailand. By selecting the experiences of these countries to illustrate the different modalities of labor politics, I do not imply that the countries themselves may be characterized and differentiated in this way, only that the different modalities of labor politics have attained differential prominence in each of these four countries.

the 1976 military coup in no way detracts from the important role of labor, not only in pushing for their enactment but just as important in garnering public support for progressive social policy that influenced future generations of political leaders.

The story of labor politics is somewhat different, however, in the post-1980's period of market reform. Despite a gradual relaxation of political controls in several countries, including broader democratic reforms in Thailand, the Philippines, South Korea, Taiwan, and (belatedly) Indonesia, organized labor has suffered a steady attenuation of influence. Dramatic exceptions certainly present themselves. Militant Korean trade unions have played a sometimes forceful role in opposing privatization, external liberalization, and labor market deregulation. Thai state-enterprise workers were able to press successfully for enactment of Thailand's important Social Security Act of 1990, and then to slow SOE privatization efforts over subsequent years.[6] More dramatically, the economic and political crisis of the 1980s in the Philippines precipitated what Rene Ofreneo terms "a rise in militant unionism whose depth and breadth has no parallels in the country's history" (Ofreneo 1995a, 3). With these and other exceptions, however, unions have generally been relegated to participant or spoiler roles at best, and to policy irrelevance at worst, especially in matters relating to social policy (Haggard and Kaufman 2008, 259–60). Available data on trade union membership, collective bargaining, and labor militancy offer support for such a conclusion.

An important indicator of the potential influence of union-based politics is to be found in union-membership densities. In the era of economic restructuring and reform, Chinese unionism has declined steadily from approximately 60 percent of the workforce in the 1980s to less than 40 percent in 1995 (Chiu and Frenkel 2000, 37) and to 22 percent in 2006 (calculated from PRC, *LSY* 2007). In Korea, the percentage of unionized workers declined from 11 percent of all employed workers in 1989 to 6 percent in 2003. Union density in Thailand declined by 7 percent during the early 1990s, in part due to the forced dissolution of public-sector unions following the 1991 military coup. It is estimated that less than 4 percent of the total workforce is now unionized in Thailand (11% of industrial workers, but more than 50% of state-enterprise workers). And, in the Philippines, approximately 5 percent of the total labor force (18% of public-sector workers and 6% of all employed workers) were unionized in early 2007 (Sibal et al. 2008). Collective bargaining agreements, a second indicator of a legally institutionalized

---

6. "EGAT Union Vows to Oppose Privatization." *Bangkok Post,* June 21, 2003.

union role, show a similar pattern. In Thailand, such agreements cover only about 5 percent of employed workers, and in the Philippines only 1 percent.[7]

It is true that membership levels are not the only determinant of union influence in shaping public policy, as seen most clearly in the institutional leverage still enjoyed by Korean unions despite low union densities. Conversely, higher-density levels may sometimes only reflect government support for co-opted unions, as is the case of China's ACFTU.[8] Nonetheless, low and declining membership levels are an important constraint on the policy influence unions might potentially wield.

While trade unions seek to influence national policy in a variety of ways, their political leverage rests ultimately either on their coalitional voice in national politics, or, more often, on their labor market and workplace bargaining power and on the credibility of the threat of a withdrawal of labor. Work stoppages and strikes are a collective, as opposed to individual, expression of that power. To what extent do workers in these countries use strikes and work stoppages to influence firms and governments? Table 8.1 presents data on levels of industrial conflict in South Korea, Thailand, and the Philippines since 1985.[9] Recognizing that cross-national differences in workdays lost to industrial conflict in part reflect differences in occupational structure, the data for salaried and waged employees are shown separately.

It goes without saying that these data must be viewed with caution. National and temporal variation in data collection and reporting makes comparisons hazardous. In addition, these data include both work stoppages and employer lockouts, although the great majority are worker-initiated work stoppages and strikes. Finally, it is clear that temporal trends in levels of industrial conflict often mirror changing political and economic circumstances that interact in complex ways that may work with or against each other in provoking labor militancy.

Recognizing these and other perils of interpretation, a few observations are nonetheless useful. First, Korean workers rely on union-based industrial militancy to influence firms and governments more often than do their counterparts in Thailand or the Philippines, and Thai workers are the least

---

7. Philippines Department of Labor and Employment, Bureau of Labor and Employment Statistics, *Key Labor Statistics,* annual. Online at http://www.bles.dole.gov.ph. Fourteen percent of registered establishments had collective agreements with at least some of their employees (Sibal et al. 2008).

8. During the protracted and well-publicized strikes by workers in Honda suppliers of China, the ACFTU-affiliated local union failed to become involved or to lend support. "Workers in China Accept Deal, Honda Says," *New York Times* (online), June 4, 2010.

9. Comparable data for China are not available.

Table 8.1   Workdays Lost to Industrial Conflict Per Thousand Employed Workers

Year	Korea		Thailand		Philippines	
	Total employed	Paid employees	Total employed	Paid employees	Total employed	Paid employees
1984	—	—	—	—	—	—
1985	4	8	0	—	124	—
1986	5	9	16	72	—	—
1987	425	755	3	12	92	208
1988	320	510	1	5	71	155
1989	362	613	3	12	44	97
1990	248	413	2	8	60	131
1991	175	289	8	—	50	109
1992	81	133	5	—	30	68
1993	68	111	7	—	29	65
1994	75	120	1	3	23	50
1995	19	—	7	—	23	50
1996	43	68	3	8	19	40
1997	21	—	5	12	24	50
1998	73	119	7	18	20	41
1999	67	109	4	18	—	16
2000	90	144	7	32	11	23
2001	50	79	0	1	7	14
2002	71	111	1	3	12	25
2003	59	90	1	3	5	9
2004	53	80	0	0	2	3
2005	37	56	1	5	4	7
2006	52	77	1	3	1	3
2007	23	34	1	1	0	1
2008	34	50	—	—	1	2
2009	27	38	—	—	0	—

Sources: Calculated from ILO, *Yearbook of Labour Statistics,* annual statistics, and Korean Ministry of Labor, *Yearbook of Labor Statistics,* 1996 and 2005. Thailand: paid employees 1999–2007 from http://laborsta.ilo.org.—: missing data.

prone of all to employ work stoppages and strikes.[10] This difference is most notable during periods of political crisis and democratic reform. Coming out of a period of strict authoritarian controls during the 1980s, Korean strikes surged from 1987 to 1989 as workers rushed to join newly formed independent unions and as new political parties competed for labor support at the beginning of a new democratic era (Koo 2001, 153–87) Similarly, Philippine workers mounted waves of strikes in support of and in response to the successful 1986 overthrow of the corrupt Marcos regime. By contrast, labor militancy in Thailand did not increase appreciably during the political liberalization and democratic transition of the mid- and late 1990s. And, in the Philippines, militancy declined continuously and substantially during the years following the 1986 revolution (Ofreneo 1995b). Further, it is notable

---

10. With notable earlier exceptions, as during 1972–75.

that in none of these countries did the late-1990's regional economic crisis provoke significant union militancy, in part because layoffs and economic hardship increased the economic vulnerability of workers.

ILO data (*YLS* 2010) suggest a further observation. In Thailand, virtually all labor militancy is to be found in the manufacturing sector, whereas in Korea the manufacturing sector accounts for only about two-thirds of all labor disputes. This difference reflects the institutional extension, less prominent in Thailand, of union-based labor politics into Korea's burgeoning modern service sector.

Explaining the Decline in Union-Based Politics

The explanation for declining union densities is to be found in political restrictions and repression, economic structural change and reform, developmental sequencing, and the temporal-historical context within which Asian economic growth has occurred. Political restrictions, the 'usual suspect' in many accounts of labor weakness, have played an important role in all these countries and across the region more generally. These restrictions have to varying degrees included police repression, incorporation into ruling-party structures, and the encouragement of organizational fragmentation.[11] In some cases, as in the Philippines, earlier periods of heightened labor conflict along with increased competitive pressures in cost-sensitive export sectors have supported antiunionism among employers (Sibal et al. 2008). Even following the overthrow of the Marcos regime, President Aquino responded to increased strike activity by invoking strict anti-strike laws enacted under Marcos (Kuruvilla et al. 2000, 32).

In other cases, as in China, official unionism, sponsored and supported by the ruling party, has largely preempted independent unionization and collective action while also ensuring a dominant official voice in union activities. Thus, while unions, now legally required in large firms, have been important in China, they have acted largely as auxiliary organs of the state. By law they must affiliate with the government-linked ACFTU, a requirement that discourages militancy and independent worker representation while confining the role of national unions to that of junior partner within the Communist Party. Further discouraging union activism is the widespread leadership of local chapters by company managers (Chiu and Frenkel 2000, 39), although this poses less of an obstacle in wholly owned foreign enterprises where

---

11. For fuller discussion see Deyo (1989) and Deyo (2006).

workers and Chinese managers may sometimes receive tacit government encouragement in confronting foreign managers.

As elsewhere (e.g., in Singapore), state-linked unions may play an important role, not only in controlling labor and preempting militancy, but also in representing workers in management and governmental policy and in organizing social programs and services for workers. But their independent political role in inserting a worker agenda into public policy is clearly inhibited by their state dependency on the one hand, and lack of membership competition with other unions on the other.[12] Such was the case for Korea's older union confederation, the FKTU, which only belatedly joined oppositional unionists in resisting labor market reforms after growing membership competition from the upstart Korean Trade Union Congress (later the Korean Confederation of Trade Unions) forced greater attentiveness to demands from the rank and file.

In Thailand, close links between the leaders of some peak union federations and particular government agencies and political coalitions encouraged collaborative, if not collusive, relations that blunted and diverted union responses to national reform policy during the 1980s and early 1990s. In addition, the same watershed 1975 Labor Relations Act that offered new support for unions and collective bargaining also imposed important restrictions on unions. As discussed by Andrew Brown, the act:

> set limits on the forms that labour organization would be allowed to take, the range of objectives these organizations were permitted to pursue and the institutional structures and processes through which workers and their unions... could seek to realize their legally defined objectives... [and]... there were numerous restrictions placed on the forms and degree to which... rights could actually be exercised. (2004, 95)

Brown goes on to note that the act precluded union involvement in other than "economic" and employment issues, thus isolating labor organizations from other groups and movements and prohibiting political engagement. Further, by greatly easing the requirements for union formation, it encouraged multiple unions in single enterprises with resulting fragmentation and vulnerability to employer manipulation (Brown 2004, 96). Finally, the act inhibited union activism through rules mandating prestrike cooling-off periods, required mediation, restrictive rules of eligibility for union office

---

12. See the discussion in Murillo (2000) of the role of union dependency on the state in muting union opposition to market reform.

holders, lack of job protection for workers seeking to establish new unions, and the like.

Over the course of the four years following Thailand's 1976 military coup, the 1975 act was suspended under a severe crackdown on organized labor. During the balance of the 1980s, and until a second military coup in 1991 that abolished parliament and dissolved the democratically elected Chatichai government, employers increasingly learned to use the 1975 act to their advantage in dealing with employees. While the 1991 coup temporarily removed state-enterprise workers from the protections of the act,[13] in large part to allow a continuation of privatization programs fiercely opposed by state workers, by the early '00s the 1975 act had become the effective foundation for Thai labor-management relations in both private and state-enterprise sectors.

Despite these various forms of political containment, it remains to be said that democratic reform and political liberalization in many countries of the region have created new political space for organized labor. Legalization of oppositional union federations and reduced restrictions on strikes have given labor greater freedom to contest reform policies of privatization, labor market deregulation, and external economic liberalization. Why then have unions and union politics declined or remained stagnant even amid democratic reform? The answer to this question is in part to be found in the labor outcomes of two decades of economic restructuring and market reform.

Economic Restructuring

In China and Thailand, employment in export-manufacturing sectors has continued to grow rapidly. As we have seen, this pattern of industrialization has been associated with the expansion of unstable and unprotected (and sometimes coercively controlled) work situations inhospitable to effective union organizing. The privatization and marketization of state enterprises has had a further negative impact. Across Asia, privatization has provoked especially sharp labor opposition. As layoffs of state-enterprise workers in China continued, and as the 2008–10 world recession brought increased layoffs in export zones, industrial disputes and informal worker demonstrations increased dramatically.[14] Thai SOE workers, whose unions and employee

---

13. In 2000 state-enterprise workers regained the right to form unions, but not to strike.

14. "Hundreds Clash as Labour Strike Widens," *South China Morning Post* (online), June 9, 2010; "Power Grows for Striking Chinese Workers," *New York Times* (online), June 8, 2010.

associations have been the backbone of Thai unionism for decades,[15] have mounted continuing opposition to ongoing privatization moves under successive governments. And, in Korea, the militant and independent KCTU, which replaced the KTUC in 1995, draws membership and support in part from workers in state enterprises threatened by privatization.[16] Despite this sustained opposition, the effectiveness of labor militancy has been compromised by the structural effects of privatization itself. In China, and to lesser degree in Thailand and the other two countries, privatization has driven labor into largely defensive collective efforts to delay privatization programs while at the same time disempowering state workers whose job security and institutional protections had, during earlier years, given them substantial bargaining power in dealings with management and the state.

In China, union decline is primarily explained by the numerical decline of the highly unionized SOE sector in favor of less-unionized foreign-invested firms. In 1995, union densities in the state-enterprise sector stood at 77 percent, as against 49 percent in collectively owned enterprises and only 35 percent in foreign-funded firms (Chiu and Frenkel 2000, 37–38).[17] In this context, privatization has had the structural effect of shifting employment from unionized to nonunionized sectors.

In private sectors, the liberalization of external trade and investment pose the primary threats, placing heightened competitive pressures on employers and weakening the bargaining power of workers and their unions. In the Korean case, increased cost competition, along with industrial upgrading out of standard production, has been associated with deindustrialization and capital flight, along with growth of modern service and R & D sectors wherein smaller firms gradually supplant the earlier predominance of large manufacturing plants. Resulting declines in average firm size in Korea and elsewhere have in turn further reduced union strength in manufacturing and other sectors, with the possible exception of core industrial sectors in Korea, where the structural foundations for independent unionism, established in the 1970s and early 1980s under industrial-deepening strategies, eventuated in the institutionalization of strong unions and government accommodation of the voice of organized labor (Deyo 1989, 144–47).[18] These disempowering structural

---

15. In 1991 Thai trade unions were banned in the state-enterprise sector then under military rule.

16. Transport workers (e.g., subway workers) have been especially prominent in this regard.

17. Chiu and Frenkel (2000) note that the union density percentage is artificially inflated by the tendency for foreign companies to overreport union formation in order to comply with national legislation requiring large firms to encourage and recognize trade unions.

18. In her analysis of a major database on historical and spatial patterns of labor unrest, Beverly Silver (2003, 38) finds strong labor movements among most workers employed in the mass

effects have, of course, been reinforced by programs of labor market deregulation in Korea and the Philippines and by social-policy and other reforms in all four countries.

If economic restructuring has thus played a critical role in reducing the political capacity of organized labor, weak economic performance has played an important further role in the Philippines. Here, industrial stagnation, widespread poverty, slack labor markets, high rates of underemployment, the escape valve provided by overseas work, and fiscally challenged governments have severely undercut the bargaining power of organized labor.

Developmental sequencing, or the temporal ordering of economic and political reform, is a third influence. Contrary to the experience in the industrially advanced countries of Latin America, where populist corporatism mobilized and politicized labor at the outset of import-substituting industrialization, authoritarian political regimes preceded rather than followed periods of rapid industrialization that typically encourage unionization.[19] In Thailand,[20] and arguably in China as well despite the disruptions of the Cultural Revolution, early industrial expansion took place in the context of established military or authoritarian rule, preempting independent union organization, sometimes in favor of government-sponsored unionism. Conversely, the early and relatively successful period of import substituting industrialization in the Philippines paralleled the Latin American experience in pairing industrialization with labor regimes (though in this instance more liberal than corporatist) that encouraged broad-based unionization and collective bargaining. Of particular importance was the instituting in the early 1950s of new labor-relations legislation patterned after the U.S. National Labor Relations Act that established organizational rights for unions and provided an important structural foundation for the labor mobilization and militancy that occurred even under martial law during the mid-1980's political crisis.

Korea, of course, stands as an exception to the more general regional pattern, inasmuch as early industrialization was accompanied by authoritarian rule but nonetheless spawned a powerful labor movement during the late 1980s. Here it may be noted that a primary instrument of labor control, a state-sponsored trade union federation, the FKTU, proved largely ineffectual

---

production phases of the automobile industry. For a similar argument applying specifically to East Asia, see Deyo (1989, 187–201).

19. As noted earlier, Indonesia, where the postcolonial regime of Sukarno enjoyed strong coalitional support from an activated labor movement, stands as an exception to this more general pattern.

20. Thailand experienced military rule during most of the period from 1947, following the overthrow of the Pridi government, until 1973, and then again from 1976 to 1980.

in its intended goal of monopolizing and managing unionization. While the more blunt instrument of state police repression often supplanted and largely replaced the FKTU in efforts to suppress labor activism, it had the unintended consequence of further radicalizing workers. This radicalization began initially among female workers in textiles and other light industries, and later spread to male-intensive, heavy-industry sectors. These latter workers ultimately created the strong and independent trade unions that assumed such an important role in Korean politics (Koo 2001). The political mobilization of labor was further encouraged by the explosive state-led growth of concentrated heavy industry and mass production beginning in the 1970s.

Finally, where the most rapid periods of industrialization occurred later, in the context of ongoing market reform, as in Thailand and China, new structures of flexible production, external-trade exposure, and extensive reliance on outsourcing and international subcontracting created a context ill-conducive to effective unionization.

Alternative Labor Politics: Social Movements and Labor NGOs

If union-based production politics has not been the primary instrument of labor struggle outside Korea, Southeast Asian SOEs, and some heavy-industry sectors, one cannot on that account dismiss labor from the politics of Asian development and reform. Rather, it is only to invite a somewhat different understanding of labor's role, as well as to acknowledge that changing political and economic circumstances encourage new agencies and arenas of conflict and new forms of struggle (Silver 2003, 19).

If trade unions have encountered political and economic structural impediments to effective representation in employment and social-policy debates, they have often sought instead to leverage their power through coalitional engagement with other popular-sector groups, including farmers' associations, women's organizations, environmentalists, and human rights groups (see Haworth and Ramsay 1984). The contrast between union-centered labor struggles and union-associated populist social politics is most evident in the contrast between Korea and Thailand. In Korea, an institutionally supported, stable workforce has used independent trade unions (especially those affiliated with the KCTU) to negotiate labor market deregulation and to retain an important collective voice in labor reform. The KCTU, more than the more conservative government-linked FKTU, has sought to engage with broader social movements in order to compensate for a weak bargaining position stemming initially from lack of governmental recognition prior to

1998.[21] This effort included increased moves to include subcontractor wages in collective bargaining with employers.[22] More generally, however, the relative strength, militancy, and institutional power of the Korean labor movement has tended to discourage union efforts to articulate with broader worker and social interests and to encourage a predominance of economic over social unionism (Koo 2001, 204).

Korea's union politics may be contrasted with the situation facing Thailand's far weaker and more fragmented unions that have, by necessity, been forced to forge political alliances with a broad range of social movements and popular-sector groups. In her study of the Thai labor movement, Napaporn Ativanichayapong (2002) documents the ascendancy of social unionism during the 1990s as a weak trade union movement turned to social alliances and NGO leadership to address issues of broad social concern. Particularly important in this context was the political mobilization of women workers as their numbers were increased structurally by growth in light export manufacturing. Female labor mobilization prior to the 1997 financial crisis had a critical influence on labor politics in encouraging greater engagement with issues relating to social reproduction and workforce protection. Two issues were of central importance in this change: the campaign for ninety days of maternity leave, and the campaign to address problems of workplace safety and health following the tragic 1993 Kader toy factory fire tragedy in which 188 workers were killed and 481 injured (Ativanichayapong 2002; Brown 2004, 114–15; also see Charoenloet 1998, cited in Brown 2004). These campaigns were instrumental in establishing legislation requiring employers to provide at least forty-five days of paid maternity leave, following which female workers could claim wages from the Social Security fund for the remaining days; in improving health and safety workplace enforcement; and in establishing the Institute for Occupational Safety and Health (Ativanichayapong 2002). Most important here, both campaigns encouraged workers to ally with other non-union activist groups including women's organizations and, for later campaigns during the '00s, the Assembly of the Poor. Social unionism was further invigorated by the establishment in 2001 of the Thai Labour Solidarity Committee, founded to bring under a single organizing umbrella both formal and informal sectors, including migrant workers. This committee, supported by the radical wing of Thai labor, has explicitly rejected an exclusive focus on workplace issues in favor of engagement in

---

21. For discussion of social movement organizing in Korea, see Chun 2009, 68–100.
22. "Federation of Korean Trade Unions Negotiating a Pay Raise Along with Subcontractors' Wage," *The Dong-A Ilbo,* December 22, 2003.

broader social and political debates involving peasants, students, and other social groups (Suttawet 1999; Brown 2004, 112–20).[23]

Similarly, state-enterprise workers, bereft of legally recognized trade union rights after 1991, were nonetheless able to delay privatization of the Electricity Generating Authority of Thailand (EGAT) and a number of other SOEs only by joining larger social movements seeking economic justice, farmers' rights, and, most important, policies of economic nationalism. Labor–civil society coalition building with NGOs, academics, health-care workers, lawyers, civil liberty groups, bureaucrats, child-welfare agencies, and others have thus provided a major avenue for addressing problems of factory health and safety. In this way, trade unions and workers have been able to address social policy and livelihood issues by inserting worker agendas into larger social movements focused on social protections and livelihood issues affecting an array of popular-sector groups partly unified by their common vulnerability to the social outcomes of market reform. While the resulting merging of social agendas has blurred and stretched strictly "labor" issues, it has provided a basis for more-inclusive social movements that have arguably posed as formidable a challenge to economic reform in Thailand as the more traditional union-based labor politics of Korea.

The Philippines offers an equally compelling case of social-movement unionism in sectors with organizationally entrenched unions that nonetheless lack substantial political leverage. In some cases, the impetus to engagement with broader social movements lies in the effort by unions to organize informal workers, thus enlarging initially narrow union agendas by engaging broader social issues (Sibal 2007, 308). During 2010, to take one example, several major trade unions joined with the Informal Sector Coalition of the Philippines to address problems faced by unorganized household and domestic workers in several major cities.[24] Here, as in Thailand, trade unions have joined larger social movements in pushing for broad social programs directed at both rural and urban poor. These efforts often entail the creation of umbrella social movements, such as the Philippine Alliance of Progressive Labor,[25] which has campaigned for policies promoting full employment, poverty alleviation, labor justice and labor rights, and a variety of social and community services. This form of political engagement is well described by Sibal in his overview of labor organizing in the Philippines:

Trade unions are reinventing themselves by uniting with or organizing other forms of workers' organizations that operate in the informal

23. "Assembly of Poor Rallies at Ubon City Hall." *Bangkok Post* January 13, 2011.
24. See http://www.tucp.org.ph/informal-sector-2.
25. See their website at http://apl.org.ph/.

sector, like guilds, crafts unions, cooperatives, [and] peoples' organizations...of vendors, farmers, drivers and other workers of similar
occupations. From these renewed forms of labor organizations, the advocacy campaign for new laws on labor standards based on good or best
practices and the formulation of industry codes among industry, community, professions and occupations can be pursued. (2007, 23–24)

In both the Philippines and Thailand, labor-oriented NGOs (vs. unions)
play a similarly important role in mobilizing workers to press both employers and government to embrace the social agendas of workers not otherwise represented by unions. This alternative labor politics is most evident
among informal-sector workers (e.g., home-based, SME, and own-account
workers) for whom unionization is especially difficult, and among workers subject to severe management controls and antiunionism (as in some
export zones) but where a more general political liberalization, often associated with democratic transition, opens new political space for civil society organizations and associations. In both countries, labor NGOs play a
prominent role in politically mobilizing and representing workers in situations that preclude or discourage union organizing. In China, on the other
hand, where unions are controlled and civil society is preemptively managed by state agencies, independent labor-oriented organizations are either
co-opted and controlled or driven underground. Co-optation is illustrated
by the proliferation of NGOs that receive government encouragement to
provide services and support for migrant workers in Shenzhen and other
industrial-export zones (Hsu 2009). Alternatively, a variety of underground
organizations that operate illegally in those same zones may play a similar
role. Here, delayed pay and numerous violations of employment law drive
workers into illegal collective associations and gangs that provide some economic support to unpaid workers and that sometimes resort to the threat
or practice of violence against employers and government officials. These
illicit organizations typically build on the informal ties of place of origin
and pose a major threat of social disorder and high levels of crime to which
local authorities and the national Chinese leadership have been forced to
respond.

Quite different is the Philippine experience, in which two different trajectories of non-union labor politics have evolved: first, the more
self-directed efforts of factory workers to establish unions in the face
of sustained employer resistance through alliances among church and
community-based groups; and second, direct non–union-mediated worker
participation in broader social movements to influence social policy

relating to poverty, basic social services, health care, and other issues. It is these latter issues that provide a mobilizing agenda for informal-sector, rural, underemployed, and poor workers. The NGO approach is best illustrated by the organizing efforts of workers in export-processing zones, many of whom are young women in electronics assembly and garment industries. As discussed by McKay (2006, 132–77), antiunion employment practices, police intervention, workforce instability, mobile capital, and high rates of unemployment have discouraged direct efforts to unionize local workers. In this context, the lead role has been assumed by local churches and labor-oriented NGOs to create organizations of workers that need not register under the restrictive rules governing trade unions but that offer a variety of forms of social assistance, training, legal help, and other support for workers. The community-based organizing efforts of these NGOs seek to embed worker grievances in broader livelihood, gender, human rights, and other struggles, and in this way to empower and embolden otherwise isolated and vulnerable groups of workers. While the intended transition to union formation and recognition is always problematic, NGO-based labor movements have won important gains for workers even in industries whose competitive strategies demand cheap, flexible, and docile labor.[26] In other firms, where innovation, rapid technological and product change, and quality considerations loom larger, unionization (where it exists) has more often succeeded without insertion in broader social movements (McKay 2006).

Social-movement unionism contrasts as well with other instances in which worker participation is largely unmediated by unions or labor-oriented NGOs, and in which worker agendas are embedded in and more fully subordinated to the agendas of popular-sector social movements. In many countries, including Korea and Thailand, governments have sought to discourage or prohibit union involvement in non–employment-related social and political issues, largely to undercut political unionism or labor radicalism. One outcome of such prohibition is to inhibit social-movement unionism as well. In the context of weak but independent unions and of legal restrictions on union involvement in politics, social-movement unionism here yields to direct worker participation in social movements, whether through electoral politics or direct actions that pursue broad social agendas relating to public health, housing, political reform, the environment, education, and the like—most suitably understood as a "citizen" politics of collective

---

26. One prominent example is GABRIELA, the National Alliance of Women in the Philippines (ALU April–June 2009).

consumption or social wage.[27] A particularly prominent example of such politics is Thailand's Assembly of the Poor, a broad coalition of impoverished farmers, environmentalists, unemployed persons, and the urban poor established in 1995 to influence national development and social policy.[28]

Each of these forms of labor politics may in principle be associated with a fifth political expression: that involving close ties to a labor-based or labor-friendly political party. In Korea, the KCTU was closely associated with the emerging Democratic Labor Party in the early '00s. This party won ten legislative seats in the 2004 national elections, but received far less support in subsequent elections (Lee 2006, 725). In 2010–11, organized labor was actively courted and supported by the Democratic Party, which among other things has pushed for the conversion of irregular workers into regular workers and an increase in the minimum wage.[29] In neither case, however, did engagement with national political parties offer an important channel of influence in national debates and policy (Lee 2011).

In Thailand, citizen politics was greatly energized in the late 1990s by the emergence of an oppositional electoral coalition of farmers, workers, and civil society groups. In 2001 this coalition was able to elect a new government under the Thai Rak Thai Party led by Prime Minister Shinawatra Thaksin,[30] and based on a populist program of debt moratorium for farmers, low-cost medical services, village development funds, small-business promotion, and protection of key factions of domestic capital from foreign interests (Hewison 2006a). The broad social movements with which both organized and unorganized Asian workers have engaged have played major political roles as well, particularly in helping to remove unpopular governments in the Philippines in the 1980s, and in Thailand and Indonesia during the late-1990's economic crisis. The sometimes violent confrontation during the '00s between poor Thai farmers, low-income urban workers, and the urban poor, on the one hand, and bureaucratic and middle classes, royalists, and the military, on the other, dramatically evidences the social and political instabilities, class conflict, and mass-populist mobilization generated by the structural outcomes of unregulated, market-driven, and uneven development,

---

27. In an interesting article on unionization among informal-sector workers in India, Agarwala (2008) describes a form of labor politics intermediate between union politics and social movements. It is one in which workers utilize unions, not so much to push employers to provide better wages and working condition as to push state governments to organize sectoral "welfare boards" to provide citizen-based benefits and protections that workers are unable to win from employers.

28. "Assembly of Poor Rallies at Ubon City Hall," *Bangkok Post* (online), January 13, 2011.

29. "DP Released New Plan on Labor Policy," http://english.hani.co.kr, March 8, 2010.

30. The party name translates "Thais Love Thais." Following repressive countermeasures during later years, this party re-emerged in the late 00's as the Pheu Thai Party.

especially in the context of democratic reform, and of the quick recourse to authoritarian measures on the part of domestic elites in the face of those instabilities.

In part, the tactical choice among these various avenues of political opposition is determined by state policy and established modes of institutionalized access to policy decision making (Lee 2006, 2011). And, in this regard, the transition to democracy has had unexpected outcomes. Democratic reform in both Thailand and the Philippines has had the effect of opening new political space for social movements, but with few institutional forms in place to limit, channel, and otherwise manage political discourse and action. But the resulting emancipatory outcomes for social movements contrast sharply with the more limited outcomes for unions. Despite ongoing political liberalization, long-established institutional constraints continue to divide, and in some case suppress, unionism—constraints that were only incrementally relaxed over subsequent years. In the case of Thailand, for example, an early abrogation of state-enterprise worker rights to unionize and to bargain collectively remained in place long after the democratic transition of 1994. By consequence of these path-dependent differences in institutional opportunities, democratic reform had the dual outcome of liberating and empowering noninstitutionalized social movements without substantially changing the political terrain of trade unionism, thus encouraging a general shift from institutionally constrained unionism to social-movement unionism, and from social-movement unionism to direct worker engagement in social movements, where collective organization and direct action encounter fewer legal obstacles. That Korean democratization did not have a similar effect in displacing union politics is further explained by another institutional legacy in that country: that of the union solidarity and organizational cohesion that emerged from early political struggles on the part of stable primary workers in heavy industry. The economic structural factors that empowered those workers, even in the face of harsh state repression, was to play a major role in driving new modes of union-focused tripartite political engagement during later years of crisis and reform.

These emergent differences in labor politics are often reinforced by corresponding differences in institutionalized modes of government–civil society interaction (Lee 2006). In Korea, governments relate to workers through unions and labor federations, tripartite councils, and other formalized institutions, an outcome of the earlier institutionalization of state-labor relations during the 1980s. By contrast, in Thailand and the Philippines the continuing weakness of trade unions alongside an explosive growth of social-movement politics encouraged other sorts of institutional accommodations to societal pressures even before the democratic transitions, giving rise to a labor politics in which unions played a less-prominent role. By consequence, governments and government agencies in those countries focus their attention less on organized labor than on NGOs, farmers' associations, environmental groups, and a variety of other civil society organizations. In China, by contrast, even those alternate modes of labor politics are largely precluded, a consequence of the political preemption of all independent forms of worker organization, both union and non-union. There, an institutional vacuum in state-labor relations reinforces a largely unfocused politics of social disorder, a final modality of influence to which I now turn.

Labor and the Politics of Social Disorder

Social disorder is an alternative public response to that of organized political opposition insofar as it manifests itself not so much in collective action as in a general breakdown of normative social control alongside disorganized social protest.[31] In Korea, for example, as the economic crisis of the late 1990s revealed new employment vulnerabilities for workers and communities, families disintegrated, crime increased, and children were abandoned to orphanages (Kang et al. 2001, 120). Similarly, Thai observers noted growing problems of family breakdown, political cynicism, and crime during the height of the crisis.

This larger trend, of course, must be tempered by recognition of substantial variation. By almost any measure of social cohesion and order, South Korea still ranks relatively high. China, by contrast, confronts social disorder of such proportions as to have become a major focus of state policy and action. China's official unionism, on the one hand, and the government's preemptive, repressive containment of autonomous civil society organizations, on the other, have largely precluded either independent unionism or organized social movements and have driven some labor-advocacy groups underground. As discussed by Ching-kwan Lee (2007), poorly coordinated and short-lived factory-based public demonstrations have been a primary means of protest, often following earlier legal efforts to elicit employer compliance with contractual obligations or existing labor law. Similarly, Cai (2006, 6) discusses the "fragmentation" of collective action among laid-off SOE factory workers. In this context, the politics of labor has largely taken the form of informal social protest, unorganized industrial action, and workforce instability. In

---

31. Andrew Brown (2004) notes a displacement of organized labor militancy by public demonstrations and protests in Thailand over recent years. For a similar account of China, see Wang (2002).

June 2010, worker suicides at Hon Hai Precision Industry Company, a huge Taiwanese contract manufacturer of electronics,[32] as well as labor unrest at several nonunion Honda supplier plants, alarmed company managers and local governments and have led to public inquiries and renewed calls for instituting corporate-responsibility programs.[33]

In part, large-scale worker protests are encouraged by the massing of workers in huge dormitory complexes and in densely populated rental areas, where workers share common grievances and discuss collective responses (Chan and Ngai 2009). These protests, typically ignored or discouraged by the ACFTU, have become very common in coastal industrial areas, particularly in Guangdong Province. Such disorder, it should be noted, often characterizes early periods of union organizing during rapid industrialization. In Korea, for example, nonunionized women workers in textile, clothing, and other industries deployed non-union-based direct action in the 1970s to redress grievances and to improve their conditions of employment (Koo 2001, 69–99), even in the face of government repression. In the Chinese context, however, the trajectory to independent union formation is forcefully blocked.

Chinese social disorder is sufficient in magnitude to alarm the national leadership, but too disorganized to pose a fundamental threat to the ruling party. This country's institutionally corrosive politics of social disorder is most evident in rapidly growing numbers of "spontaneous" riots and protests, especially in rural areas where farmers have challenged the corruption of local officials. Rural riots against land seizures, environmental damage, and local corruption have become commonplace across China.[34] Another politically charged issue is the virtual dismantling of the *danwei*-based health-care system as millions of workers have been laid off by state enterprises and as rural collectives have been dissolved,[35] leading to public outrage and riots at hospitals.[36]

Riots and protests are common as well among urban workers who face a variety of problems including nonpayment of wages, violations of health and

---

32. An initial, and poorly received, response proposed by Hon Hai management was to install safety nets on high-rise dormitories in order to prevent further suicides. See "Suicides Spark Inquiries," *Wall Street Journal* (online), May 27, 2010.

33. "Workers, Unionists Clash at Honda Plant in Foshan," *South China Morning Post* (online), June 1, 2010. "Striking Workers in China Win Wave of Raises, New Clout," *Wall Street Journal* (online), June 9, 2010.

34. "Thousands of Chinese Villagers Protest Factory Pollution," *New York Times,* April 13, 2005.

35. "A Quiet Revolution Begins: Reinventing China's Farms," *South China Morning Post,* February 12, 2003.

36. "In China, Preventive Medicine Pits Doctor Against System," *Wall Street Journal,* January 16, 2007.

safety laws in factories, and even physical abuse at the hands of factory officials and hired thugs. In response to these problems, workers often seek legal
redress through labor courts or appeal to national party officials to intervene
in local affairs. Official statistics show that the country's courts handled more
than 280,000 labor disputes in 2008 alone.[37] And, as international NGOs and
politically active Chinese lawyers have brought these problems to international attention,[38] there has been some effort by national leaders to prod local
governments to respond.

But given the common failure of legal appeals or public petitions to resolve the problems facing workers, it is not surprising that street protests
have escalated sharply. Smith, Brocher, and Costello (2006) find that whereas
the Ministry of Public Security typically reported roughly 10,000 annual
collective-labor protests during the mid-1990s, figures have mounted sharply,
to 74,000 in 2004, and 87,000 in 2005. Worker protests further escalated
during 2008–9 as factories closed and wages were often not paid.[39] It is estimated in this regard that the recession led to the shuttering of over 670,000
labor-intensive factories and to the firing of 25 million migrant workers in
the coastal cities of Guangzhou, Dongguan, and Shenzhen alone.[40]

Disaggregating National Labor Politics: Sectoral Specificities

While much of the discussion has thus far been directed to national-level
reform, I have also emphasized that sectoral differences in technology, the nature of market pressures, skill requirements, and organizational characteristics
play an important role in influencing the competitive strategies of firms and
thus also in shaping labor systems and labor politics. The foregoing account
of cross-national differences in labor politics is intended less to characterize
national economies than to illustrate important modalities of Asian labor politics through case studies drawn from labor systems that have played critical
developmental and political roles in these four countries. Stated differently, it
is clear that even though particular modalities of labor politics are especially
prominent in particular countries, all four modalities coexist within each
country. But having said this, it is also the case that economic structures,
and the particular mix of labor systems with which they are associated, tend

37. "The Next China," *Economist,* July 31, 2010, 48.

38. *New York Times,* March 22, 2006; *New York Times Magazine,* October 15, 2006.

39. For more recent increases in protests and "mass incidents," see "Wave of Unrest Rocks
China," *Wall Street Journal,* June 14, 2011 (A1).

40. "The Next China," *Economist,* July 31, 2010, 49.

to shape the emergence of social regulatory regimes and labor politics that present important cross-national differences. Jessop (2002, 24–28) usefully captures this point in his discussion of the "ecological dominance" of particular modes of economic (and thus sectoral) organization in shaping the logic and organizational paradigms of national regulatory regimes.[41] It is in this sense that macroregulatory regimes, labor systems, and labor politics do, in fact, show continuing, path-dependent national differences despite significant intersectoral differentiation.

To take a prominent example, Korea's urban-based heavy industry, extensive workforce proletarianization, high level of regulatory formalization, and rising skill levels initially encouraged the development of stable primary labor systems and, with them, union-based labor politics that in turn played the major role in shaping national industrial relations institutions and policies. This is not to say that Korean workers employed in other sectors (e.g., low-skill sunset industries, petty services, modern service sectors, or farming) did not participate in quite different labor systems or adopt other modalities of labor politics: only that the national regime of labor and social regulation within which those alternate modalities played out was most decisively shaped by union-based labor politics and that other, less economically and politically dominant sectors and labor systems were relatively less influential in shaping national institutions and policies.

In summary, in this chapter I have questioned a union-centric view of Asian labor politics that too often marginalizes the role of labor through its failure to embrace a broad range of modalities of labor influence. A fuller understanding of those diverse modalities of labor politics supports the view that Korean workers are not alone in finding ways to influence policy and trajectories of economic reform. The alternative modalities of labor politics identified here, modalities that are in each case influenced by economic structures, political constraints, and institutional legacies, have all to varying degrees been able to insert social agendas into reform policies. I return to the question of the actual outcomes of labor politics in chapter 12.

---

41. Fligstein's (2001) account similarly foregrounds the role of regulatory logics in shaping national regulatory regimes.

PART IV

Addressing the
Tensions of Reform

```
≋ CHAPTER 9
```

The Reregulatory Face of Labor Reform

Institutionalization, Social Compensation, and
Developmental Augmentation

> No society could stand the effects of such a system of
> crude fictions [e.g., that labor is a commodity] even
> for the shortest stretch of time unless its human and
> natural substance...was protected against the ravages
> of this satanic mill....Indeed, human society would
> have been annihilated but for protective counter-
> moves which blunted the action of this self-destructive
> mechanism.
>
> —Karl Polanyi, 2001 [1944] 76, 79

> Governments around the world share the goal of hav-
> ing more and better jobs for their citizens. Jobs are
> the main source of income for people—and the main
> pathway out of poverty.... Crafting an investment
> climate that provides firms with the opportunities and
> incentives to expand is fundamental to meeting this
> challenge. Government policies affecting the labor
> market play a critical role in this effort by helping to
> connect people to jobs.
>
> —World Bank, *WDR* 2005, 136

Insofar as deregulatory market reform has been
associated with disruptive market failures, it has encouraged new institutional
efforts to make markets work. And insofar as reform has engendered social
and political disruptions, it has spawned Asia's societal "countermovement,"
especially following the regional financial crisis of the late 1990s (Mok and
Forrest 2009). In some cases, these compensatory responses have been largely
reactive as reform tensions have become ever more apparent and disruptive.[1] In
other cases, the responses have been more *anticipatory* in nature, as elites have
attempted to pre-empt or manage the disruptions of reform. And in most

---

1. The most dramatic and regionally unsettling political outcome of the crisis was the 1998 collapse of the Suharto regime in Indonesia.

instances, the responses have been strongly path dependent, taking as their starting point a range of existing structures and institutions that are adapted to new circumstances (Peck and Tickell 2002, 388).

Chapter 9 explores this newer phase of re-regulation and social accommodation as it relates to labor markets and social policy, while chapter 10 focuses on the labor process. Chapter 11 assesses the role of small industry policy in addressing the developmental deficits of reform, while chapter 12 returns to the earlier discussion of labor politics to assess its often-ignored impact on reform trajectories. Given the great importance of the late 1990's financial crisis in forcing a rethinking of Asian reform policy, I emphasize the post-crisis years in my discussion of the reregulatory period of Asian reform.

In some cases, an initial response to the social and political disruptions of the late 1990's crisis was to slow reform itself. To take a prominent example, Thailand's Thaksin government, responding to antireform pressures from domestic businesses, labor, academics, and a host of social movements, slowed Thai privatization[2] and liberalization, placed new restrictions on foreign investment in newly privatized state enterprises, moved to protect major domestic banks and industrial firms from bankruptcy, and largely ignored several reform timetables that had been negotiated with the IMF by the former government (Hewison 2006a: 125–26). Similarly, Cai (2006, 118) notes a slowing of privatization and of bankruptcy proceedings against failing state enterprises in China during the early '00s for fear of social instability.

But these short-term measures did not detract from a longer-term Thai commitment to market reform, including administrative decentralization, state-enterprise privatization (Hewison 2006a, 126), and external liberalization of trade and investment, albeit with new protections for domestic capital.[3] This longer-term commitment to ongoing reform, despite short-term reversals and political compromises, characterizes all the countries in this study.[4]

That Asian reform has not proven as vulnerable to political opposition as that in Latin America and elsewhere may be attributed to several interregional differences. First, much of Asia has experienced long-term, rapid growth over a period of three decades. That growth has brought economic gains to a broad range of elite groups, thus muting elite factional opposition to reform.[5] Second, that dominant industries and economic sectors have been

---

2. "State Firms Won't be Sold Off, says Thaksin," *Bangkok Post,* July 10, 2003.

3. This included negotiation of a new U.S.-Korea bilateral free trade agreement. *Seoul Times,* 2009.

4. "Economic Woes Will Not Restrain Reform Drive," *Korea Times,* May 21, 2003. "Lee Calls for Unwavering Reforms," *Korea Herald* (online), November 30, 2008.

5. Here, as elsewhere, important exceptions exist, as in the Philippines in the mid-1980s and in Thailand in the first decade of the 2000s.

able to compete so successfully in global markets has partially blunted the edge of opposition to external-trade liberalization.

Third, if expanding income and wealth have been unequally distributed, many Asian workers have nonetheless fared relatively better in absolute terms than their counterparts elsewhere, as seen most dramatically in continuing reductions in the numbers of families living below the poverty line. World Bank data show a continuing decline during the first decade of the 2000s in the percentage of the population living on less than two dollars per day: from 51 percent (2002) to 36 percent (2005) in China;[6] and from 15 percent (2002) to 12 percent (2004) in Thailand.[7] As elsewhere, the Philippines remains the outlier, at 44–45 percent below this international poverty line in both 2002 and 2004 (WB, *WDI* 2010).

Fourth, continuing economic growth and a relative invulnerability to external debt and stabilization pressures provide the material resources (Haggard and Kaufman 2008, 2, 11–12) and strategic opportunity for Asian governments to respond more robustly and independently to institutional and social tensions, even in the face of contrary pressures (as during the crisis) from the IMF and other international lenders.

And finally is the importance of the world-historical timing of Asian reforms, which generally occurred after the harsh market-fundamentalist phase of worldwide economic restructuring during the 1980s, and instead in the more supportive context of the augmented Washington consensus that increasingly seeks to address its major disruptions at the very outset of reform.

As noted earlier, to the extent there was a shared watershed moment in Asian reform, that moment is to be found in the late-1990's regional financial crisis, when economic vulnerabilities on the one hand, and social dislocations and insecurities on the other, loomed large in the political and economic agendas of national elites, and when economic stimulus programs brought renewed emphasis on social policy (ADB *Outlook* 2010, 134–35, 227). While Asia's countermovement clearly spans that important historical divide, there can be little question that the trauma of the late 1990s, during which rising unemployment brought increased labor militancy and social conflict, had a powerful transformative impact on public policy there and elsewhere.

---

6. World Bank estimates, based on "consumption poverty," suggest that roughly 85% of the Chinese population lived in poverty in the early 1980s. See *China Daily*, April 8, 2009. In Korea, only a negligible percentage of the population lives in poverty as defined here.

7. Some estimates suggest that over 40% of Thais lived below this poverty line in the 1970s. See "Many Thai Workers, Now Out of Poverty, Are in Dissent," *Washington Post* (online), June 9, 2010. On the Philippines, see "Campaign a Cakewalk Compared with Tasks Winner Aquino Must Face," *Manila Times* (online), May 16, 2010.

How, then, have Asian governments sought to manage the tensions of deregulatory policies by redirecting, institutionally consolidating, and socially buffering economic reform? I begin with efforts to enhance the functioning of labor markets.

Contractualizing Flexible Labor Markets

Earlier discussion noted efforts to regulate increasingly fluid labor markets through legally enforceable contracts. Such contracts, which bring the rule of law to employment relations, are multifaceted in their intent and outcome. Contractualization may be seen as supporting efforts to deregulate formal-sector labor markets by transitioning from a substantive focus on mandated terms of employment to procedural and enforcement issues relating to privately negotiated terms of employment. The elaboration of employment-contract law has had the further effect of partially supplanting collective labor-management agreements with individual employment contracts better adapted to the requirements of labor market and production flexibility, while also incrementally undercutting the power of trade unions by shifting the arena of contestation from factories and streets to the more manageable setting of mediation committees and courts.

But contractualization plays a socially stabilizing role as well. The institutional encouragement of individual contracts, most dramatically seen in China and Korea, provides legal standing and protection for workers otherwise exposed to the heightened risks and instabilities of fluid labor markets. For employers, contractualization combines flexibility and mutuality in the employment relation by offering job security for a specified term of duty, in many cases with the possibility of renewal or advancement to regular work status. Such protected fixed-term employment is especially common among skilled and technical workers in skill-intensive industrial sectors where changing technology and the requirements of production flexibility increase the costs and liabilities of older systems of long-term employment security. China presents the most dramatic instance of the turn to contractualization through its enactment first of the 1995 Labor Law that requires labor contracts for all employees (Chiu and Frenkel 2000, 35–36),[8] and then of the 2008 Labor Contracts Law that establishes an enforceable legal basis for grievances and arbitration in cases of contract violation by employers.

---

8. In considering the impact of this legislation, problems of local implementation and enforcement must also be taken into account.

Instituting Active Labor Market Policies

If earlier functionalist and modernization theorists saw "traditional" institutions and networks as creating inefficiency-generating frictions in labor and other markets, and if an earlier market-fundamentalist reform agenda sought to socially disembed and thus "free" labor markets from a host of institutional and political constraints, post-crisis Asian reform attends as well to a different sort of labor market friction: that associated with an absence of positive institutional supports for flexible labor markets and a corresponding need to re-embed labor markets in new institutional structures that enhance the allocative efficiencies of those markets. Of particular importance are efforts to meet the informational, risk-management, retraining, and job-matching requirements of economic transition.

If labor market restructuring and reform have sometimes outrun the capacity of other support institutions to manage the transition to more fluid employment and the movement of workers from declining to expanding sectors, gradualism and stepwise implementation may be the preferred initial response while long-term institutional strategies are developed.[9] Chinese labor law provides a prime example. There, a continuing, if diminished, enforcement of *houkou* residency restrictions has imbued labor markets with sufficient stickiness to reduce the strain that more rapid and unrestricted labor mobility might have created for urban social institutions and policy. Similarly, while SOE workers hired after 1986 lacked many of the protections and securities enjoyed by earlier hires, older workers, with fewer long-term options, have received transitional compensations and allowances (Ho 2007, 218).

Having said this, however, nowhere are the more general transitional difficulties of deregulation and economic transition more apparent than in China, where millions of rural migrant and laid-off state-enterprise workers have been denied the earlier protections of residency and state service and are forced to fend for themselves amid the disorderly emergence of labor markets. Confronting the social instability resulting from this massive transition, and with the encouragement and assistance of the World Bank, the Chinese government has instituted a variety of programs offering transitional assistance and retraining for workers, loans to small businesses, tax incentives for firms to hire unemployed workers, and reemployment programs for laid-off SOE workers (Ho 2007). In this regard, Chen and Hou estimate that of the 28 million SOE workers laid off between 1998 and 2005, 19 million were

---

9. It will be recalled that Polanyi saw the speed of institutional change as a critical determinant of the capacity of society to contain and respond to its disruptive consequences.

then reemployed with the assistance of their former employer (Chen and Hou 2008). These various social accommodations were in part driven by fear of social instability and in part by continuing ideological debates between idealists and realists in the Communist Party leadership itself (Ho 2007).

Especially important is the network of government reemployment centers, sometimes created within SOEs themselves, to provide monthly pay and benefits along with retraining, outplacement, and job location services for laid-off SOE workers for up to three years, followed by public relief and basic subsistence available to impoverished urban residents (Reutersward 2002; Ho 2007). Also important have been new efforts to facilitate and support a more orderly entry of rural workers into urban employment, including increased access on the part of migrant workers to urban education, health services, training facilities, and housing. By 2010, Guangdong's migrant workers were permitted on an experimental basis to apply for permanent residency in small- and medium-sized provincial cities, although workers from other provinces were barred from participation.[10] These policies, which have facilitated a continued easing of *houkou* residency restrictions and thus an increased flexibility of labor markets, have encouraged incorporation of workers into full-time employment while at the same time providing important social services.

South Korea's active labor market policy is arguably the most comprehensive in all of developing Asia. At its core is the Employment Insurance System (EIS), designed both to cushion unemployment and to hasten the reincorporation of unemployed workers into new employment. If OECD countries show marked variation in their relative emphasis on income security and job reentry, the Korean EIS leans toward the more-restrictive U.S. approach in providing a minimal social safety net for laid-off workers (90–240 days of unemployment benefits) along with other policies designed to get workers back to work.[11] While major provisions of the EIS, which by 2005 covered 81 percent of all workers (Lee and Yoo 2008, 225), deal with employment creation and retention, they also include an array of measures that provide for information, job counseling, and placement services; monetary incentives to workers who actively seek out new jobs; support for vocational training; requirements that firms consult with unions prior to retrenchment and give advance warning of layoffs (thus allowing workers to begin their job search

---

10. "Migrant Workers Get Chance for Urban Residency," *South China Morning Post* (online), June 9, 2010.

11. The "flexicurity" model of Denmark, for example, combines flexible labor markets with income support and extensive retraining for laid-off workers.

before termination); and incentives for firms to hire workers laid off by other firms (Kang et al. 2001). The EIS, along with other vocational education and training initiatives and short-term livelihood support, facilitates the rapid redeployment of workers from sunset industries to expanding economic sectors, thereby providing an institutional foundation for both labor market flexibility and worker reentry into gainful employment (Jayasuriya 2006).

While these measures, especially from 1998, may be viewed as an outcome of the social tensions of the crisis, they are more than just countercyclical policies. Rather, they are best seen as institutional responses to long-term tensions of structural transformation and reform that were both augmented and politicized by the crisis. Building on similar, though only minimally funded, earlier programs, these interventions were sharply augmented during the financial crisis. If in 1997–8, government employment services assisted only 5.8 percent of those actually finding work (Kang et al. 2001, 122–23),[12] in 1999, EIS-funding supported the activities of some five hundred vocational training institutes and 200,000 workers (41% involving in-plant training and 51% "other" educational training) (102). In the larger context of a rise in government social expenditures from 5.2 percent of GDP in 1997 to 11.8 percent the following year (Jayasuriya 2006, 119), expenditures on labor market programs rose from negligible levels in the mid-1990s to 2.2 percent of total GDP in 1998 (Kang et al. 2001, 109).

Thailand and the Philippines differ from Korea in their relatively greater focus on the huge informal sectors characterizing their economies and on the volatile social movements that have emerged in those sectors in response to problems of uneven development and poverty. While both countries have instituted active labor market policies to deal with the new instabilities of more fluid formal-sector labor markets, those policies have not been pursued with the vigor or resources of their Korean counterpart. In the Philippines, it is true, a panoply of job placement, job information, and retraining schemes suggests strong commitment to enhancing labor market efficiencies. Particularly important is the Public Employment Service Office (PESO), first established in 1992 in the wake of late-1980's labor market reforms and then augmented in the wake of the crisis, in 1999. This office provides job information and employment services for workers and local businesses. At the national level, a manpower and registry system pools and disseminates labor market information to local labor offices. But given that the major employment problem here is as much one of continuing high levels of structural

---

12. This figure does not include job assistance provided by publicly supported or licensed private employment agencies.

unemployment and underemployment, especially in the informal sector, as it is of the frictional unemployment more centrally addressed by active labor market policy, the resources and focus of government action are more often directed at job creation through small-business development, subcontracting, and flexi-work (Sibal et al. 2008), on the one hand, and compensatory social policy (discussed below), on the other.

Similarly, Thailand has provided increased funding for worker-training programs to help workers stay abreast of changing technology and job requirements and to find new work. The government has also expanded programs of income support and social services for the unemployed, and community-based job-placement services and job-vacancy information for laid-off workers (Behrman et al. 2000; Siengthai 2008). These programs, initially underfunded and serving only small numbers of workers, were subsequently expanded under the Thaksin administration (2001–5). Firms were now required to provide advance notification of planned retrenchments, worker training was expanded, and social security unemployment benefits (which permitted workers to pursue retraining and job search) were extended from six months to twelve (TDRI 2002).

Incomes Policy

The adequacy of household income comprises a critical foundation for meeting the basic livelihood needs of workers and their families, and thus too the economic requirements of workforce social reproduction. As I noted in chapter 6, minimum-wage legislation has been only marginally effective in improving the living standards of the low-wage workers it nominally seeks to protect—an inadequacy rooted in the downward wage pressures associated with early stage EOI, the decentralization of minimum-wage setting to business-dominated local governments, and a tendency to prioritize economic agendas over considerations of social livelihood and welfare under productivist welfare regimes.

Having said this, however, important cross-national and temporal exceptions present themselves. First, Korea's industrial advance into high-skill, high-value economic niches, alongside its political vulnerability to demands from organized labor, have encouraged greater attention to incomes policy than in other developing countries of the region (Kim 2007, 57–58). Second, the postcrisis ascendancy of social policy across the region more generally has carried over into incomes policy as well. In China, for example, the first minimum-wage law applicable to the entire employed population was enacted in 2004. And, in the context of growing worker protest, especially during the recession in the late '00s, local and provincial governments have themselves enacted dramatic minimum-wage increases.[13]

In Thailand, a tripartite minimum-wage commission was first established in 1972–3 amid a wave of prodemocracy street demonstrations and strikes that ended military rule and ushered in democratic rule. This legislation established the guiding principle that the wage rate should be "sufficient for the employee and two additional family members to dwell in the society" (Imudom 2000, 1). This provision was later amended in 1976 to require only that the minimum wage be sufficient for the individual employed person. In both cases, the primary consideration was that of providing a livelihood safety net, an outcome of escalating political pressures during the early 1970s. The more restrictive minimum-wage guidelines of 1976 largely reflected the impact of the 1976 military crackdown on public protest and labor militancy. In subsequent years, especially during the 1997–98 crisis, the minimum wage offered some protection for employed, low-skill workers in the formal sector, although its outcomes for employment levels and for informal-sector workers are less uncertain. For the 1976–99 period as a whole, Imudom concludes that increases in the Thai minimum wage were marginally higher than corresponding rates of inflation. Sununta Siengthai (2008, 326–27), on the other hand, argues that the real minimum wage declined modestly during the late 1990s. She notes in this regard that roughly 36 percent of all employees, particularly in small firms, were working at or below the legal minimum wage in 2003, mainly due to widespread nonenforcement. On the other hand, minimum-wage increases accelerated sharply in later years, culminating in a very large increase in 2010 in the run-up to national elections and in the face of heightened political mobilization among rural populations and the urban poor.[14]

Regulating International Labor Markets

The internationalization of trade and capital has been associated as well with vast movements of labor, both skilled and unskilled, across national boundaries. Indeed, there has been some discussion of ways in which the General Agreement on Trade in Services (GATS), which encourages the unimpeded access of service-providing firms (e.g., banks and retailers) to international markets, might be broadened to include the international movement of

---

13. "Striking Workers in China Win Wage Raises, New Clout," *Wall Street Journal,* June 9, 2010.

14. "Thailand to Raise Minimum Wage," *Thailand Business News* (online), April 10, 2010.

"natural persons" as well (Imperial 2003, 12–13). It is clear that international agreements in this area, whether at the global or regional level, would have to provide regulatory safeguards against the job displacement of nationals in more-developed countries, such as Korea, and for less-developed countries, such as the Philippines, against both brain drain and the exploitation of lesser-skilled overseas workers (Sumano 2010). That much labor migration has to this point taken place outside the regulatory overview of states is suggested by the magnitude, and the growing political sensitivity, of undocumented and "illegal" workers seeking employment in countries with more advanced economies and higher wages. It is in the context of this widespread, unregulated movement of undocumented workers that new regulatory efforts have emerged.

Earl Brown (2003) estimates that nearly three million workers, or roughly 10 percent of the total Thai labor force, are undocumented migrant workers, many from Burma working near the Thai-Burmese border.[15] Other studies based on higher estimates of worker in-migration, suggest that roughly 80 percent (1.2 million) of all Thai construction workers are from Myanmar, Laos, and Cambodia, including 500,000 unregistered workers.[16] These workers typically earn less than one-third the pay of Thai workers, a factor of great importance to employers in construction, garment and other cost-sensitive industries. Labor emigration, conversely, has long been a household subsistence strategy for rural Thai families (particularly in the impoverished Northeast).

Beginning in the mid-1990s, the Thai government began introducing stricter registration and higher levies on foreign workers, in part to more closely articulate immigration and economic policy (Athukorala 2000, 78). During the financial crisis, foreign workers were encouraged, and sometimes coercively forced, to return home in order to increase job opportunities for unemployed Thai workers. In 2001 the government began more rigorously to enforce registration of foreign workers, a difficult task in the large informal sectors of construction, services, and small-scale industry. These efforts were augmented in 2004 by a new work-permit system under which cross-border migration was more closely monitored, and again in 2010 as the government sought to increase surveillance and suppression of illegal immigration from Myanmar,[17] Laos, and Cambodia (Corben 2010). A further example of an increasingly systematic linkage of immigration and economic policy is seen in

---

15. "Thailand: Cynical Ploy on Burmese Migrant Workers," *Nation,* December 11, 2006.
16. *Nation* (online), June 22, 2005.
17. "Desperate Burmese Labor in Thailand," *Wall Street Journal,* October 13–14, 2007.

efforts beginning in the mid-'00s to establish new economic zones, primarily along the Myanmar, Cambodian, and Laotian borders, within which numerical restrictions on foreign labor would be suspended in favor of tighter registration procedures.[18]

Current Thai debates in this area center on further revising immigration policies to encourage economic upgrading and restructuring out of low-skill, cost-driven sectors into higher-value activities. As long ago as the mid-1990s, more selective immigration policies sought to reduce inflows of low-skilled workers in favor of technical contract workers required for industrial upgrading.

In the more economically challenged Philippines, labor *exports* have played the more dominant role. Here, inbound remittances from the roughly 10 percent of the population working overseas account for approximately 10 percent of GDP,[19] providing a countercyclical offset to periodic economic downturns as unemployed workers turn to overseas work opportunities (Hutchison 2006, 45).[20] During the 2008–10 world recession, overseas labor deployment increased by 15.1 percent from 2008 levels to 1.4 million workers.[21]

If, as McKay notes, "the Philippines' development strategy is really a labor market strategy, built around what it considers its comparative advantage: cheap, skilled, English-speaking labor" (75), labor exportation in turn comprises a strategic transnational rescaling of labor systems based on the domestic social reproduction of labor for insertion via internationally regulated transborder labor markets into overseas labor processes. Receiving countries, such as the United States, Korea, and Hong Kong, greatly benefit from this international transfer of human capital.

Of course, even the more traditional EOI strategies may themselves be understood in part as labor-export programs insofar as they are primarily

---

18. "Thailand's Cynical Ploy on Burmese Migrant Workers," *Asia News Network,* November 12, 2006 (http://www.asianewsnet.net). "The Burma Connection," *Wall Street Journal,* October 13–14, 2007. Takao Tsuneishi, "Development of Border Economic Zones in Thailand," Institute of Developing Economies, *Discussion Paper* #153 (May 2008).

19. Employing a more-inclusive classification, Hutchison (2006, 45) estimates that roughly 25% of the employed domestic workforce was employed overseas in the early 2000s. It is estimated that foreign remittances make up over 10% of national GDP. "Wandering Workers," *Economist,* January 20, 2007, 54.

20. "Manila Banks on Its Expats," *Wall Street Journal,* December 8, 2008. The World Bank estimates remittances from overseas workers to the Philippines at US$5.4 billion in 1995, $8.7 billion in 2001, and $19.8 billion in 2009. By contrast, Thailand received only $1.6 billion in 2009 (World Bank *WDR* online 2011).

21. "OFW Remittances Growing above Forecast," *Manila Times* (online), April 17, 2010. Also see Philippine Overseas Employment Administration statistics at http://www.peoa.gov.ph/stats.

organized around the insertion of domestic labor into international circuits of production, finance, world markets, and organizational networks.[22] The growth of service outsourcing in both India and the Philippines, based in large measure on the ready availability of well-educated, cheap, English-speaking labor, is but a more recent extension of these more traditional labor-export strategies. But the systematic, policy-based export of labor to other countries in order to address balance-of-payment deficits, provide employment, and address poverty through foreign remittances is less often included in discussions of national employment. What distinguishes the Philippines from many other countries, then, is official acknowledgment of the role of labor exports in national development policy (Scott 2009). Since the 1970s, the Philippine government has offered substantial assistance in placing domestic workers in overseas employment. Particularly important in this regard is the Philippine Overseas Employment Administration, which overseas, mediates, and monitors foreign recruitment (U.S. Department of Labor 2003b; also see Rodriquez 2010). The regulatory efforts of the Philippine government include long-standing agreements with governments in Asia, the United States, and elsewhere regarding employee placement, work visas, and worker protections. An example of such an agreement is a 2009 memorandum of understanding under which Korea agreed to hire eight thousand Filipinos each year for three years.[23] Central to the labor agreement is the continuing restriction, pursuant to a 1995 bilateral accord,[24] of low-skill Philippine labor to two-year (extendable) "trainee" contracts with Korean businesses to address shortages of low-cost labor available to small businesses, along with other restrictions applying to higher-skilled workers that seek to minimize job competition with skilled Korean workers. For the Philippines, this and other labor-export programs provide a source of remittances and an important social safety net in a country unable to impose costly social insurance requirements on competitively challenged companies or to afford a substantial government-funded social wage (Ignacio-Esteban 2003).[25]

Government regulation of international labor markets suggests a further way in which positive state intervention may enhance, rather than only restrain, labor market flexibility. As Asian governments have now twice confronted economic crisis in roughly one decade, the management of flows of

---

22. Whether through FDI or international contracting.

23. "South Korea to Hire 8000 Filipino Workers until 2011," *Manila Times* (online), June 1, 2009.

24. The 1995 Migratory Workers and Overseas Filipinos Act.

25. Ibid.

workers, both inward and outward, has become a tool of crisis management itself. In the case of the Philippines, encouragement of labor emigration has provided an important social safety value amid chronic domestic economic stagnation. In other cases, the regulation of immigrant labor has similarly provided a means of tempering labor market instability, as seen most dramatically in changing Thai policy toward low-skilled immigrant workers. During the world recession of 2008–10, the Thai government implemented a new migrant-labor policy, one that has eventuated in a marked increase in police sweeps and raids on factories that employ workers from Myanmar, Laos, and Cambodia.[26] Similarly, immigration policy has provided to the Korean government an important instrument for meeting the needs of domestic businesses for lower-skilled workers unprotected by employment laws enjoyed by domestic workers. In all these instances, labor market flexibility has been encouraged through a comparable flexibility in immigration policy.

Workforce Social Protections

If the contractualization of labor markets and active labor market policies seek to institutionalize and enhance the functioning of flexible labor markets in order to improve competitive efficiencies, policies of social protection are oriented as well to a concern for economic livelihood and political stability. These latter policies may either mandate that firms offer particular benefits or compensations or more directly provide compensatory citizen-based, rather than employment-linked, social safety nets. In either case, they seek to balance and integrate often-competing social and economic agendas. I begin by discussing mandated, employment-linked social protections—most notably those provided through social insurance programs.

Addressing Livelihood Insecurity: Social Insurance

Social insurance, while in principle establishing a minimal baseline of livelihood security and socialization of market risk, is in fact consonant with market-oriented reform insofar as it institutionalizes worker protections in legally enforceable private employment contracts and is primarily funded by employers and workers rather than by the state. Partly for this reason, social insurance programs have been strongly encouraged not only by the ILO but by the World Bank and the Asian Development Bank as well. Social

---

26. "Thailand's New Migrant Labor Laws Spark Fear, Criticism," VoANews.com, July 7, 2010.

insurance, it is argued, fosters labor market flexibility, provides short-term support as workers seek alternate training and employment,[27] and replaces a direct government fiscal role with a more indirect regulatory role.

But having said this, it is clear that social insurance is also market *displacing* insofar as it goes beyond providing a legal framework for the functioning of markets to imposing substantive provisions in legally permissible terms of employment. Most common are requirements that firms, usually above a specified minimum size, participate in government-regulated programs relating to job security, loss of employment, health insurance, and worker compensation. Further, a regional pattern of growth between 1995 and 2008–9 in the percentage of GDP accounted for by government expenditure on social security and welfare (ADB *KI* 2010) suggests the possibility of market *displacement* as much as of market consolidation.

China's 11th Five-Year (Reform and Development) Plan (2006–10) was quite explicit in emphasizing "people first" and the need for a "harmonious society." In pursuit of this goal, China is developing a rudimentary social security system, including a pension system, unemployment insurance, basic medical insurance, worker compensation, and maternity insurance. These programs are primarily available to formal-sector workers (Yu 1999; Saunders and Ping 2000), especially in state and collective enterprises, and are intended to supplant failing work-unit-based systems (Reutersward 2002).[28] Indeed, it has been reported that SOE privatization has been driven in part by the need to *fund* expanding pension and other social welfare programs. The pension system, though still small, has increased its coverage from 85 million workers in 1998 to 166 million in 2008.[29] Population coverage under the Basic Medical Insurance program has grown dramatically, from fewer than 8 million persons in 1995 to 318 million in 2008. During those same years, work-injury insurance grew from 26 million contributors to 138 million contributors, while unemployment insurance increased its coverage from 82 million to 124 million workers.

China's 1995 Labor Law required private-sector firms to participate in various national social insurance schemes, but left implementation to local and municipal governments (Chiu and Frenkel 2000, 35). Since then, the government has moved aggressively to preempt labor unrest by expanding worker protections. For the period 1995 to 2005, Solinger (2009, 170)

---

27. Unemployment insurance, financed by contributions from employers and employees, is the preferred mode of livelihood protection for the ILO.

28. Also see "Urban Discontent," *Economist*, June 15, 2002.

29. This and subsequent statistics from *China Labor Statistics Yearbook 2009*.

documents a dramatic sixfold increase in social security expenditures as a percentage of total government expenditures, from 0.017 percent to 0.109 percent, with the steepest gains occurring in 1997–99, the years of regional crisis.[30] Correspondingly, Chinese government expenditures on social security and welfare rose from 0.2 percent of GDP in 1995 to 2.2 percent in 2008 (ADB *KI* 2010). It should be noted that the three major programs developed during the 1990s, unemployment insurance for laid-off workers, provision of a basic living allowance for retrenched SOE workers, and a minimal livelihood subsidy for the very poor, mainly targeted urban and state-enterprise workers and offered little assistance to the millions of migrant workers who entered urban areas to accept short-term work (Chen 2003).

During the '00s, public funding for pensions and health insurance has increasingly supplemented these social insurance programs. As discussed by Solinger (2009), these and other worker protections were developed largely in anticipation of the harsh social outcomes of external liberalization, increased international competition, and a host of new rules linked to WTO membership. In particular, official statements during this period repeatedly stressed the need to compensate workers for new privations in order to maintain social stability and to forestall social turmoil (192).

The longer-standing social insurance programs in the Philippines and Thailand are similarly largely restricted to workers in the relatively small formal sectors of those countries. The Philippines instituted a national social security system as long ago as 1959. This contributory social insurance program, loosely patterned after the U.S. system, covers old age, disability, unemployment, health, and worker compensation, and is supplemented by a redistributive, noncontributory program of social pensions and welfare.

In Thailand, the Labor Protection Act of 1998, instituted in the wake of massive and politically destabilizing layoffs during the late 1990's crisis, requires that all firms offer their workers twenty-five days' severance pay; injury compensation for permanent workers; and a range of additional benefits, including holiday pay, overtime pay, sick leave, pregnancy/maternity pay, and payment priority in case of bankruptcy (Brown 2003, 258–59). This social security program is funded by a 4 percent payroll tax along with a 2 percent government contribution from general revenues. Reliance on mandatory severance pay, while reducing labor market flexibility by imposing

---

30. The importance of the late 1990's regional economic crisis for social policy is further reflected in changes in the percentage of total Chinese health expenditures accounted for by health insurance programs: from 47 percent in 1978, to 39 percent in 1990 and 26 percent in 2000, to 35 percent in 2008 (PRC *CSY* 2010).

costs on firms that dismiss regular workers, is justified as reducing public pressure for unemployment relief, a rationale often voiced in the Philippines as well. Later, Thailand's Thaksin government went further in increasing severance pay requirements for firms while also enlarging the coverage of the social security fund to include nearly 7.8 million workers in 2004 (Alpha Research Co. Ltd. 2005). In the context of the 2008–10 global recession and heightened political opposition in the run-up to national elections, the Democratic Party proposed an increase in the minimum wage, a national retirement scheme,[31] and a battery of new programs to address poverty and social inequality.

But it is South Korea, with its open endorsement of principles of social protection, that offers the most dramatic experience of new protections for workers. In 1988, and following dramatic labor uprisings beginning the year before, the government established a national pension program (Tang 2000, 17, 138) intended eventually to cover nearly the entire workforce. Under Korea's earlier described employment insurance program, laid-off workers receive modest pay for a designated period of time, conditional on their availability for retraining and job placement. In 1995, unemployment insurance covered roughly 40 percent of all manufacturing workers, rising subsequently to 64 percent in 2004.[32] Similarly, the percentage of Korean manufacturing workers covered by injury-compensation insurance rose from 64 percent in 1988 to 68 percent in 2004, with a corresponding increase in coverage for the entire workforce from 34 percent in 1988 to 46 percent in 2004.[33]

Increasing Regulatory Scope: Reaching beyond the Formal Sector

By the late 1990s, reform thinking increasingly acknowledged that a degree of economic compensation against market instability is necessary so that "losers" under liberalization not pose a political threat to the social order or to continuing reform itself (Kapstein 1999, 134; Stiglitz 2000; World Bank 2002, 150). This new thinking, reflected in the augmented Washington consensus, has largely responded to new political pressures (sometimes augmented by democratic transitions) in shaping social policy in the region. Beyond social insurance and livelihood protection limited to public servants, state-enterprise workers, and formal-sector workers, Asian governments have

---

31. "National Retirement Scheme Set for 2011 Launch," *Bangkok Post* (online), April 13, 2010.

32. Korea, *Yearbook of Labor Statistics* 2005.

33. This includes medical care, sick leave, disability insurance, survivors' benefits, and funeral benefits.

traditionally eschewed compensatory social safety nets in favor of reliance on employment-generating economic growth, and on families and communities for residual social protection. To the extent social safety nets were instituted, they offered only minimal support,[34] and mainly during times of economic crisis (Islam and Chowdhury 2000, 230).

Huck-ju Kwon (2002, 2005a, 2005b) and others have pointed to the postcrisis expansion of income maintenance and social welfare programs in Korea and elsewhere in Asia, a change often attributed to escalating political pressures and democratic reform (Ramesh 2003; Wong 2004; Haggard and Kaufman 2008). This pattern, suggestive of the influence of economic crisis on regional social policy, is further highlighted by temporal trends in government social expenditures. Between 1995 and 2001, two years that bracket the period of the late 1990's crisis, government expenditures on social security and welfare as a percentage of total GDP grew by a factor of 6 in China, 4 in Thailand, 3 in Korea, and 2.5 in the Philippines (ADB *KI* 2010). Most dramatic, perhaps, are new policies that seek to broaden the scope of worker protections beyond the ranks of formal-sector employment, in some cases building on existing social insurance programs, in other cases through creation of new citizen-based entitlements.

It was noted that if social insurance and pension programs, encouraged by the ILO and funded largely through payroll taxes on employers and employees, offer varying levels of protection to formal-sector workers, they often fail to reach the large numbers of unregistered, informal-sector, low-income, and rural workers whose needs are often far greater (Tang 2000, 154).[35] Korea's social insurance schemes, including pensions, health insurance, unemployment insurance, and severance pay, are largely funded by payroll contributions by registered firms and "regular" employees, most of whom are now covered. By contrast, only 10 to 16 percent of temporary workers, and roughly half of dispatch workers, were initially covered under social insurance programs (Yang and Moon 2005). Similarly, Thailand's National Economic and Social Development Board estimates that in 2002 roughly 72 percent of the workforce was in the informal sector, mostly unprotected under existing labor law and social insurance programs that mainly apply to workers in registered

---

34. Korea provides something of an exception, given its greater provision than elsewhere in developing Asia for formal-sector job security and social insurance even before the crisis. The World Bank has generally promoted social security systems along with welfare assistance circumscribed by targeting, means testing, and confinement to basic essentials. See Asia-Europe Meeting, "China—Social Strategy Framework" (November 1999), http://www.worldbank.org/eapsocial/ASEM/region/china.ht, accessed March 23, 2003.

35. For Thailand, see Siengthai (2008).

places of business. Later estimates for 2010–11 suggest that as many as 24 million persons still live outside those protections,[36] while two-thirds of the population lack a formal retirement plan.[37] This problem is only deepened during periodic economic crises when large numbers of workers must leave formal-sector employment to find part-time and informal jobs.

In China, where rapid growth of the informal sector has brought heightened awareness of the close relationship between economic reform and livelihood vulnerability, there has been increased effort to establish a basic livelihood floor for impoverished persons. Particularly important is the 1997 Minimum Livelihood Guarantee scheme for the disabled and poor, an experimental program instituted in the wake of sustained protests among laid-off SOE workers (Mun 2010).[38]

As alarming is the growing and politically troublesome income gap between rural and urban workers. As rural protests directed at official corruption, government-organized land seizures for development, and environmental damage have become ever-more frequent and sometimes violent, efforts have mounted to reduce the urban-rural income gap and to incorporate rural development more fully into national economic planning.[39] Attention has been focused especially on relieving the debt burden facing local governments, encouraging greater investment in rural and western provinces, reducing school and medical fees, cracking down on corruption, and reducing the tax burden on China's 750 million rural residents.

The exceptional difficulties faced by rural migrants in relatively unregulated economic zones has in part been addressed by the earlier mentioned experimental program, initially limited to only a few provinces, under which migrants receive rights to housing, education, employment, vocational training, medical care, and social security equivalent to that enjoyed by urban residents.[40]

In Thailand, in recognition of the important economic role of informal-sector businesses that generate roughly 44 percent of GDP, the Thaksin government proposed tax credits to encourage registration of small

---

36. "Korn Touts Pracha Wiwat," *Bangkok Post* (online), January 8, 2011.

37. "FPO: National Retirement Scheme Set for 2011 Launch," *Bangkok Post* (online), April 13, 2010.

38. Mun (2010) notes, however, that this program has failed adequately to address the problems faced by these former SOE workers.

39. "China Plans to Invest More in Rural Sector to Close the Wealth Gap," *Wall Street Journal*, February 28, 2006. "Beijing Reorders Priorities," *Wall Street Journal*, March 12, 2008.

40. See "China to Drop Urbanite-Peasant Legal Differences," *New York Times* (online edition), November 3, 2005. "Migrant Workers Get Chance for Urban Residency," *South China Morning Post*, September 6, 2010.

businesses,[41] while at the same time extending social security coverage to very small firms.[42] In 2004 unemployment insurance was extended to self-employed workers (Siengthai 2008, 339–40), and at decade's end, a national pension scheme was established to include, on a voluntary basis, self-employed and informal-sector workers, including most importantly agricultural workers, with the government contributing fifty baht for every one hundred baht worker contribution.[43] Finally, in the wake of mass demonstrations and protests by low-paid workers and rural groups in the streets of Bangkok during 2009–10, and in anticipation of upcoming national elections scheduled for 2011, Prime Minister Abhisit Vejjajiva's Democrat Party government prepared to introduce a large number of social welfare measures under a comprehensive national "People's Agenda" scheme, to include low-cost housing, cost-of-living measures for low-income workers, forgiveness of farmers' debts, and an expanded pension program, all intended to reach out to informal workers and poor families nationwide.[44]

In South Korea, growing concern about chronic structural unemployment and increasing casual and irregular employment led to a 1998 extension of EIS coverage to "atypical," irregular, part-time, and dismissed workers as well as to SMEs (Ramesh 2003; also see World Bank *WDR* 2005, 152–53). While this extension was in part undermined by contributions avoidance among non-regular and low-paid workers, as well as among self-employed workers (Yang and Moon 2005, 87), it did extend EIS benefits to over 12 percent of unemployed non-regular workers in 1999 (Kang et al. 2001, 108, 118–19). While it is clear this expansion in the scope of the EIS program, as well as expanded social security programs more generally, was strongly influenced by political pressures (Ramesh 2003), economic considerations played a further role in its enactment. In particular, its strong emphasis on vocational training and job reentry rather than mainly income replacement is signaled by its very title, which refers not to *unemployment* but rather to *employment*. In any event, the EIS is now most commonly justified not only for its role in providing a social safety net for workers experiencing increasing job instability, but more broadly as a means through which to bolster labor market participation and flexibility.

---

41. "Informal Economy: 23m Workers Need Help: NESDB," *Nation* (online), June 25, 2004.

42. Which is to say, these small firms have in part been effectively formalized.

43. "Mending the Safety Net," *Bangkok Post,* September 5, 2011; "FPO: National Retirement Scheme Set for 2011 Launch," *Bangkok Post,* April 13, 2010.

44. "B9bn Pracha Wiwat Scheme Gets Go-Ahead from Cabinet," *Bangkok Post,* January 12, 2011.

In addition, Korea has provided one of the region's only significant, if limited, social welfare programs for the general population. For those unable to work (the elderly, disabled, or young), a livelihood protection program, initially established in 1961, was expanded in 1998 to cover 2.5 percent of the population, and subsequently enlarged in 2000 into the Program for Ensuring People's Basic Living Standards. This program, which covered about 760,000 recipients in 1999, provides modest living assistance and loans for persons not eligible for EIS assistance (Kang et al. 2001, 118–19). In 2004, a Worker's Basic Welfare Act was enacted to assist low-income workers in small firms. Finally, the National Pension Service was amended, first in 1999 to expand coverage to previously excluded and informal-sector groups, and later still to include more than 85 percent of the national population by the end of 2009.[45] It was estimated that over 85 percent of all Korean workers aged fifteen and older were covered by one of the four public pension programs in 2009.[46]

In the Philippines, in response in part to the political mobilization efforts of NGOs, the government has instituted a variety of programs designed to offer new social protections to previously excluded groups, especially those in rural and informal sectors. These include microbusiness development programs, small-farmer support schemes, a variety of poverty alleviation programs, and financial and other support for social service cooperatives in both rural and urban areas (Sibal 2007). The latter efforts to encourage cooperatives has long been promoted by religious groups, labor NGOs, and other civil society advocacy groups.

Health Care

Health care bridges the gap between social reproduction and social protection. Primary health care, especially for children, largely addresses the need for social reproduction. Comprehensive health insurance schemes, on the other hand, both maintain the work-ready population and parallel other social protections that buffer the risks of involuntary loss of employment. If in many cases early health care reform generally relied on employment-linked contributory social insurance for formal-sector workers, later policies reached out to informal-sector workers in more direct ways.

---

45. "Subscribers to Public Pensions Top 20 Million," *Korea Herald* (online), April 11, 2010.
46. This figure refers to formal coverage only. Actual, or effective, coverage is lower due mainly to employer evasion in smaller to medium-sized firms.

In China, roughly two-thirds of the population had no health insurance at the dawn of the twenty-first century.[47] This contrasts strikingly with the prereform situation. In the 1970s, Chinese citizens enjoyed almost universal access to (variably) adequate programs of health care through collectives, work units, and state enterprises. This system was then incrementally dismantled by the structural reforms of the early 1980s under which collective farming gave way to the household responsibility system, and public and collective social protections were dismantled. The resulting gap between a shrinking proportion of workers either covered under state programs or able meet their own medical costs, and growing numbers of workers and families not able to access family health care, created growing social tensions. The official response has been uneven. In 1998 the central government introduced a new national basic health insurance scheme of employment-linked insurance funded by payroll deductions (6% employer, 2% employee) (Blomqvist and Qian 2008, 9). Gaps in this program are huge. As noted earlier, the program effectively reaches only formal-sector workers, and even then it does not cover dependent family members. Workers may voluntarily purchase health insurance for their children through their schools, but most cannot afford to do this. And due to lax enforcement, many private employers simply ignore new requirements to provide health insurance to employees, so that a majority of private-sector workers still have no coverage. By consequence of these gaps, it was estimated that by the late '00s, only about 30 percent of registered urban residents were covered by the new law (Blomqvist and Qian 2008, 11).

Corresponding to this largely urban-based social insurance plan, the New Co-operative Medical System (CMS) was established in 2002 to fill the gap left by the earlier dissolution of rural collectives and the social benefit programs they provided for rural populations. While enrollment in the CMS is voluntary, enrollment has expanded very rapidly,[48] reaching nearly one-half of rural residents in the mid-'00s (Blomqvist and Qian 2008, 15). Parallel to the CMS, provincial and national governments have funded expanded medical training and local health stations to provide public primary health services for local populations.[49] And, in response to the growing and politi-

---

47. This and the remainder of the paragraph is based on "China's Workers See Thin Protections in Insurance Plans," *Wall Street Journal,* December 30, 2005.

48. Official statistics suggest a ten-fold increase in enrollment in this program between 2004 and 2009 (PRC *CSY* 2010).

49. Chou and Hou (2008) estimate that roughly 138 million persons were covered by this plan in 2005. Between 2004 and 2008, the number of registered community health stations increased from 5,096 to 11,617, with a corresponding six-fold growth in numbers of visits by patients (PRC *CSY* 2010).

cally explosive problems of health costs, the national government unveiled an ambitious plan in 2008 to expand universal health insurance to extend health coverage to 90 percent of the population within two years, and to the entire population by 2020.[50]

While questions have been raised regarding funding and implementation, including the problematic issue of the respective roles of central and local governments, it is clear that the new programs reflect increasing official concern about the social and political implications of continuing neglect in this area.[51]

For some years Thailand pursued a course of devolution of health services to private-sector providers on the assumption that the private sector is more efficient and more responsive to changing local needs. More recently, however, state-funded national health programs have grown dramatically. Beginning in 2002, and propelled in part by the revised 1997 Constitution that guarantees a variety of "social rights," including health and education, to the entire national population (Dressel 2009), Thailand offers universal health coverage through its thirty-baht-per-visit program in public hospitals, a program that especially targets the poor and uninsured. This dramatic change in health-care policy is reflected in national health expenditure statistics. Between 2004 and 2008, the government share in total national health expenditures rose from less than 64 percent to 73 percent. As noted earlier, it is unclear how effective or fiscally sustainable Thailand's national health insurance program will be.[52]

By consequence of this health policy turnaround, Thai health coverage has increased dramatically. Whereas in 1999 only about one-third of the population was covered by medical insurance, by 2003 this coverage had increased to 95 percent (World Bank *WDI* 2006, 146). Thailand's National Statistical Office reports that in 2005–6, more than 47 million persons (out of a total population of just over 65 million) received treatment under this

---

50. "Beijing Plans Health Care for Everyone," *Wall Street Journal*, October 20, 2008.

51. In the early 1980s, Whyte and Parish (1984, 372–74) had already pointed to a growing tension between the requirements of efficiency and growth, on the one hand, and those of social cohesion and equity, on the other.

52. The social security fund covers only a small percentage of the total workforce (6 million of a total of 33.08 million in 2000, 7 million in 2003). The National Health Insurance Bill in fact undercuts the social security fund's health coverage through a proposal to replace the fund's health insurance with the national health-care program with its substantially reduced benefits. See "Budget Chief Wants Wealthy Out of Scheme," *Bangkok Post*, January 4, 2002. Also see "Labour Leaders Dead against Government Social Security Plan," *Bangkok Post*, February 2, 2002; and "Second-Class Scheme for Poor Picked," *Bangkok Post*, February 16, 2002. For a more general assessment of the sustainability of these programs, see "Government Given Thumbs-Down," *Bangkok Post*, February 4, 2002. Also "Welfare Levy to Rise," *Nation*, January 6, 2003.

program (KOT, *SYT* 2007).[53] This new medical program has assumed so prominent a social role that it has become politically difficult to contain its escalating costs. Following a 2006 military coup that replaced the Thai Rak Thai populist government that introduced this program, there was new discussion of dismantling it. But political protest, especially in rural areas, ensured not only a continuance of the popular program but discussion of elimination of the thirty baht fee as well!

Korea presents an equally dramatic example of increased public involvement in health care, although here the government's role was less provisionary and more regulatory. As discussed by Ramesh (2004), a national health insurance scheme, first established in the late 1970s, mandated that large firms provide health insurance for their workers. Contributory insurance was subsequently extended to smaller firms, to self-employed workers, and to the families of employed workers, and eventually included very poor families under a heavily subsidized Medicaid program. In the late 1990s and early '00s, the disparate regional, occupational, and organizational insurance schemes that had previously functioned somewhat independently of one another were brought into a unified governance structure under the National Health Insurance Corporation. This new national scheme imposes a uniform premium structure and has eventuated in the extension of health coverage to nearly the entire national population (U.S. Department of Labor 2003a).[54] While many Korean hospitals are run by private nonprofit organizations,[55] rules now permit for-profit entities to participate in health-care delivery. This provision responds in part to demands for increased access by foreign investors to domestic service sectors. While the insurance programs coordinated by the National Health Insurance Corporation are largely funded by payroll taxes on employers and employees, it is noteworthy that private health expenditures as a percent of the total declined sharply between the mid-1990s and the early '00s (World Bank *WDI* 2002), as noted below.

In The Philippines, formal-sector employment is estimated at only 18 percent of the employed workforce (Sibal 2007). For this reason, employment-based social insurance programs fail to reach the vast majority of workers and their families. In this context, the government established a national

---

53. The World Bank estimates that the Thai government pays for around 73% of total health expenditures in that country, a figure that exceeds that even of Korea (55%). The corresponding percentage for China is 45%, and only 35% for the Philippines. For Thailand, also see KOT, *SYT* 2007.

54. Most authors view Korea's expansive health insurance system as a response to political pressures following democratic reform (see, e.g., Wong 2005).

55. "For Profit Entities to be Allowed to Run Hospitals," *Korean Herald* (online edition), May 15, 2005.

health insurance program, PhilHealth, in 1996, to act as an umbrella regulatory and coordinating structure for a host of public- and private-sector
health organizations and providers, with the eventual goal of extending
health coverage to most of the population. It is estimated that PhilHealth
currently covers approximately 80 percent of the national population, although means testing and uneven enforcement diminishes the effectiveness
of this program.[56] And, by contrast with Thailand and Korea, where private
outlays for health expenditures constitute a far lower percent of the total,
those in the Philippines made up 60 percent of total health expenditures in
2005 (ROP *SY* 2005).

The growth of nationally organized health programs signals a turn to
social compensation and protection in order to sustain both reform agendas
and political legitimacy. As in the case of social security and welfare, but with
the exception of China, the late 1990's financial crisis was associated with
an increased government role in health provision. Between 1996 and 2001,
public health expenditures as a percentage of total health expenditures rose
from 40 percent to 52 percent in Korea, from 41 percent to 44 percent in
the Philippines, and from 47 percent to 56 percent (64 percent in 2002) in
Thailand. By 2008, these percentages had grown further: in China (from
38 percent in 2000) to 50 percent, in Korea to 54 percent, and in Thailand
to 76 percent, while declining modestly to 35 percent in the Philippines
(WB *WDI* 2011). Correspondingly, out-of-pocket expenditures (nongovernmental and not covered by social insurance) had declined to 44 percent
in China, 35 percent in Korea, and most dramatically, to only 18 percent in
Thailand.[57] Again the outlier, out-of-pocket health expenditures in the Philippines comprised more than half (54 percent) of the total there. In the case
of China, the late 1990's reversal is evident as well in data on the percentage
of total government expenditure allocated to health: 32 percent in 1978,
25 percent in 1990, and only 15 percent in 2000, thereafter rising to 25 percent in 2008 (PRC *CSY* 2010).

If the national provision of health care to formal-sector workers responded
to both economic and political requirements, its extension to informal sectors
and rural populations attended most clearly to politics (Wong 2004). I return
to the political drivers of new reform policies in chapter 12.

---

56. Philippine Health Insurance Corporation, http://www.philhealth.gov.ph/about_us/index.
htm.

57. By 2005, more than 8 percent of total Thai government expenditures (vs. only 1% in Korea)
went to health care (IMF *GFS* 2006).

Job Creation and Livelihood Protection through Small Business Development

Small-enterprise development programs, widespread in developing countries, are a further instrument of social protection and compensation for informal-sector workers and rural populations. A major impetus for the early launching of SME-focused antipoverty programs was the Grameen Bank microcredit program developed in Bangladesh in the 1970s and subsequently extended to India and elsewhere.[58] The apparent success of that program, which provided loans on a rotating basis to small groups of rural women, led to widespread inclusion of microcredit programs in the antipoverty efforts of NGOs, governments, and international financial institutions, including the World Bank and ADB. SME development programs have had the additional effect of formalizing small-firm employment sectors by drawing them into government assistance programs.

Encouragement of SME development to compensate for the uneven employment and livelihood outcomes of market-oriented reform was dramatically evidenced in the success of national efforts in China to encourage local development of township and village enterprises following the introduction there of the household responsibility system in the early 1980s. While the TVEs are more famously known for their remarkable contribution to economic development, and while they in fact tended to cluster near urban centers in the East rather than in rural areas further inland (Whyte and Parish 1984), their role in providing alternative employment for displaced rural labor must also be recognized.

In Thailand, many SME development programs, especially those targeting rural and small businesses, address the related goals of employment creation and poverty reduction (Deyo 2002, 17; Hewison 2006b). These include labor-intensive infrastructure-creating public works projects, credit schemes for the self-employed, and other income-replacement efforts. Given the focus of these Thai programs on short-term cyclical (vs. structural) unemployment, their emphasis would seem more social than economic, especially during times of recession. While not as comprehensive as comparable programs of employment creation in Korea, where public works programs employed roughly 76 percent of 1.7 million unemployed workers at the height of the crisis in 1999 (Betcherman and Islam 2001, 20–24), Thailand's employment-creating policies nonetheless provided important assistance to rural communities during the course of the crisis. Similar in function are Philippine SME

---

58. "India's Small Loans Yield Big Markets," *Wall Street Journal*, May 25, 2005.

assistance programs that target informal-sector firms in that country (Herrin and Pernia 2003, 292).

Social Capital as Social Protection

Given the problems of embracing informal-sector and non-regular workers under social protection schemes designed largely for workers employed in larger, formal-sector firms, there is growing pressure to establish or expand alternative social protections. The World Bank in particular has encouraged and supported a variety of needs-based income-support schemes, including public works projects, rural and small business assistance, and microcredit programs (World Bank 2002a, 112–20). These programs converge with and build on parallel efforts by NGOs to encourage cooperative ventures and informal-sector livelihood projects among poor and rural populations.

As these various top-down and bottom-up initiatives have increasingly interpenetrated and commingled, they have resulted in a proliferation of state-initiated and financed, but locally implemented, development projects that have drawn community groups and NGOs into "partnerships" with government agencies. During prereform decades, community development programs functioned largely to complement national-development policies. Under market reform, these social capital programs have been expanded, with the state role largely confined to facilitation and start-up or partial funding. In this context, civil society has assumed an ever-greater role in compensating market risk. This is true for both urban and rural areas. In urban China, Xinping Guan (2000) notes that government has in part addressed the social dislocations associated with the declining efficacy of collective and SOE-based social safety nets by "societalizing" (vs. privatizing) social welfare systems through supporting the work of nonprofit NGOs, especially those officially recognized as "resident community associations."[59] This approach, it should be noted, has not escaped criticism. In particular, the partnership and self-help programs that have proliferated under this approach have sometimes been viewed as only constructing a new "economy of the poor," within which impoverished groups manage themselves on the economic margins and thus absolve both state and capital of responsibility for social livelihood (Fontan and Shragge 2000, 6).

Thailand perhaps best illustrates the social capital–building approach. Here a moderately autonomous, economically viable rural community base

---

59. It is ironic that the earlier dissolution of rural collectives undermined social capital that the state seeks now to recreate.

and vibrant networks of local social institutions, including NGOs, provide a supportive social environment for new government initiatives. Following the initial impact of the late-1990's crisis, and assisted by World Bank and ADB "social investment" funds, the Thai government launched community-based infrastructure and village development projects, including block development grants to 78,000 villages, support for agricultural diversification (to hedge market risk), provision of debt relief for farmers, establishment of community banks, strengthening of local communities under an expanded community forestry program,[60] and expansion of microcredit and SME business-development programs. The social capacity–building approach, institutionally located in the operations of the Ministry of Social Development and Human Security,[61] has been strongly supported by the King himself as part of his "self-sufficiency" movement. This approach is evident in community empowerment programs promoted by the Thai National Reform Assembly, a government advisory body to address problems of inequality and poverty.[62]

Combining Labor Market Policy and Social Policy: The New Worker Entrepreneurialism

In chapter 3 I discussed emergent efforts to transform workers into what Jessop termed "enterprising subjects," capable of navigating uncertain and unstable labor markets and of adapting to the requirements of continual job mobility and self-reinvention (also see Jessop and Sum 2006, 183). It was noted in this regard that active labor market policies, expanded training opportunities, and adequate livelihood protections to compensate for periods of unemployment and job transition form essential structural supports for the new worker identities and capacities required by new conditions of employment.

Korea's flexicurity approach, as embodied in the Employment Insurance System, seeks to address these requirements by shifting the emphasis from short-term job placement and reskilling to longer-term upskilling that may keep workers out of work for longer periods of time but that supports the

---

60. The community forestry programs constitute a partial reversal of previous policies under which farmers were simply evicted from government forest reserves. "Alternatives Needed to National Parks: Hurting Villagers Living around Forests," *Bangkok Post*, January 6, 2002; "Displaced Farmers to Get Previously Allocated Land: New Approach to Reform Welcomed," *Bangkok Post*, January 7, 2002. The self-sufficiency movement has led to renewed interest in environmental protection of Thailand's dwindling forests, as previously languishing community forestry programs have received growing official support.

61. "Three More Ministries to Join Line-Up," *Bangkok Post*, January 10, 2002.

62. "NRA Proposes Reform Package," *Bangkok Post* (online), March 25, 2011.

growth of new knowledge-based industries (Jessop 2002, 156–57). Support-ive of this approach is Korea's Vocational Training Promotion Act (1997), which goes beyond skill training to "ability-development whose purpose is to make workers themselves more flexible and self-responsible in continually adapting to economic change" (for discussion see Moore 2007).

That such a program, which demands relatively expensive long-term live-lihood support for workers undergoing training, has been adopted in Korea but not, say, in Thailand or the Philippines is in part attributable to Korea's relatively stronger unions, which, though declining in numerical strength, are still able to negotiate these and other high road labor policies. Similarly, the continued threat to political stability posed by displaced SOE workers in China has indirectly empowered those workers to demand continued postemployment support and training, though there the emphasis has been less developmental and more focused on enabling workers to find *any* kind of work in the growing private sector. Also important in Korea, Taiwan, and Hong Kong, and to a lesser degree even in Thailand, are the national health insurance programs that encourage workers to risk withdrawal from work in order to undergo further education and training, or even to start up their own small or family businesses (Castells 2000 [1996], 204).

If the developmental sidelining and upskilling of workers presupposes a favorable opportunity structure for workers, other policies and programs have emphasized the subjective side of the new worker entrepreneurialism: building new identities and motivations that encourage the seizing of those opportunities. At the most general level, this encouragement is embodied in neoliberal discourses of freedom, market empowerment, individualism, and self-responsibility that are the counterparts of parallel discourses of consum-erism. In some cases, as in Singapore, strict meritocratic standards for pro-motion are accompanied by public and union-based campaigns promoting hard work and individual responsibility. In Indonesia, as reported by Daromir Rudnycky (2008), *spiritual* training has been harnessed to the goals of privati-zation and increased productivity, and of "preparing employees to participate in a commodity market [as] self-governing, entrepreneurial subject[s], exer-cising what one manager described as 'built-in control . . . and taking respon-sibility for one's actions at work and being proactive in one's career'" (75). Rudnycky goes on to note that "concordant with a shift to the conditions of global neoliberal markets, development was reconfigured as a matter of individual accountability and spiritual practice" (79).

The new worker entrepreneurism has also in part been institutionalized in the gradual shift in China, Korea, and elsewhere from collective to individual employment contracts, a shift that forces on workers the responsibility not only to negotiate their own fixed-term contracts with firms but also to continually improve the diversity and depth of their technical and interpersonal skills, proactively construct their own careers, assume greater responsibility for their livelihood security, and in some cases seize the interludes of unemployment to create startup microbusinesses of their own.

In Korea, efforts to encourage new worker subjectivities have been explicit. As the late-1990's financial crisis gradually enlarged the pool of unemployed university-educated youth seeking their first full-time jobs, and as it became increasingly apparent that an entrepreneurial knowledge-based economy was beginning to displace the concentrated, chaebol-dominated economy of the 1970s and 1980s, there was recognition that new entrants to the labor force would need to become less risk averse and more entrepreneurial, self-directed, flexible, and self-invested in terms of seeking out new opportunities and acquiring new skills and capabilities. In her discussion of welfare and employment programs directed at Korea's underemployed youth, Jesook Song (2009, chap. 4) notes a decisive shift in welfare and employment policy during the presidency of Kim Dae Jung—from a traditional welfare-as-compensation model to an approach emphasizing initiative and self-responsibility, particularly among technology-savvy college graduates who might be expected to start dot-com companies in emerging technologies. Similarly, Seo Dong Jin (2005) discusses the centrality of the cultivation of autonomy and responsibility, and of a new embrace of "enterprising labor," in Korea's training and vocational educational programs during the mid-'00s. I return to this topic in chapter 11.

Social Reproduction: Education and Training

In the domain of social and labor protections, economic and social agendas often conflict, as the demands of labor market flexibility clash with the requirements of livelihood security. It is here that one finds the most intractable social and political conflicts in the reform-driven restructuring of labor systems. I have noted in this regard that the rapid development of contributory social insurance programs has sought to resolve this conflict.

Quite different is the domain of social reproduction, where social agendas and economic requirements more often coincide, if only in the long run. Insofar as some aspects of social reproduction are closely and directly linked to the requirements of productive efficiencies and economic growth (e.g., education, training, primary health care), developmental and strategic factors at least in part displace class politics in influencing policy trajectories, especially in the more economically dynamic East Asian economies.

It is generally observed that East Asian social policy has traditionally, and increasingly, stressed education, training, and other elements of "human capital formation," particularly in South Korea and other developmental states, thus leading Chan and Ngai (2009), Holliday (2000), Holiday and Wilding (2003), and others to characterize East Asian social policy as strongly "productivist" in nature (Lee 2007, 1–6). It is notable that government expenditures on education as a percentage of GDP have risen steadily since the mid-1990s: in China from 2 percent (1995) to 3.5 percent in 2008, in Korea from 2.4 percent (1995) to 3.7 percent (2009), and in Thailand from 2.9 percent (1995) to 4.4 percent (2009). Only in the developmentally challenged Philippines has this percentage declined during that same period: from 3.2 percent to 2.9 percent[63] (all figures from ADB *KI* 2010). These changes in educational outlays, undertaken in the context of EOI developmental upgrading and market reform, have both anticipated later developmental requirements and created strong institutional path dependencies on which policymakers could later build in responding to the new challenges of reform.

The Korean experience provides a prime example of the Asian productivist model. There, public spending on education began its upward ascent as early as the 1970s, later increasing even faster in response to new economic requirements and as an alternative to reliance on immigrant workers for skilled and professional labor.[64] As seen in Table 9.1 below, Korea has a clear lead in educational enrollments at both secondary and tertiary levels, as well as very high and still increasing enrollments at the tertiary level.[65]

As important here is the level of support given technical, engineering, and science-based education. Following a 1974 policy decision to place greater emphasis on vocational education, the Korean government enacted the Basic Law for Vocational Training in 1976. This law required large firms to provide in-house training for workers, in the absence of which firms were required to pay a training levy of at least 6 percent of the total wage bill to be used

---

63. In the case of the Philippines, a UNDP report notes a corresponding decline between 2007 and 2008 in classrooms, books, teachers, and enrollment in public basic (primary) education, alongside continued enrollment gains in private schools. "Education Crisis Looms: UNDP Blames Falling Enrolment, Shortages," *Manila Times,* May 21, 2009.

64. Another factor pushing states into a more central role in labor force enskillment is that industries that were more important during first-stage EOI, such as wearing apparel and shoes, required skills that were most often taught at home, while the higher value-added industries that have increasingly replaced those earlier industries rely on formal instruction outside the home, thus bringing the state more fully into the picture. See Caraway (2006, 29).

65. This section on educational reform draws extensively on the comprehensive survey of education in Asia by the Asian Development Bank (*KI,* 2003).

Table 9.1   Educational Attainment

Country	Mean years of schooling[a] 2000	Percentage in secondary enrollment[b] (net) (%) 1999	2009	Percentage in tertiary enrollment (gross) (%) 1999	2009
China	7	—	78[c]	6	25
Korea	11	97	95	66	98
Thailand	7	—	71	32	45
Philippines	8	50	61	29	29

[a] World Bank: *World Development Report 2006* (table 2.13) and *World Development Indicators*, 2002 and 2011.
[b] Secondary and tertiary enrollments from World Bank, *World Development Indicators 2011*. *Gross* enrollment: all enrollees, regardless of age. *Net* enrollment: only appropriate-age enrollees. —: missing data.
[c] Gross enrollment.

to promote vocational training in government-sponsored training schools (ADB *KI* 2003, 8).[66] In 1996 the government went further by establishing the Korea Research Institute for Vocational Educational Training. This organization, assisted and advised by a range of international institutions, including the ILO, Asia Pacific Economic Cooperation Forum, the OECD, and UNESCO, supports Korean vocational education programs and human resource development more generally through institutional research and coordination. Operationally, the Ministry of Labor assumed supervisory control of private vocational training in 1997, while the Ministry of Education was given centralized control of vocational education in schools, vocational institutes, polytechnic institutes, and universities. Since 1998 government has played a directive role in vocational education and training on a national scale, a role further strengthened and formalized under the 2001 Goals and Strategies of National Human Resources Policy. This expanded role was driven by the competitive pressures on Korean firms associated with liberalization of external trade and investment. Those pressures had two important outcomes to which vocational education sought to respond: first, the need to move into higher-value market niches in response to cost-based competition from China and elsewhere; and second, the necessity of providing continuing vocational training and retraining to facilitate increased labor market flexibility. Such retraining, it may be noted, while addressing requirements for flexibility and upgrading, responds as well to sociopolitical pressures for institutional protection from the risks and instabilities of global markets. And, most important, these programs help compensate for training disincentives

66. This law was formally similar to the earlier-established Singaporean Skills Development Fund.

to firms resulting from the increasing prevalence of contract and contingent employment. It may also be noted in this regard that as Korea deindustrializes in favor of modern service industries and regionally outsources its manufacturing production, its earlier strong emphasis on secondary-level vocational education will likely wane as well. Indeed, by the late 1990s, Korea's early lead in secondary vocational enrollments had already been challenged, particularly by China where secondary vocational enrollments increased from just 2 percent of the total in 1980 to 15 percent in the late 1990s, not far below Korea's 20 percent level (ADB *KI* 2003). The dramatic increase in Chinese secondary vocational enrollments reflects official concern about growing shortages of technically skilled workers. In Guangzhou, for example, 42 percent of firms surveyed in 2005 indicated they were unable to fill vacancies for skilled technicians.[67]

At the tertiary level, Korea's relative standing in technical and science-based education has also been challenged by China, which by the mid-1990s exceeded Korea in the percentage of higher education students enrolled in science and engineering (ADB *KI* 2003). By way of contrast, it may be noted that the vast majority of tertiary students in the Philippines continue to enroll in nontechnical disciplines.[68] Other available data suggest massive Chinese investments in education and in research and development,[69] especially following the announcement of "The Decision on Accelerating Scientific and Technological Progress" at the 1995 Third National Conference on Science and Technology (Appelbaum 2009, 66). Together, these initiatives have reinforced the gradual increase in China's technical and research workforce,[70] although Korea maintains a strong lead in actual numbers of practicing R & D workers.[71]

Korea's strong commitment to industrial upgrading, signaled in 2008 by the establishment of the new Ministry of Knowledge Economy, is further evidenced by relatively high levels of R & D expenditure. From 1987 to 1997, total Korean expenditures on research and development activities stood at 2.82 percent of gross national income (GNI), as against 0.66 percent in

---

67. "Train More Blue Collar Workers, City Warned," *South China Morning Press,* March 22, 2005.

68. In 2009–10, only 14% of tertiary students in the Philippines were enrolled in natural science, mathematics, computer science, or engineering and technology. NSCB, *Philippine Statistical Yearbook,* 2010.

69. Chinese R & D expenditures as a percent of GDP were 0.9% in 2000 and 1.42% in 2006. *China Statistical Yearbook,* 2007.

70. "Chinese Spending for Research Outpaces the U.S," *Wall Street Journal,* September 29, 2006.

71. In the mid-'00s, Korea employed 720 R & D technicians per one million people vs. 160 in Thailand and only 10 in the Philippines (World Bank *WDI* 2011).

China, 0.22 percent in the Philippines, and 0.13 percent in Thailand[72] (World Bank *WDI* 2001). By the mid-'00s, however, that lead had been substantially reduced. Studies by the OECD estimate that R & D expenditures made up 3.22 percent of Korea's total GDP in 2006, as compared with 1.49 percent in China in 2003.[73] Other OECD data show that businesses accounted for over 70 percent of total 2007 R & D expenditures in both Korea and China, although China relied more heavily than did Korea on the R & D activities of locally operating foreign firms.

While an emphasis on vocational training and science-based education (as in Korea and China) is most often attributed to a growing demand for skilled and technical labor, a further important consideration relates to the need to maintain high levels of employment in the face of increasing wage pressures through productivity improvements and industrial upgrading. Such labor market pressures, seen earlier in Korea, are now most pressing in China. Between 1997 and 2007, the average wage rose from 6,470 to 24,932 yuan. The corresponding average *real wage index,* based on 1978 = 100, rose during those same years from 218 to 700 (PRC, *Population and Employment Statistics* 2008).[74] Conversely, such wage pressures have not presented themselves in the Philippines, where job creation has failed to keep pace with growth in the labor force.[75]

Finally, I noted in chapter 6 that economic reform in these four countries has included a very mixed experience of partial, selective, and gradualistic engagement with neoliberal policies of market deregulation. The present chapter, on the *re*regulatory face of reform, has further documented this region's cautious and nonlinear encounter with neoliberalism by emphasizing ways in which the tensions of deregulatory reform have been varyingly addressed through a variety of compensating institutional, social, and developmental interventions. I return to this latter, developmental, dimension in chapter 11.

---

72. "R & D Spending Needed to Escape 'Middle-Income Trap'," *Bangkok Post*, August 19, 2010.

73. OECD, *Main Science and Technology Indicators 2009* and *Science and Engineering Indicators 2010*). Correspondingly, World Bank data suggest a relatively stronger government role in R & D expenditures in Korea than in the other countries: at 3.2 percent in Korea, 1.4% in China, 0.25% in Thailand, and only 0.12% in the Philippines (WB *WDI* 2011). Also see "China's Spending for Research Outpaces the U.S." *Wall Street Journal*, September 29, 2006.

74. Comparable data reported by the *Wall Street Journal* shows real wage increases averaging 10% per annum during 2002–8. "World Bank: Wages Can Rise in China," *Wall Street Journal*, June 19, 2010. The *Economist* similarly reports a tripling of Chinese labor costs during the decade after 1995." The Rising Power of the Chinese Worker," *Economist*, July 31, 2010, 9.

75. "Unemployment a 'Time Bomb' for RP, Warns ADB," *Manila Times* (online), April 20, 2010.

CHAPTER 10

Disciplining Labor and Rebuilding the Labor Process

> This most recent phase of "roll-out" neoliberalism... is increasingly associated with the aggressive reregulation, disciplining, and containment of those marginalized or dispossessed by the neoliberalization of the 1980s.
>
> —Peck and Tickell 2002, 389

> Since February (2011), Chinese leaders have repeatedly called for new approaches to what they call "social management"—meaning local authorities are under pressure to find new ways to prevent, or contain, unrest.
>
> —"China Stamps Out Southern Rioting," *Wall Street Journal,* June 15, 2011

I have argued that policies relating to workforce social reproduction tend to provoke less intense conflict than policies of social protection, where labor costs are more often seen as competing with rather than augmenting competitiveness and labor market flexibility. Even more conflictual is the labor process, in which regulatory regimes and policies must more directly address the structural disparities between the livelihood agendas of workers and the accumulation strategies of firms and states. Here questions of pay, work discipline, job control, work organization, and accepted avenues of worker representation pose especially contentious issues in which common ground is often difficult to find. Managing this conflict becomes harder still under the intensified competitive pressures of market reform.

Insofar as economic structural change, labor market deregulation, and social-policy reform have generated follow-on tensions and conflicts in the labor processes of manufacturing firms (as discussed in chapter 7), how have those tensions been addressed by employers and states? I focus here on six common strategies: coercion, social pyramiding, the institutional segregation of incompatible labor systems, mutual commitment employment practices, new mechanisms of collective conflict resolution, and worker-participation programs. The first of these, despotic and coercive controls, differs from the others in seeking mainly to repress or contain conflict rather to manage or confront its underlying causes.

Imposing Worker Discipline

When de jure or de facto deregulation has provoked worker opposition, firms and governments have moved quickly to reestablish worker discipline. That discipline may in turn rely on the power of markets, psychological pressure, or physical coercion. Market discipline entails a fusing of external labor markets with the labor process itself through heightened reliance on piece-rate and performance-based remuneration within "clean" wage systems, detailed pay incentives and penalties based on specified worker behavior (cleanliness, courtesy, punctuality, etc.), and the threat of dismissal.[1] A primary reliance on market discipline is found most prominently among casualized workers in the export zones of coastal China, Thailand, and the Philippines.

Parallels may be found in the changing labor practices of China's reformed SOE sector. Chan (2001) finds that as government enterprises have faced greater market competition, while at the same time being granted increased latitude in their internal employment practices,[2] they have begun to adopt some of the same disciplinary practices found among private and joint venture firms, including increased reliance on casual, vulnerable labor and resort to harsh pay regimes (13–15, 42) (also see Taylor 2002). Chiu, in her study of worker outcomes of SOE reform, similarly found that many SEO workers reported increased strictness in managerial practices during the late 1990's reforms (Chiu 2005, 684).

When market sanctions prove inadequate for controlling workers, employers may resort to various forms of coercion. It will be recalled that the earlier development of export-processing zones in Taiwan and elsewhere was accompanied by increased reliance on police power to maintain industrial

---

1. While bearing similarities to Frederick Taylor's scientific management (relating especially to a fine division of labor, separation of mental and manual tasks, and reliance on individual material inducements), market discipline in Chinese and other Asian export factories has not generally been associated with the systematic, science-based organization of production he espoused. Indeed, and apart from the infamous time-and-motion studies to which unions vigorously reacted, such science-based management was rarely fully realized in the United States during the height of its popularity there in the 1920s (Jaffee 2001, 59–60).

2. Beginning with the Regulation on Transforming the Management Mechanism of State-Owned Industrial Enterprises Act of 1992.

discipline. That pattern has repeated itself in other countries of the region. Coercive controls are currently most prominent in China's export-processing zones, where many low-skill workers are subject to dormitory surveillance and lock-ins, confiscation of work permits, humiliation, and physical abuse (Chan 2001, 270). The need for such controls to prevent workers from *quitting* suggests the power of cost competition in international markets to encourage employers to push compensation levels below even minimal market-clearing levels.[3] Such coercive discipline is often reinforced by local authorities, especially if municipalities are co-invested in joint ventures with foreign companies. Of particular importance in this regard is the discretionary police role in managing and enforcing the residency-based work-permit system. For their part, companies may enhance their disciplinary power through loans to workers for the purchase of work permits, demands for an advance deposit from newly hired workers against the risk of their quitting before completing their contract, and the sequestering of permits and identity papers for the duration of contracts. Such practices by police and employers often culminate in what Anita Chan describes as a loose equivalent of labor bondage (2001, 20, 143). Similarly, Chan and Ngai (2009, 291) note how much disciplinary leverage "dormitory labor regimes" give managers in large Chinese factories.

These harsh labor regimes are most common and most successful when they are supported by a broader state authoritarianism. And, indeed, as governments have confronted political and economic crises, they have often reinforced disciplinary labor practices at the level of the firm. Most notable perhaps is the authoritarian turn in China following the 1989 Tiananmen Square protests by students and workers.[4] And again in 2011, the Chinese government met increased militancy among migrant workers with harsh police suppression.[5] In Thailand, following the late 1990's financial crisis, the new populist Thaksin government, as well as the military-backed government that replaced it in the wake of political upheavals in 2006, pursued an authoritarian path (Hewison 2006a, 125), culminating, under a new government, in a 2007 constitution that largely restored elite rule while restricting the political activities of dissident groups of farmers and workers (Dressel 2009). Similarly, following the 1986 popular uprising against President Marcos of the Philippines, and amid increased labor militancy in 1986–87, the

---

3. It is only very recently, in the mid-'00s, that labor scarcities have forced employers into wage bidding to attract workers, especially those with scarce skills.

4. "Containing Unrest: The Government Moves Swiftly to Stop Protest Spreading," *Economist,* January 16, 2003.

5. "Wave of Unrest Rocks China: Threats to Social Order Increasingly Hit Cities, Bringing Iron-Fist Response," *Wall Street Journal,* June 14, 2011.

successor Aquino and Ramos administrations both reinstated strict rules on strikes and labor protests.

The Korean experience has been quite different. There, particularly during the 1980s, factory workers were subject to coercive state controls, including police surveillance and intervention in strikes or other collective action, suppression of efforts to form independent unions, and mandatory registration of existing unions within the state-controlled FKTU. Such coercive controls were most dramatically employed in response to the explosion of Korean labor militancy in 1987–88 (Kang et al. 2001, 104; Koo 2001). In the subsequent years of democratization and labor market deregulation, coercive political regulation gave way to increased liberalization, including official recognition of the oppositional labor federation (the KCTU) (Lee 2006), relaxation of restrictions on labor organizations and collective action, and recognition of the right of teachers and civil servants to organize. It should be noted, however, that these progressive changes did not entirely eliminate earlier abuses. The ILO notes the selective refusal to register new unions and the occasional arrest of militant trade unionists, including the KCTU president himself in 2002.

Social Pyramiding

Social pyramiding, a somewhat different strategy for stabilizing the labor process, is most closely linked to social capital approaches. This strategy seeks to embed (or re-embed) workplace discipline in social networks of family, business, and community. As used by employers, pyramiding offers a means by which partially to shift the burden of discipline to external networks and organizations by tapping the bonds of mutual dependency and normative obligation that constitute them. For example, Japanese and other foreign investors in China typically delegate personnel management to local Chinese managers who are better able to utilize social networks, union contacts, and political connections to reinforce workplace authority (Taylor 1999). Similarly, Ching-kwan Lee's (1998) insightful account of labor controls among young female workers in a Chinese export-processing factory shows that as production was gradually relocated from Hong Kong to one of China's export-processing zones, the employer was able successfully to rely for recruitment and shop-floor discipline on locality-based social networks of women employees. Chiu and Frenkel (2000, 40) note the importance placed by foreign investors on the cultivation of good relations with local officials, even to the extent of locating factory operations in their familial places of origin in China. And Philip Kelly (2001), in his study of Philippine industrial zones, reports the great efforts of foreign managers to cultivate close relations with community leaders, local officials, and family heads as a means of maintaining effective control over locally recruited workers.

A final example of pyramiding is to be found in outsourcing strategies themselves, strategies that devolve workplace control to workshops and family businesses where patriarchal and personalistic discipline provides an effective alternative to factory-based managerial controls.

Institutional Segregation

A third approach to reconstructing the labor process addresses the earlier-discussed problem of normative conflict among workers who must interact on the job but who are institutionally located in a variety of different labor systems that collectively make up the actual production process. I have noted that the articulation of different labor systems within shared workplaces, especially where labor practices sharply distinguish stable regular workers from contingent and non-regular workers, generates disruptive conflicts and inhibits the information sharing and cooperation so necessary for new forms of flexible production. This conflict may invoke efforts to institutionally segregate these diverse labor systems or at least to find a better balance between the often-opposed needs for their operational articulation, on the one hand, and their institutional segmentation, on the other.[6] Of particular importance is the need to institutionalize, and thus legitimate, differential terms of employment so as to reduce the disruptive consequences of the inequities those differences create.

In some cases, the institutional segregation of incompatible labor systems is rooted in government policy, as illustrated by the official demarcation in Chinese job-placement services between "labor" markets for ordinary workers and "human resource" markets for technical school and university graduates (Meng 2002). Immigration policy defines another important context for institutional segregation, as in the case of the earlier-mentioned Philippine immigrant workers in Korea. Here, nationality differences and intergovernmental agreements create legitimating markers that distinguish privileged (Korean) workers from less privileged (short-term, immigrant) workers, whose terms of employment differ sharply from those enjoyed by Korean workers. The Taiwanese government goes even further in using immigrant

---

6. Reliance on meritocratic arguments or ideologies asserting that those enjoying superior employment conditions and pay have earned these rewards through superior performance fail adequately to justify the numerous cases of equally skilled workers doing comparable work but receiving lesser rewards.

subidentities to demarcate labor systems, by applying gender, age, nationality, and skill criteria to its immigration controls and work-eligibility rules. Construction work, for example, draws heavily on young males from Thailand. Once recruited, these Thai workers typically find their compensation levels and terms of employment markedly inferior to those of the domestic crews with whom they work. However, the potential conflicts and disruptions those inequities might otherwise provoke are effectively diminished by their incorporation into a contractual framework that offers a legitimating rationale and legal codification of differential employment practices and entitlements.

Efforts to effect institutional segregation are most evident at the enterprise level, where managers may seek to institutionalize and legitimate labor market segmentation and associated differences in employment conditions, pay, and benefits. In part, the gradual shift from collective to individual contracts legalizes the differential treatment of workers between "regular" workers and workers hired under fixed-term contracts, and also among contract workers themselves, with their individually negotiated terms of employment.

But other approaches are important as well. In Thailand, where contract workers or workers from supply firms work alongside regular workers, distinctions are highlighted by differences in uniforms or hat color (Deyo 1996, 149). Labor segmentation is furthered by a clear demarcation between "women's work" and work done by men. Here, the gender divide, sometimes irrespective of similarities in required skills and the content of work, defines a socially accepted boundary marker relating to work conditions, expectations, and rewards. Such an institutionalized gendering of labor is perhaps most evident in the employment practices of firms that preferentially hire young women for light export-assembly work, thus confining despotic labor controls to the ranks of young, transitory, and more easily disciplined females. Alternately, efforts may be made to *physically* separate different categories of workers while at the same time functionally reintegrating their work through computer networking. In all these instances, differences in work conditions and rewards are institutionalized and formalized so as to clarify and legitimate them.

Deep, hierarchically differentiated Japanese supply chains seek to enhance workforce and institutional homogeneity within plants and workplaces while allocating diverse but complementary labor systems across plants and firms.[7]

---

7. Hierarchical differentiation is often achieved through creation by large Japanese firms of multitiered supply chains in which workers employed in higher-tier firms enjoy privileged access to training and work benefits. For discussion, see Deyo (1996).

Of course, the very act of outsourcing service and manufacturing tasks to other firms, or of hiring temporary help from dispatch agencies, utilizes *organizational* boundaries to demarcate differentially employed groups of workers, although coordination may be compromised in such cases. In cases of international subcontracting, diverse labor systems are dispersed as well across national boundaries.

Honda's Guangdong auto assembly plant, to take one example, tries to preserve institutional homogeneity and mutual commitment employment practices among core factory staff by physically separating different operations, not hiring migrant labor in its core plants, separately employing a buffer of temporary workers (both skilled and unskilled), and subcontracting many lower-skilled activities to other firms. Insofar as some of the temporary workers are hired through placement agencies, they are largely viewed as guest workers or outsiders.

Beverly Silver usefully frames this question of institutional boundaries, noting their function in balancing the often-competing agendas of profitability and legitimacy, by demarcating those groups to whom concessions and favorable terms are to be offered and, conversely, those groups who will not be so favored (2003, 20–25, 156). Such a demarcation typically brings politically important groups (e.g., unionized Korean workers) into supportive networks and relations while denying expensive concessions to politically less-consequential groups.

Promoting Consensual Labor Regimes

If coercive containment is one approach to dealing with social opposition and labor unrest in Asia, other responses have become more prominent during recent years. This change is attributable to several factors. First, rapid economic growth in the East Asian region has partially muted social opposition, augmented the material resources for expanded social programs and services, and given ruling groups leeway to develop alternative responses. The socially disruptive outcomes of periodic regional economic crises lends support to this suggested link between growth and social order. Second, short-term, developmentally self-defeating, and ultimately costly, attempts to forcefully contain worker dissent have led to new government efforts to encourage less-harsh labor regimes. Such efforts have been especially apparent where new social policies have afforded workers a degree of livelihood protection, thus reducing the market dependency of workers and forcing employers to turn to less-despotic labor practices (Burawoy 1985). Third, growing labor scarcities in some areas, such as China's Guangdong export zones, give workers increased bargaining power in their dealings with employers. Fourth, efforts by firms to move into higher value-added product niches have encouraged new labor practices intended to supplant unwilling compliance with fuller and more willing work involvement. Fifth, political liberalization has, in some countries in the region, rendered less acceptable and less effective a continued reliance on harsh work discipline. And sixth, there is growing recognition by governments that harsh labor practices and repressive state labor controls create their own problems of escalating conflict and political instability.

For these and other reasons, elites have been both encouraged and required to turn to less-despotic and more consensual labor practices. This change is perhaps most dramatically seen in the growing adoption by regional firms and suppliers of new codes of conduct under corporate social responsibility (CSR) programs. CSR programs involve self-policing in such areas as environmental protection, consumer-product safety, and fair labor practices. In China's relatively unregulated export industrial zones, it is often said that CSR programs are one of the few effective social governance institutions, apart from the state-controlled ACFTU and NGOs, to encourage labor protections and compliance with national labor standards. Typically, and often with host-government encouragement, major outsourcing firms in the United States and Europe commit to maintaining labor and environmental standards down their supply chains to factories in developing countries such as China, Thailand, and the Philippines. Those factories participate in CSR programs by hosting a CSR representative from the outsourcing company, permitting periodic inspections by impartial third-party observers, and preparing periodic reports on the extent of local compliance with CSR codes and standards. Rene Ofreneo (2009) notes the way in which some garment producers in Philippine firms have instituted CSR programs to attract investments and export contracts from European and North American companies.

CSR programs are now widespread in the foreign-invested export sectors of China and elsewhere in Asia and Latin America. That these programs are strongly market driven is clear. First, consumer and investor pressures and downstream buyer firms in developed-country markets have pushed their suppliers and foreign subsidiaries to adopt these programs, even to the extent of supporting the formation of unions, as in Reebok/China (Luce and Bonacich 2009). In the case of the May 2010 suicides of Hon Hai Precision Industry workers in China, Apple and Hewlett-Packard have pushed hard for a quick inquiry into working conditions there.[8] Relatedly, the new ISO 26000 guidelines on social responsibility, which came into effect in 2010, have encouraged the development of CSR labor standards designed in part to facilitate continued access to European markets.[9]

Second, critical production processes in some industries can no longer rely solely on the sullen obedience of alienated workers. Managers I interviewed at the Guangdong Honda assembly plant noted the great importance of teamwork and worker initiative, not only in securing labor peace, but more importantly in maintaining the high standards of quality necessary for entering world markets. CSR programs signal, at least in principle, a general commitment to improved labor practices and compliance with legal standards in dealings with workers, although many scholars tend to dismiss these programs as what Chris Chan (2010, 11) terms "window dressing."

But what can we say more specifically about the ways firms are actually responding to new pressures for improved labor practices? Recognizing that many firms, particularly those in cost-driven sectors, continue to rely on the harsh practices of the past, I note here ways in which some firms have begun to move away from those practices, particularly in their dealings with skilled and technical workers.

Establishing Mutual Commitment Employment Systems

While labor market deregulation, alongside a generally diminished role for trade unions, offers employers increased latitude in determining their own employment practices, it is broadly recognized that economic upgrading and development cannot sustainably rest on a foundation of mutual distrust and overt conflict between managers and workers. An established industrial relations literature points to the ways in which high-morale mutual commitment employment practices, based on job security and benefits, joint labor-management consultation, internal labor markets and job advancement possibilities, worker participation and team-based production, adequate pay, and mutual respect, can foster self-responsibility, initiative, and worker commitment to the firm's economic success. Such practices, it is clear, most appropriately apply to the ranks of skilled workers, among whom firms encourage enhanced productivity and long-term commitment.

---

8. Jason Dean and Ting-I Tsai, "Suicides Spark Inquiries: Apple, H-P to Examine Asian Supplier after String of Deaths at Factory," *Wall Street Journal*, May 27, 2010.

9. "Top 100 Companies Not Ready to Meet Social Responsibility," *Korea Herald*, January 26, 2010.

Korea provides the best example of these new managerial initiatives. Following the late-1980's labor struggles, large firms sought, with government support, to move away from the harsh, authoritarian employer practices of earlier years in order to establish more stable, cooperative industrial relations. Of particular importance in this regard was their support of "responsible" enterprise trade unions and efforts to create a new company culture of familism and paternalism (Koo 2001, 190–93).

To the extent that high-morale developmental labor systems must at least in part be bought through expensive wage and benefit packages, thus linking the labor process to supportive practices in the realms of labor reproduction and protection, the heightened competitive pressures associated with reform and external economic liberalization often undermine the attempted transition to these more worker-friendly employment practices. These practices tend, by consequence, to be confined to narrow segments of the workforce, particularly to skilled and technical workers engaged in the core functions of large firms. Most other workers, by contrast, experience job insecurity,[10] more restricted training and career opportunities, and disadvantaged status in negotiating compensation levels and working conditions.

While individual firms are unlikely to unilaterally institute expensive, high-morale labor practices, given that such an approach would directly and immediately undercut their competitiveness relative to other firms, governments often assume a lead role in this regard. In exceptional cases, governments may seek to reposition entire economies in such a way as to encourage firms to adopt new labor practices and to compete in new ways, as when Singapore mandated pay increases in 1979 that led many firms to relocate to lower-wage countries. While the Singapore solution defines an extreme policy response to the developmental trap posed by economic reliance on low wages and footloose industry (as in the Philippines), governments can intervene in other, less draconian ways. Although external cost pressures cannot entirely be avoided, domestic employment practices can be leveled up in sectors that show developmental potential, so that improved labor practices undertaken by a few firms will not disadvantage them in their competition with other domestic firms. It is here that employment legislation relating to pay, benefits, working conditions, social insurance, and training can play an important role. That such legislation may have the partial effect of reducing

---

10. Amid the slowdown of automobile sales in the early 2009 recession, Honda announced a policy of releasing most of its temporary workers in order to honor is commitment not to release regular workers.

labor market flexibility only points to a trade-off between short-term market flexibility and longer-term structural development.

Given that governments in several of the rapidly growing Asian countries have been more consistently guided by the long-term requirements of development than have countries in other regions where market reform has played a more pressing and disruptive role, it is not altogether surprising that trajectories of Asian social policy have tended to hedge and buffer policies of labor market deregulation. As discussed in earlier chapters, Korean labor market deregulation has been balanced by a wide range of social protections, including minimum wages, social insurance, and national health insurance. In Thailand, there has been movement to institute new employment protections for workers, including the 1998 Labor Protection Act, which covers working hours, employment of women and children, holidays and overtime, health and safety, and labor inspections (Brown et al. 2002). In China, the national government and the ACFTU have encouraged adoption of corporate codes of conduct establishing basic standards relating to work conditions, health and safety, hours of work, wage bargaining, and environmental practices, although more growth-focused local governments sometimes undermine these efforts.

But it remains the case that mutual commitment employment practices confront the contrary pressures of reform and external liberalization. In particular, the instituting of more flexible labor markets has undermined a critical foundation for such systems through its incremental displacement of stable primary employment in favor of contingent labor. As expensive morale-building but flexibility-compromising employment becomes more narrowly confined to skilled and technical workers in the core activities of firms and among upper-tier suppliers, its costs are subsidized by increased cost pressures on other workers and lower-tier suppliers (cf. Kalleberg 2007, 168). This outcome actually reverses developmental initiatives at these lower levels, ultimately undercutting and contradicting quality and innovation efforts at higher levels of supply chains, while also sharpening existing employment dualism and inequalities. It is in this sense that sharpened competition may have an anti-developmental effect in these economies, encouraging companies to concentrate on increased efficiencies within existing cheap-labor niches rather than undertaking longer-term investments in training, R & D, and organizational innovation that might move them to higher-value niches in world markets.

In response to these pressures, employers and governments have sought to institute morale-building practices more appropriate to situations of contingent employment. As stable primary employment has been increasingly displaced by fixed-duration contractual employment of skilled and technical workers, worker involvement, commitment, training, and initiative can no longer be secured through firm-level labor policies predicated on long-term employment. Rather, in the context of shorter fixed-term employment, firms must rely on broader institutional supports that offer other sorts of incentives for workers to engage in continued skill development and must seek new ways to enhance the productivity and competitiveness of their current employees. These broader supports are to be found in the collaborative training and R & D programs organized by businesses and occupational and professional associations as well as in supportive government policies and programs. Associations, and the informal social networks they nurture, offer important performance incentives for skilled, technical, and professional workers through cross-firm information sharing regarding the successes of employees and work teams in particular firms. Such information provides a means of reputation building and career advancement for skilled contract workers who no longer participate in internal labor markets. Insofar as governments, particularly at local levels, encourage interfirm and occupational and professional networks and associations, or at least the industrial and high-tech infrastructures wherein those networks tend to flourish, they may play an important facilitative role in the consolidation of developmentally dynamic labor systems. I return to this possibility in the discussion of industrial parks in chapter 11.

Union Recognition and Collective Bargaining

Given the inevitability of labor-management conflict in the labor process, the institutionalization of labor-relations machinery assumes a major role in national and sectoral labor regimes. Governments and formal-sector employers have in some instances sought to restabilize labor relations by instituting union-based collective bargaining and other forms of employee consultation and representation.[11] While the formation of unions is always problematic, particularly as it may flow largely from managerial impulses to contain, control, or preempt rather than to institutionalize and manage conflict,[12] it is clear that this is one of several chosen options in China, where the government

---

11. Based on the findings of cross-national research, Frenkel concludes that the state and political institutions have played a key role in influencing patterns of trade unionism and collective bargaining in the Asia-Pacific region (Frenkel 1993, 333).

12. Depending in part on the extent to which this approach in taken in response to pressure from below rather than preemptively from above (Dong 2000; Islam and Chowdhury 2000, 152).

has sought to increase the reach of an increasingly marginalized ACFTU to private and nonorganized employment sectors (Chiu and Frenkel 2000, 37). Under 1990's legislation, increasingly implemented in the late years of the decade, Chinese and foreign firms employing more than one hundred workers are required to establish ACFTU union chapters.[13] Government statistics on numbers of registered "grassroots unions" confirm a U-shaped trajectory over the 1990s and '00s: declining from 606,000 in 1990 to 509,000 in 1999, and then sharply increasing to 859,000 in 2000, and to 1,845,000 in 2009. Corresponding to this year-2000 reversal, total union membership declined from 101.4 million in 1990 to 86.9 million in 1999, and then increased by 10.4 million in 2000 and 22.6 million in 2009 (PRC *CSY* 2010).

In the past, union officials were often drawn from the ranks of management,[14] thus ensuring effective management control. At its auto assembly plant in Guangdong, for example, Honda sponsored a very active union whose vice president and informal head was a high-level manager. But, as part of efforts to stabilize industrial relations and to establish greater union credibility in the eyes of workers, new legislation now prohibits the "principle officials" of companies from assuming union-leadership posts. This, however, does not preclude the union appointment of managers who vacate their official management positions for the duration of their term as union heads.

Government efforts to reinvigorate trade unionism have paralleled more general efforts in China to institutionalize, mediate, and regulate industrial conflict. Under legislation enacted in the mid-1990s,[15] new mediation and arbitration machinery was established[16] to handle the growing number of labor disputes, both collective and individual, relating to nonpayment of wages and a variety of other violations of employment contracts. Chan and Ngai (2009) note in this regard the rapid growth in the number of labor disputes submitted for arbitration, from 135,000 in 2000 to 314,000 in 2005, followed by further increases. This earlier legislation was later supplemented by a 2008 arbitration law that allows workers to bring complaints to the courts free of charge (Silver and Zhang 2009, 176), a change followed by a further sharp

---

13. In the early years of the '00s, the ACFTU represented about 30 percent of formal-sector workers outside the government sector (Smith et al. 2006), and it is estimated that 30 percent of foreign-funded firms now have union branches. Even Walmart, strongly anti-union in its U.S. operations, has unionized its Chinese employees, partly in response to government pressure. See "China to Press More Firms to Unionize," *Wall Street Journal*, October 13, 2006. Also "Chinese Union Furthers Reach," *Wall Street Journal*, July 6, 2007.

14. A practice I observed in visits to several Taiwanese companies in the late 1990s.

15. Regulations for Handling Enterprise Labor Disputes (1993) and a revised 1995 Labor Law.

16. "China's Labour Dispute Resolution system." 2011. In *China Labour Bulletin*, http://www.China.labour.org.hk (accessed September 2011).

increase in arbitrated disputes: from 350,182 in 2007 to 684,379 in 2009 (PRC *CSY* 2010). It is notable that a substantial and growing percentage of arbitration decisions have favored workers rather than employers.

As well, the Chinese government has sought through the 2008 Labor Contracts Law to encourage collective, as well as individual, contracts, although collective bargaining machinery had not been fully developed as of 2010. There has been increased reliance on employment law and employment courts in managing the grievances of migrant workers as well.

It should finally be noted that union-focused efforts to stabilize labor relations and the labor process are most appropriate among regular workers in stable primary-labor systems, as in the case of Thai state-enterprise workers, whose rights to be represented by unions were restored in 2000 under the State Enterprises Labor Relations Act. Quite different are the circumstances of primary-contract workers, from whom firms seek levels of work involvement and initiative comparable to those of regular workers but whose fixed-duration contracts undermine long-term commitments or union organizing. Among those workers, union-focused approaches give way to greater reliance on individual representation in labor courts.

Instituting Worker Participation

Sponsored unionism overlaps with another approach to stabilizing labor relations, creation of joint-consultation committees through which worker agendas can be represented in managerial deliberations. In China, Staff and Workers' Representative Congresses (to be distinguished from trade unions) were strengthened in 1988 and given legal standing to participate in decisions relating to employee welfare, housing, and distribution of wages and bonuses (Zhu and Chan 2005). At the Guangdong Honda plant, the union's governing board includes worker representatives who are included in discussion and planning of new projects. All production workers at that plant are employed under a union-negotiated contract.[17]

In Korea, confrontational labor-management relations encouraged the government to mandate more participative labor relations within firms. Particularly important is the Act Concerning the Promotion of Worker Participation and Cooperation, promulgated in 1997 to address matters relating to productivity, worker welfare, and educational and training. The local councils through which this participation is organized have a national-level counterpart,

---

17. Interviews by author at plant.

the Central Labor–Management–Government Council, to deliberate on labor policies and their relationship to economic and social policy (Kang et al. 2001, 105). This Central Council is to be distinguished from the Tripartite Commission in its emphasis on consensual participation rather than collective bargaining and wage deliberation. The Tripartite Commission, by contrast, was established to encourage agreement between unions and companies regarding burden sharing during the financial crisis and as a means through which to negotiate and implement flexibility-enhancing labor laws deemed important for company restructuring (including mergers and acquisitions), and for attracting increased foreign investment. The commission thus sought consensus on such matters as layoffs, work hours, and social protections. As noted earlier, following difficult and often aborted negotiations, the commission ultimately reached an agreement in 1999 under which flexibility-enhancing labor reform legislation was adopted in exchange for government concessions relating to the unionization rights of teachers and civil servants and unemployed workers, and to the institutional standing of trade unions.[18] More generally, the government role in labor-management relations has shifted from direct intervention to facilitation and mediation.[19]

In the Philippines there has been increased encouragement of labor-management councils at the plant level and of tripartite consultations at all levels of government (Kelly 2001). By contrast, Thai labor-relations policy has historically vacillated between repression (often associated with military rule following a coup) and accommodation (during interludes of parliamentary government). Following the labor militancy of the early 1970s and the establishment of democratic politics in 1973, the Thai parliament passed the 1975 Labor Relations Act under which worker associations and unions received legal recognition along with rights to collectively bargain and to strike (Brown 2004, 85–86). This act, which remains an important point of reference in labor affairs today, created national-level tripartite institutions for labor participation in wage setting and other labor matters, while also expanding mediation services for industrial disputes.

In sum, if policies of social protection have largely addressed the adverse social distributional and livelihood outcomes of labor market change, labor-relations policy has addressed quite different and equally problematic outcomes relating to authority and conflict in the workplace. Under first-stage

---

18. The Danish model of flexicurity, noted earlier, similarly pairs labor market flexibility with support for effective unions.

19. "Labor Management," *Korea Times*, April 17, 2003.

EOI, the initial regulatory response was one of deepened coercive controls in support of cost-based competitive strategies. Regulatory change, driven by the sometimes incompatible pressures of industrial upgrading, growing employment contingency, increased labor conflict, and the unintended outcomes of expanded worker protections, has had the effect of re-engaging government in enterprise-labor practices and in the labor process more generally.

CHAPTER 11

Small Enterprises, Supplier Networks, and Industrial Parks

Creating High-Skill Developmental Labor Systems

> The "developmental space" for diversification and upgrading policies in developing countries is being shrunk behind the rhetorical commitment to universal liberalization and privatization. The rules being written into multilateral (e.g., WTO free trade)... agreements actively prevent developing countries from pursuing the kinds of industrial and technology policies adopted by the newly developed countries of East Asia... aimed at accelerating the "internal" articulation of the economy... (and) limits... their rise up the value chain.
>
> —Robert Wade 2007, 277–78

> Under neoliberal globalization, regulatory states like the Philippines are downloaded with the responsibility for reproduction and stability but do not gain the real power or "transformative capacity" to improve their position with the global economic system.
>
> —Steven McKay, 2006, 223

Successful regimes of social and labor regulation must address a host of reform-driven institutional deficits relating to the social reproduction of an educated, work-ready, and well-trained workforce; creation of an institutional and motivational infrastructure within which flexible labor markets can function successfully; meeting essential requirements of workforce social protection; and managing or redirecting conflicts within the labor process and in the broader workforce. They must do this in ways that also engage the economic agendas and developmental goals of dominant elites. That these multiple and sometimes conflicting requirements would seem to present impossible institutional demands is clear. Indeed, the very impossibility of attending to them all explains the incessant experimentation and vacillation of national regulatory regimes. Yet, in the continuing search for the requisite institutional fixes to manage and partially reconcile the contradictory impulses and conflicting agendas of state policy, it is in the area of small-enterprise policy that one finds a likely candidate.

In this chapter, I examine three foci of SME policy: small business or SME development; the promotion of supplier networks linking local firms (and especially domestic SMEs) to larger downstream firms; and the creation of industrial parks. In each case, earlier policies that predated the major reform programs of the 1990s and that sought both to improve rural livelihoods and (particularly in urban areas) to promote industrial development have retained their developmental thrust even as they have been adapted to changing economic circumstances and regulatory regimes.

Small-Enterprise Policy

Asian governments have pursued a variety of policies designed to foster and energize small and medium-sized enterprises. In most cases, those efforts were directed toward creating employment and supplementing the incomes of rural and poor families. This has been especially apparent in the Philippines, where employment generation and poverty reduction have been the primary goals of SME policy (Tolentino 2007). Significantly, since 2004, substantial financing for the Philippine National SME Development Plan has come from the social security system's pension fund,[1] thus underscoring the primarily social emphasis of SME promotion. More recently, in the late '00s, special tax exemptions and other assistance were offered to registered cooperatives under the Cooperative Development Authority.[2]

In other cases, SME programs have been more explicitly developmental in nature—seeking to encourage domestic entrepreneurship, including start-up SMEs by skilled and enterprising persons formerly employed in larger firms, and to enhance economic growth through business growth and exports, in some cases as suppliers to larger firms.[3] In Taiwan, for example, first-stage EOI was in part led by local networks of small family-based factories and household production units, variably organized by import-export firms, government agencies, and multinational buyers of light consumer goods. This pattern was encouraged in the 1970s under two government programs that encouraged young married women to engage in home-based production.

---

1. "SULONG Program Beneficiaries Hit 150,000 Smes," *Manila Times,* December 11, 2009.

2. "Cooperatives Receive Full Exemptions," *Manila Standard Today* (online), January 26, 2010.

3. In the mid-'00s, these efforts led to regional proposals, supported by the ADB, to set up an SME development fund among ASEAN countries. See "ASEAN SME Fund Due: But Process May Take Years to Complete," *Bangkok Post* (online), July 2, 2010.

These "mothers' workshops" and "living rooms as factories" programs not only permitted women simultaneously to fulfill productive and reproductive roles but also bolstered labor discipline by pyramiding on patriarchal authority in household production (Deyo 1989).

In Korea and China, SME policy was less direct and more driven by economic structural factors and the strategies of firms. Korean SMEs were largely bypassed in the 1970s and early 1980s when large diversified companies (chaebols) accounted for much industrial growth. Koo documents a dramatic decline during the 1970s in the percentage of workers employed in small firms alongside a corresponding increase in the percentage of workers in large firms (2001, 37).[4] But, beginning in the 1980s, this trend slowed as the government sought to reduce the political and economic power of chaebols through divestiture of captive or equity-controlled supplier companies (Tipton 1998), as small supply companies responded both to increased government support (Weiss 2003, 25) and to new international opportunities generated by external-trade liberalization and foreign investment, and as large-scale mass production was increasingly supplanted by technology-intensive and small-batch production and by a displacement of direct production with R & D and business services. These changes were reflected in ever-larger percentages of workers in small firms, fewer workers in very large firms,[5] and declining average manufacturing firm size, beginning in the 1990s.[6] These trends are corroborated by Kim (2007, 27–29), who found a decline in the percentage of workers employed in large firms (from 17.2% of all workers in 1993 to 8.7% in 2005), with a corresponding increase in the percentage of workers in firms with fewer than fifty employees (increasing from 60.7% to 69.4% in that same time period). Kim also notes in this regard the importance of the outsourcing strategies of downstream firms and supplier linkage policies in explaining this change.

During the 1980s and 1990s, the many small- and medium-sized TVEs that were established in China's rural towns were an outcome of the gradual dissolution of agricultural communes, the increased availability of unemployed workers, and government efforts to create new rural employment

---

4. Koo's figures show a decline in the percentage of workers in firms that had fewer than twenty employees—from 22% in 1968 to 7.5%—and an increase in the percentage of workers in firms with more than five hundred employees—from 31.3% to 43.9% during those same years.

5. From 1992 to 2004, the percentage of all Korean manufacturing workers in firms with fifty or fewer employees increased from 32% to 46%, while the corresponding percentage in firms of more than five hundred declined from 28% to 19%. These figures are calculated, with adjustments to take into account the inclusion, in 1999, of microenterprises of fewer than five workers (ROK, *YLS* 20; UNIDO *Yearbook* 2009).

6. Data drawn from the annual *Mining and Manufacturing Survey* as reported in UNIDO, *YIS.*

opportunities (Solinger 1999, 155–61; Zhu 2003, 147).[7] During those years, TVE industrial employment grew dramatically, from 30 million in 1980 to 128 million in 2000, followed by somewhat slower growth to 155 million in 2008. These enterprises tended to be relatively small, with a mean firm size of only thirty-nine employees in 1980, thirteen in 1990, nineteen in 2000, and twenty-one in 2008.[8]

In the 1990s, it is true, SOE reform tended to target small and medium-sized state enterprises for divesture or bankruptcy (Zhu 2003, 155–56). But the presumably augmenting effect this size-selective SOE policy would otherwise have had on mean firm size was countered by other overriding changes. Primary among these were the increasing numbers of displaced workers seeking a livelihood on their own account and in family-run businesses, and a dramatic proliferation of small private-sector export-manufacturing firms, many established by investors from Taiwan and Hong Kong. Further, specialized industrial clusters became widespread in China's eastern provinces.[9] Those clusters are in turn predominantly populated by small labor-intensive firms that work closely together in industrially specialized districts, in many cases producing garments and other low-technology goods for export.[10]

In part by consequence of these trends, firm size in China shows a persistent decline after 1994. Between 1998 and 2004, mean firm size fell from 345 to 221 workers (PRC, *CSY* 2005), thereafter declining yet further to 195 workers (UNIDO *Yearbook* 2011).[11] While very large manufacturing and supplier firms have certainly played an important role in Chinese export manufacturing (Appelbaum 2009, 77), it is estimated that small-business activity now accounts for roughly 60 percent of the national economy and for 80 percent of all jobs.[12]

The data for the Philippines, by contrast, suggest a growing bifurcation between small and large enterprises. There, periodic enterprise censuses show a gradual increase in the percentage of manufacturing workers in firms of fewer than 10 employees, reaching the relatively high level of 34 percent in

---

7. Solinger (1999, 167–69) also notes, however, that most TVE development occurred not in the impoverished interior but in the more prosperous eastern provinces.

8. PRC *LSY,* 2009.

9. Palat (2010) notes the growth of a number of industrial districts in eastern China, in many cases specializing in the production of components for specific products.

10. Andrew Batson, "Rising Wages Rattle China's Small Manufacturers," *Wall Street Journal,* August 2, 2010. Also see "Bamboo Capitalism," *Economist,* March 12–18, 2011.

11. This takes into account a 1997 change in statistical methodology. The Chinese data are problematic in matters of survey coverage and data comparability over time, but nonetheless they suggest a fairly clear picture of overall decline since 1998.

12. Andrew Batson, "Rising Wages Rattle China's Small Manufacturers," *Wall Street Journal,* August 2, 2010.

2003. Conversely, average mean size also remains relatively high, at around 150,[13] and increasing somewhat to 192 in 2006 (UNIDO *Yearbook* 2011). These findings can be understood as reflecting parallel policy agendas of support for small enterprises to address problems of poverty and joblessness alongside encouragement of labor-intensive manufacturing (e.g., electronics) and other large-scale enterprises.

By contrast with the other three cases, Thailand has seen little change in the percentage of workers in very small firms, or in mean firm size.[14] Unfortunately, the available Thai data fail to isolate manufacturing employment for separate consideration, and for this reason they are less useful for comparison with the other countries. It is clear, however, that in both Thailand and the Philippines, the national economies have long been characterized by a substantial presence of small family enterprises. And, in both countries, SME policies have played a significant role over several decades and are largely oriented to social agendas of employment creation, improved social livelihood, and poverty reduction. In Thailand, this largely social orientation of SME policy was further reinforced by the late-1990's crisis, as efforts mounted to address economic and employment disruptions. Those efforts prominently targeted small businesses. They included direct government financial assistance, selective tax incentives,[15] expanded SME lending by the Bank for Agriculture and Agricultural Cooperatives, creation of an SME bank authorized to accept land, machinery, and even occupancy rights to the use of public land as loan collateral, establishment of an SME institute at the new Rangsit campus of Thammasat University, and creation of a national oversight committee, the SME Supervisory Committee, chaired personally by the prime minister. This array of SME support initiatives helped bolster the popularity of the Thaksin government, much of whose support came from rural provinces.[16]

Supplier-Linkage Programs

As important have been economic policies supporting backward linkages from large international manufacturers and retailers to local SME suppliers of

---

13. Philippines, *Census of Establishments* and *Census of Philippine Business and Industry,* partially reproduced in UNIDO, *Yearbook.*

14. As calculated from Thailand, *YLS* and *Yearbook of Labor Protection and Welfare Statistics 2004.*

15. Under new legislation, SMEs may even enjoy a negative income tax. "SMEs May Get Tax Breaks," *Nation* (online), June 28, 2005.

16. See "MOI Confident of Giving Full Support to SMEs This Year," *Pattaya Mail,* January 21, 2002; "Launch a Big Hit with Small Firms: Thousands Queue for Help from New Fund," *Bangkok Post,* January 17, 2002; "BOI Says Tariff Cuts Must Not Be Delayed," *Bangkok Post,* January 12, 2002.

parts, consumer goods, equipment, and support services. Korea, for example, has created new incentives for major companies to develop the capabilities of supplier firms under a "shared-growth" program linking large and small firms.[17]

From the standpoint of labor systems, what is most critical here is the extent to which these policies permit or encourage downstream companies to cultivate domestic suppliers that compete mainly on cost, or, alternatively, to develop quality-focused and technologically innovative local suppliers. In many industrial sectors, of course, government policy incentives may not be critical in determining the supply strategies of buyer firms. In the auto industry, for example, major assemblers often depend critically on the capabilities of their upper-tier suppliers. To take an example from Thailand: Aapico, a joint venture firm with investors from Malaysia and Singapore, is a dynamic, technologically advanced producer of assembly jigs and other auto parts for regional auto assemblers.[18] The success of this company derives in large measure from the variety of cooperative networks and linkages it has developed with assemblers and other suppliers. These networks encourage engineering collaboration, joint production agreements, industry representation before the Ministry of Industry, and cooperative training programs. The advantages these networks present from the standpoints of skill development, recruitment, R & D, and technology learning are viewed by management as critical for the success of this small company in achieving ISO certification in areas demanded by assemblers.

While the Thai auto industry highlights the importance of sectoral and technological factors in shaping domestic supply chains, government policy has played an important, if secondary, role. Unlike Korea, Thailand's auto industry is heavily dependent on Japanese and other foreign companies for capital, technology, access to export markets, and, most important, supply-chain coordination by major assemblers like Toyota and Honda. As part of their investment licensing agreement with the Thai Board of Investments, these companies have until recently been committed, under domestic content requirements, to using domestic suppliers for many of their local assembly operations, although in practice much of their first-tier outsourcing is directed to Japanese supplier transplants in Thailand. These linkages were initially promoted under the Board of Investments Unit for Industrial Linkage Development (BUILD) program, established in 1991. As the inadequacies of this program were subsequently realized, the follow-up National Supplier

17. "Big Businesses Come Up With 'Shared Growth' Plans," *Korea Herald* (online), March 7, 2011.

18. This paragraph draws from Deyo and Doner (2001).

Development program was launched in 1994,[19] followed in 1995 by the sectoral multiagency Master Plan for the Development of Supportive Industries (Doner 2009, 121). More recently, in 2010, The Thai Office of Small and Medium Enterprise announced increased assistance to domestic SMEs in their efforts to export to regional buyers,[20] in many cases as supplier, thus taking advantage of new opportunities presented by ASEAN regional trade liberalization.[21] While these various policy efforts have achieved only mixed results,[22] their encouragement of training, R & D, technology transfer, and technical cooperation suggests growing recognition of the close relationship between economic and social dimensions, even of economic policy itself, as seen in the emphasis on human resource development in Thai industrial policy (Doner 2009, 251).

In other industries, buyer firms may feel less compelled to cultivate developmentally dynamic local supply chains. This applies both to cost-driven industries like wearing apparel and to high-technology industries like electronics. The Philippines illustrates both of these. In the context of the declining garment industry, Ofreneo (2009, 544) notes the lack of backward linkage to local textile or supplier firms, given that many garment factories rely overwhelmingly on imported materials. In the case of electronics, rapid growth has been associated less with the augmentation of local technical skills than with a reliance on semiskilled labor in both assembly plants and the local supply firms serving those plants. In this context, government incentives become critically important in nurturing dynamic, skill- and technology-intensive domestic supply chains.

These considerations return us to Robert Wade's concern (at the beginning of this chapter) about the impact of trade liberalization agreements on development policy. Insofar as supplier development programs have traditionally embraced a variety of import replacement, domestic content, technology transfer, and trade protection policies that are increasingly prohibited under ever tighter restrictions on market distorting trade and technology policies, the "development space" for more supplier upgrading and other industrial policies has indeed been diminished (Wade 2007). This constraint

---

19. "New Fund to Help Makers of Auto Parts." *Bangkok Post,* August 12, 2003.

20. For more recent efforts, see "Govt Comes Up With 5-Year Export Plan," *Nation-Business,* January 26, 2010.

21. "B100m Budget to Help SMEs Enter Asean," *Bangkok Post* (online), March 5, 2010.

22. This statement must be qualified by recognition of the excessive dependency of Thailand's auto industry on foreign suppliers and its vulnerability to global financial turbulence, as witnessed during the financial crisis of the late 1990s when many Thai auto suppliers collapsed or were purchased by foreign companies (Doner 2009).

forces governments to "quietly (push) ahead to encourage new activities in ways that by-pass or go under-the-radar of the international agreements" (Wade 2003, 290). One such avenue is increased emphasis on "supply-side" policies relating to R & D, education, training, and R & D support, as discussed earlier. More generally, following Jessop:

> the scope of economic policy has been massively widened and deepened because of the increased importance for capital accumulation of what was previously regarded as being "extra-economic"... [especially]... where these policies concern... labor market policy, education and training.... national states still have major roles in shaping how the economic and social reproduction requirements of capital are met. (Jessop 2002, 251, 269; also see McKay 2006, 1–43)

If social and labor policy has thus assumed an increased role in the development efforts of states, this is nowhere more evident than in Asia's growing industrial parks.

Industrial Parks

Precursors

SME development programs are often associated with efforts to energize local capital, encourage entrepreneurship, and create institutional mechanisms to facilitate technology development, skill development, and technology transfer to local firms. Such goals may often be associated, as well, with regulatory innovation. To take an example of this latter possibility, it is useful to look at the industrial park established in 1992 by the Chinese and Singapore governments in the city of Suzhou, Jiangsu Province (Pereira 2003). This park was explicitly intended to support institutional learning. As described in 2001 by Singapore's then deputy prime minister, Lee Hsien Loong, "The significance of SIP [Suzhou Industrial Park] was not just to be another industrial park in China but to be a vehicle for transferring the software of economic development and management for testing out, adapting and applying Singaporean methods of economic management in China," and thus in attracting foreign investment by offering an attractive, predictable local administrative infrastructure in an otherwise difficult operating environment (1).

Particularly instructive in this regard were the policies and institutions relating to employment within the park, a matter dealt with by the Suzhou Industrial Park Administrative Committee, one of whose key functions was to manage and regulate human resources and to provide worker training (Pereira 2003, 55). As described by the vice-governor of Jiangsu, "What we need is to train a team of people who will master international economic management, gather practical experience and have creativity and a pragmatic attitude." As for workers more specifically, the Suzhou Industrial Park Human Resource Company assumed responsibility for recruitment through a "talent exchange centre" (68) that helped match job applicants with local companies. Unlike the situation in other industrial zones, worker selection was to be based on qualifications and aptitudes without reference to residency status, so that non-Suzhou residents were not disadvantaged in their efforts to find work or to avail themselves of locally available educational, health, and housing facilities (69). While in practice this exception was applied mainly to highly skilled technical and professional workers, it did allow for a testing of the waters for the later gradual easing of residency rules elsewhere. Following the Singapore model, the company also instituted a contributions-based retirement provident fund and built housing complexes for employees (71).

These programs encouraged foreign companies to hire large numbers of regular, full-time employees to engage in quality-focused production. While Singapore's participation in this joint venture was substantially curtailed in 2002, it does offer an excellent example of the use of social policy to encourage industrial upgrading in an economy otherwise focused on cost-based, low-skill production.

High-Tech Industrial Parks

Among Asia's more dynamic economies, especially Taiwan, high-tech industrial zones were an important instrument of industrial upgrading as developmental states sought during the 1970s and 1980s to build on the successes of early labor-intensive EOI. Taiwan's high-tech industrial zones, including most famously the Hsinchu Science Industrial Park, were important early precursors of the high-tech industrial parks established across the region over the past twenty years (Jessop and Sum 2006, 178–84). Here, as described by Lin (2010), an ensemble of large electronics firms and small high-tech suppliers that were facing high levels of worker turnover among both operators and engineers were assisted in stabilizing and managing local labor markets by government programs that addressed a broad range of shared problems relating to all phases of production. These included an employment services center that combined job placement and assistance with training and R & D activities. As well, special tax incentives were introduced to allow companies to use stock bonuses to attract and retain engineers, and an Industrial Technology

Research Institute was established to encourage professional collaboration and networking among engineers and technical workers and to foster technology transfer from foreign companies.

This industry science park, established in 1980, was followed in 2001 by the building of a second such park, the Southern Taiwan Science Park (Lin 2010). While this second park also endeavored to address the collective requirements of technology-focused companies, the imprint of neoliberal reform can be seen in the ways in which those requirements were met. First, firms in the new park relied more extensively on contract labor than did their counterparts in the first park. Second, the new park was largely administered and controlled by local government, rather than by the national government as was the case with the first park. And third, private temporary-placement companies, rather than government employment agencies, played the major role in managing both labor markets and training in the context of the more fluid labor markets in this newer park. In these and other ways, the second park constructed its labor regime in a way more reflective of the new currents of reform thinking. In both cases, it should be added, technical networks and recruitment were greatly bolstered by the several technological institutes and colleges whose local presence had itself influenced the initial decision to establish the parks.

Though Taiwan set a high bar in its instituting of developmental labor systems in high-tech industrial parks, other countries pursued a similar approach (e.g., the Singapore Science Park) during those early years of high-growth industrialization. In Korea, Daedeok Science Town, located in Daejeon, hosts 232 research and education institutes (18 government-supported), including three major technology universities that produce large numbers of technical and engineering graduates, many at the PhD level. This science zone, first established in 1973 to spearhead research, is now a major locus of innovation and product development in such areas as telecommunications, biotechnology, and atomic energy. Collectively, the many research institutes in this park provide an important venue for professional collaboration, mutual learning, job placement, and joint research and production ventures among locally established high-tech firms—many quite small.

In 1988, the Chinese government gave official recognition and support to the Zhongguancun Science and Technology Park, modeled in part after the joint venture SIP and sometimes dubbed China's Silicon Valley. This park benefits from the research activities and science training of nearby Peking and Tsinghua universities to provide research workers and to promote technology transfer and development for industrial exports (Shin 2001; Cao 2004). Again following the Singapore model, this park provides a broad range of community, employment, housing, training, and other facilities to support the activities of the many small private firms that populate the park and its immediate surroundings. Chinese policy has to this point focused on technology transfer and adaptation rather than more fundamental innovation as in Korea. This may be seen in China's national patent development strategy (2011–20), which places less emphasis on "inventions" than on more mundane "utility model" patents applicable to the operations of manufacturing suppliers.[23] For this reason, much effort has gone into attracting such international IT firms as IBM, Microsoft, HP, Oracle, Cisco, Lucent Bell Labs, and Sumitomo to collaborate with and utilize local suppliers that have located in this park.

If China's low- and medium-technology industrial clusters of firms encourage collaboration, mutual subcontracting, shared logistics, and a pooling of resources to help reduce production costs,[24] they also provide the sorts of mobility networks, job referrals, and contacts that technical and skilled workers utilize in high-tech parks in Taiwan, Korea, and elsewhere. Although these networks do not as often eventuate in the dramatic developmental outcomes of their counterparts in those industrially more advanced countries, they nonetheless play an important role in lubricating the flexible labor markets on which cluster firms rely.

Returning to Korea and Taiwan, how may a long history of government support for technology-based industrial parks in those relatively advanced economies assist in adapting economic structures and labor systems to the requirements and tensions of market reform? The answer is in part to be found in the social policies and regulatory regimes they foster.

Jessop's (2002) discussion of the role of social policy in reform-era industrial-development policy helps to clarify the relationship between labor systems, small industry, and industrial parks policy. Of particular importance is his discussion of the "competition state," which, he argues, seeks to "secure economic growth within its borders and/or to secure competitive advantages for capitals based in its borders . . . by promoting the economic and extra-economic conditions that are currently deemed vital for success in competition with economic actors and spaces located in other states" (96). Social policy and social institutions, he continues, constitute particularly important supply-side conditions for the competitive success of firms and working populations. And, in the context of the emerging knowledge-based economy with its increased reliance on intellectual labor, the role of the competition

---

23. "When Innovation, Too, Is Made in China," *New York Times,* January 2, 2011.
24. "Developer Pushes China Cluster Model," *Bangkok Post* (online), March 19, 2001.

state focuses on the mobilization and expansion of soft social resources such as knowledge; social capital; interfirm collaboration; R & D networking; and increased capacities for technology transfer, collective learning, and entrepreneurship. Insofar as the competition state seeks proactively to advance those innovative capacities essential for sectoral upgrading into higher value-added niches in global production networks and world markets, Jessop argues, it subsumes more and more domains of social life into the discursive and policy space of the market economy itself. Given the important role of East Asian governments in attending to the socioinstitutional requisites of industrial advance through support for high-tech industrial districts and parks, it is clear that Jessop's argument applies with special force to the cases thus far examined in this chapter.

The Lesser Dragons

Asia's second-tier industrializers, including Indonesia, Malaysia, and Thailand, have sought to emulate the industrial successes of Korea and Taiwan, though with more mixed results. In Thailand, the Thaksin government sought, though with only partial success,[25] to promote industrial clusters[26] as part of a return to industry policy and sector-specific development planning (Doner 2009, 232). In part, that effort built on the earlier experience of the Industrial Estate Authority in establishing the Hi-Tech Industrial Estate north of Bangkok. This industrial park provides a range of housing, educational, health care, and other services for resident firms and workers. But, while the park was initially intended to promote export-oriented, environmentally clean, high-technology industries, it has in practice offered midlevel technical and general training, along with placement of local employees in standard production work. As in the case of China, there is strong reliance on foreign firms (e.g., Canon) in securing the technology, training, and high-level technical workforce needed for local operations.

While the Hi-Tech Industrial Estate does contribute to ongoing efforts to shift Thailand's export-manufacturing base into higher value products, there is little effort to promote the cutting-edge technological innovation found in the science parks of Korea or Taiwan. In part in response to this disappointing outcome, Thailand's National Science and Technology Development Agency

---

25. That is, they had little success in the context of continuing political conflict.

26. "SMEs Encouraged to Form Clusters to Bid in State Contracts," *Bangkok Post,* August 15, 2003. Also see "Developer Pushes China Cluster Model," *Bangkok Post,* March 19, 2011.

established the Thailand Science Park in 2002,[27] where they are seeking more explicitly to support technology-intensive businesses through R & D collaboration with researchers at nearby universities, including the Asian Institute of Technology and four other national research institutes. With this park the government seeks a proactive role in encouraging private firms to engage in more extensive R & D activities.[28] Whether, given Thailand's political and institutional weaknesses, this park will achieve its stated goals is uncertain.

Informalization?

Many accounts of developing-country economies assume a close empirical relationship between small firms and the informal sector. But has declining firm size in China and Korea been associated with growth in informal-sector employment? In the case of China, such a possibility is in fact suggested by the simultaneity of two trends: declining firm size and the continuing growth of the informal sector. But what of Korea? It is true that in that country, own-account, family, and unpaid workers are almost all engaged in firms with fewer than ten workers, while regular workers (along with temporary workers) predominate in larger firms (*Korea Yearbook of Labor Statistics* 2006; ROK, YLS 2006). On the other hand, in Korea for sure, but in Thailand and the Philippines as well, earlier cited data support a finding of *increased* formal-sector employment, thus calling into question the assumption that the growth of small firms may be associated with corresponding growth of informal employment.

In order to reconcile findings of declining firm size with formal-sector growth in three of the four countries of interest here, one must clearly look beyond firm size alone and attend to the evolving nature of SMEs. Here I return to the earlier discussion of the ways in which new SME policies, as well as new patterns of SME growth, place many of these increasingly numerous small firms directly in the formal sector. Returning to the earlier cited data on Korean firm size and employment status, it turns out that the majority of workers in firms of fewer than thirty workers are in fact "regular" workers. It is likely that a similar table constructed in the 1970s or 1980s would have shown smaller percentages of regular workers in these small firms. Second,

---

27. "Science Park Opens Up a Platform for Innovation: Another Big Step for Cluster Development," *Bangkok Post*, June 18, 2003.

28. "Technology Agency Hopes to Boost R & D by Expanding Thailand Science Park," *Nation* (online), May 12, 2009.

if one takes into account the important role of small-supplier, R & D, and specialist-service firms in the expanding knowledge-based Korean economy, it is clear that many start-up small firms are situated squarely within the modern, formal sector. Indeed, as I argued earlier, many small firms in this economically advanced economy play critical roles in the production chains of modern, technologically advanced companies.

Third, while it is not reflected in these Korean statistics, under a more inclusive definition of the formal sector as embracing firms and employment that fall within the regulatory purview of the state, I again emphasize the increasing scope of (formal) state regulation to include ever-smaller firms, especially as labor laws and social protections are extended to smaller firms and as SME development programs become more readily accessible. Firms receiving bank loans, and developmentally promoted firms receiving any sort of government assistance, are by necessity government registered, in Korea and elsewhere, including Thailand and the Philippines. The outcome of this trend is that of formalizing the small-firm sector.

Relatedly, I suggested earlier that labor market deregulation has been associated with an *informalization* of formal-sector firms and employment, where such informalization refers not to reduced regulatory scope (which in fact increased) but rather to a diminution of regulatory *depth*. This suggests a growing convergence in overall degrees of formality between what are traditionally seen as informal and formal sectors, on the one hand, and between small and large firms, on the other.

But what of China, where I suggested that regulatory scope has itself been in retreat in the face of a rapid growth of guerilla capitalists in small private-sector export businesses? Here, declining firm size may well have followed the more familiar pathway of increased informality, as is suggested in many accounts.

SMEs, Supply Linkages, and Industrial Parks: Creating High-Skill Developmental Labor Systems

I now turn to a consideration of the ways in which the SME and micro-industry policies discussed in this chapter may potentially or actually influence the four phases of labor systems from the standpoint of their adequacy to address the economic, social, and political tensions of reform. I argue that small-enterprise policies offer elites a particularly useful means by which, at least in part, to reconcile or manage a variety of conflicting pressures—to achieve, in other words, a sustainable institutional fix within a neoliberal order. At the outset, it must be recognized that the reform experience of these four countries points to a very uneven record of success.[29] For this reason, the following discussion should be read as a suggestion of positive possibilities alongside a history of only limited realization.

As contingent employment has incrementally displaced regular employment among skilled and technical workers, occupational and professional networks and associations have become increasingly important to mobile employees in negotiating their own career paths. In principle at least, those networks can provide opportunities for information sharing, technical collaboration, professional development, reputation building, and job networking (Kalleberg 2007, 172). Indeed, Annalee Saxenian (1994) and others note the *positive* role of high levels of job turnover, especially among technicians and engineers, in augmenting the communication of new ideas and technologies among firms.

Governments, at both national and local levels, can play an important facilitative role in encouraging these networks. Particularly important in this regard are technology transfer requirements, agreements under which international companies undertake to provide training for in-house or supply-chain technical staff, and institutional encouragement of collaborative R & D in product development and technology upgrading. These networks may perhaps most directly be encouraged in technology-based industrial parks, where information sharing, contacts with local tertiary institutions, collaborative production and research, technical conferences and seminars, and other activities both benefit participating firms (Appelbaum 2009, 77) and encourage professional networking and entrepreneurial ventures among skilled, technical, and professional workers.

Training, Technology Transfer, and the Entrepreneurial Worker

In chapter 9 I described a variety of policies designed to provide or promote training, a critical function of industrial labor systems from the standpoint both of employers and workers. This function has become increasingly important and problematic in the context of organizational deverticalization, growing economic turbulence, market segmentation, new technologies favoring small dynamic firms, and the growth of contingent and contractual work across all skill groups, including professionals. In the Korean case, in particular, increasingly prevalent fixed-duration contracts among skilled and

---

29. Both mainstream and critical regulationists have recognized the possibility of failure in their accounts of institutional change.

technical workers and among non-regular workers (whether formal or not) has so foreshortened the time horizon for returns to training, and so increased the risks of the poaching of ones already trained workers by other firms, that an important institutional foundation for that country's industrial training system has been threatened.[30] In this context, a new set of institutional incentives is required, incentives that reside less in the institutional structures of firms themselves and more in broader, encompassing institutional supports that transcend firms. The state's role in creating or facilitating the development of industrial parks can play an important role in this regard.

As important are the entrepreneurial incentives and opportunities SME promotional policies create for workers. As noted, worker entrepreneurialism is important for the efficient functioning of flexible labor markets, for the success of training initiatives, and for the livelihood security of workers and their families. Of particular interest here are opportunities for technical and engineering workers to start new businesses, in some cases as spin-off firms supported or sponsored by their former employers.

While high-tech industrial parks provide the most likely venue for encouraging worker entrepreneurism and developmental advance, supply-chain development offers a further possibility, one more accessible for countries that lack the technological, educational, and industrial infrastructure of an advanced country like Korea, and that are more dependent on foreign capital for their industrial development. Here, career opportunities and incentives may be somewhat diminished, but then so too may be the developmental requirements for workers and labor systems. For a country like Thailand, it is helpful to set aside a restricted focus on Schumpeterian innovation and to take more seriously the continuing developmental potential afforded by technology transfer and incremental improvement, as lesser economies seek to achieve upward mobility in international production networks and world markets.[31] If Korea, Taiwan, and Singapore are to assume full status in the core of the world economy by capturing the economic rents of foundational innovation, they must institutionalize new innovative capacities that go beyond the learning and adaptation of technologies invented elsewhere (Castells 2000 [1996], 124). Less demanding are the requirements of upward mobility facing

---

30. An example of this problem is to be found in the experience of Toyota's Thailand assembly plant, where strong reliance on contingent labor discourages plant-level training (Richard Doner, personal communication).

31. Richard Doner has suggested in a personal communication that this distinction may be too stark, that innovation may only be a late culmination of earlier steps, beginning with reverse engineering and other initiatives best understood as incremental adaptations. This said, the distinction does point to very real cross-national and sectoral differences in technological and learning capacities.

China, Thailand, or the Philippines, where technology transfer and adaptation, rather than foundational innovation, offer continuing possibilities for economic advance within the middle ranks of the world economy.[32] In this lesser context, the developmental promotion of domestic supplier networks assumes particular importance.[33]

Disempowering Trade Unions and Reducing Worker Militancy

A hallmark of a neoliberal economy is the dissolution of corporatist bargaining among unions, employers, and governments, and its replacement with individual competition and contractual negotiation. The trend away from collective worker representation is reinforced when workers must assume greater responsibility for their own livelihoods and careers in the context of contingent employment, and when increasing numbers of workers must find employment in smaller firms, as in Korea and China during recent years. In a small-firm context, multiple organizational boundaries intercept the horizontal social relations fostered within larger production units, thus making it less likely that workers will embrace their class identities and solidarities or find structural encouragement for unionization.

But these structural changes are in fact double-edged in their implications for labor, for as the focus of labor market participation and career competition shifts incrementally from internal to external labor markets, those professional and occupational networks and associations that may be established among skilled and technical workers in small firms, and especially in industrial parks, acquire special importance in potentially compensating workers for the disempowering outcomes of deregulation and union decline. If lesser-skilled workers must rely on a multitude of nonunion solidarities and political modalities, as I suggested earlier, skilled and technical workers find compensating strengths in non-union occupational and professional networks that enhance individual or group labor market strategies of mutual assistance, information sharing, collaborative learning, career mobility, and individual entrepreneurship, all within an economic context that partially frees them from the tyranny of dependence on a particular firm or employer. Relatedly, those same networks offer corresponding new

---

32. For discussion of this difference, see Sachs (2000).

33. As noted by Doner (4), different levels of development require different institutional tasks and capabilities corresponding to different levels of difficulty.

freedoms for voicing shared grievances and for contesting the policies of local governments.

While these emergent possibilities, available mainly to highly trained technical and professional workers, are only sometimes realized, and while they may only exacerbate the unequal opportunities available to workers within dualistic and segmented labor markets, they nonetheless remain as empowering possibilities, if only for advantaged workers.

CHAPTER 12

Contesting Reform

The Influence of Labor Politics

> The problem with most of the literature on labour
> and globalisation is that it tends to conceive of labour
> as [a] passive victim of the new trends, the malleable
> material from which globalization will construct its
> new world order. Capital is seen as an active, mobile,
> forward-looking player... while labour is seen as
> static, passive, and basically reactive.
>
> —Ronaldo Munck 2002, 67–68

Influenced in part by a now-dated literature on
Asian developmental states, studies of regional reform trajectories over the
past thirty years have attended largely to the interests and strategies of elites
and elite coalitions. By consequence, much of this literature has emphasized
government developmental strategies, the nature and influence of existing
state institutions and political regimes, the power and interests of competing elite factions, the economic requirements of growth, and the constraints
and opportunities associated with the differential location of Asia's national
economies in global markets and interstate relations. But with the important
exception of Korea, Asian workers are only infrequently acknowledged as key
players in the politics of reform.

This tendency to marginalize the political role of Asian labor contrasts
sharply with accounts of market reform in Latin America and eastern Europe, as well as in the wealthy OECD countries of Europe and in the United
States.[1] In part this difference is rooted in the factually weaker coalitional
and political role of Asian labor movements than that of their counterparts

---

1. This is not to say that Asian labor and labor struggles have been ignored, only that the political
influence of labor has been insufficiently recognized.

elsewhere.[2] If the political economy of market reform cannot ignore the important role of workers and labor movements in, say, Brazil, Argentina, or Poland, it seemingly can more credibly ignore labor's role in China, Thailand, Malaysia, Indonesia, and Singapore. To the extent labor *is* brought into political accounts of Asian economic reform, workers and their representative organizations are often seen largely as recalcitrant victims of elite strategies—able to mount sufficient resistance to slow or cushion the impact of particular reform programs but rarely (arguably with the exception of Korea) able to secure a recognized place in national policymaking.

In this book I suggest a different view: one that sees Asian labor as playing a somewhat more forceful role in national policymaking than is usually acknowledged (cf. Boyer 2005, 516–19). While elite strategies and factional conflicts, economic constraints, institutional requirements, and international pressures figure prominently in this account (see figure 2.1), I have argued that there remains sufficient discretionary space and institutional looseness in actually existing political economies to afford subordinated groups an opportunity to influence the strategic choices of elites and the reform trajectories those choices inform. It is at this point that labor politics and popular-sector contestation enters the picture.

To the extent labor politics and class conflict do substantially influence state policy and trajectories of social change, one might expect that influence to be most salient in the realm of labor relations and social policy. If the play of interests and power among elites and elite factions plays the dominant role in many other policy domains, elite conflict is less salient in matters relating to labor market policy, labor relations, and worker training that tend more often to unite employers and governments in their collective, oppositional dealings with labor—except, of course, when labor is drawn in as a coalitional ally in elite conflicts themselves (Lee 2011). How then, and to what extent, have workers influenced trajectories of social regulatory reform?

We must first distinguish between two types of "labor" influence on social-reform policy: the first functional-institutional; the second political, taken here in the broad sense of referring to social action intended to influence policy. The first of these influences, and the one emphasized in much of the earlier discussion in this book, sees labor not as a political or social actor, but rather as a variably institutionalized *social process* through which labor

---

2. Haggard and Kaufman (2008, 10, 196–200) note the importance of legacies of social entitlement in Latin America and eastern Europe in strengthening redistributive coalitions among existing social-policy beneficiaries, and the relative lack of such beneficiary coalitions in East Asia.

power is transformed into realized labor. This elite-centric institutional/strategic understanding of labor foregrounds the economic tensions of labor systems, along with labor surpluses or scarcities, in explaining labor policies and changing labor regimes.

The second understanding of labor, and the one I pursue in this chapter, relates not to this economic institutional role of labor, nor to the productivist or developmentalist social-labor regimes with which such a role is associated, but rather to its political role in pushing for labor-centric social policies relating especially to social protections and the labor process.[3] Reference here is to the ability (or lack thereof) to translate labor market scarcities, strategic locations in the production process, ecological advantages (e.g., of residential or workplace concentrations), organizational capacities, collective solidarities, value commitments, and other resources into effective voice in firm-level and governmental decision making. All of these resources play a role in determining labor's political capacity to influence policy. At the same time, differences in the nature of the social agendas pursued by particular groups of workers in part reflect the corresponding diversity in the labor systems in which workers are employed, and in the variety of forms of political contestation with which those systems are associated.

It is important at the outset of this discussion to note the important distinction between the technical and professional workers who were the focus of chapter 11 and the lesser-skilled workers who are of primary concern here. The strong skills and qualifications of technical and professional workers place them in an advantaged position in labor markets,[4] thus encouraging individual market strategies, career building, and professional networking as avenues of career advance. The relatively weaker market-based bargaining power (Silver 2003) of unskilled and semiskilled workers encourages collective rather than individual livelihood strategies and an increased emphasis on political action to compensate for labor market weakness, to gain state protections against employer abuse and to enhance the social protections and citizen entitlements that buffer economic dependence on labor markets and continued employment. In this chapter, I focus on the ways in which these

---

3. Lee (2011) similarly notes the tendency for discussions of Asian labor unions and movements to focus on their economic significance, and calls for greater attention to their political role, particularly under democratization.

4. Beverly J. Silver (2003) usefully distinguishes between "market-based" and "structural" bargaining power, a distinction further discussed in Silver and Zhang (2009). In the present context, market-based labor market scarcities importantly distinguish technical and professional workers, discussed in chapter 11, from less-skilled workers, the primary focus of this chapter.

less-skilled workers have been successful in influencing government policies and national regulatory regimes.

In chapter 8 I identified six general patterns of labor politics that are of particular importance in these four countries: the first based on trade union activism, the second on social movement unionism, the third on non–union-based labor organizations and NGOs, the fourth on direct worker participation in broader popular-sector social movements, the fifth on participation in labor-oriented political parties, and the sixth on a generalized threat of social disorder. Union politics, it was seen, revolve around employment-related issues of terms of employment, social protection, and the labor process that are of particular interest to workers. Social movement unionism focuses less on the labor process per se and embeds labor issues in broader appeals to affiliated or supportive networks and organizations. Nonunion organizations, especially labor-oriented NGOs, extend more traditional union concerns to informal-sector and unorganized workers, including the self-employed. Social movements with substantial direct worker participation attend to more general issues of collective consumption, the social wage, and political reform. Political party involvement seeks to insert labor agendas directly into national political debates. And finally, the politics of social disorder contrasts with the others in being defined less by a coherent agenda than by an absence of well defined organizational forms through which to address social concerns. Each form of labor politics has both influenced and been shaped by economic and political reform, and each may usefully be located in the particular national jurisdictions, economic sectors, and labor systems in which it has assumed an important role.

Influencing Social Policy

The various modalities of labor politics have played a significant role in shaping elite responses to the tensions of reform. In Korea, following the massive organizational drives of the late 1980s, unions have been important players in national debates relating to matters of employment and labor law, rather than in policy areas more remote from the direct interests of formal-sector workers. There, union leaders have focused on labor market reform, union rights and organizational strength, and the negotiation of a social pact in the context of the late-1990's financial crisis. While the tripartite negotiations leading up to that pact lacked the institutional coherence, centrality, and policy influence of tripartite institutions in, say, Singapore (Kuruvilla and Liu 2008), the outcomes for labor and social policy were nonetheless important.

While the more militant of the two major national labor federations, the KCTU, participated only intermittently in the tripartite talks, the FKTU was more regularly involved. But this is not to diminish the influence of the more militant KCTU. Indeed, it was partly the government need for KCTU agreement in order to establish the legitimacy of the pact for workers that empowered the KCTU to use its continuing threat of withdrawal as a bargaining chip in pushing the government to accept important worker demands. In any event, the outcome of the talks was an accord that endorsed a program of labor market deregulation as demanded by employers, but only in exchange for other major concessions, including the requirement of prior notification in cases of worker layoffs; restrictions on mass dismissals; and new legislation expanding the organizational rights of teachers, civil servants, and other previously excluded groups. In addition, the pact laid the groundwork for a range of social-policy initiatives, including the extension of the employment insurance system to non-regular workers, increased social security coverage, a number of employment-creating public works, and further development of the national pension system. More recently, union-based tripartism has been revived since 2006 to deal with emergent issues relating to multiple unionism, pensions, education, training, and problems facing non-regular workers (Kuruvilla and Liu 2008).

It is true, of course, that Korean unions have shared with their counterparts in other countries a gradual diminution in membership and political leverage. Eroding strength has reflected multiple changes, including deindustrialization, rapid growth of the service sector, the absence of coalitional representation through a strong political party (Lee forthcoming), intensified global competition, increasing numbers of contingent workers, declining firm size, and, of course, the effects of labor market reform itself. Union decline has in turn eventuated in tripartite union bargaining from a position of relative weakness. Thus, while some organizational gains were realized in the 1998 negotiations over labor market reform, the substantive outcome of those negotiations was to consolidate flexible labor markets and to further subordinate traditional forms of social welfare to the harsher provisions of the Employment Insurance System in addressing the problem of unemployment (Jayasuriya 2006, 112–18). But what nonetheless stands out here is the important role of organized labor in *negotiating* the terms of the new (market-conforming) social pact, a role subsequently reinforced by organizational concessions to unions. In this process, of course, the concerns of non-regular, nonunionized workers have been given relatively short shrift.

Union politics outside Korea has played a lesser role. In both Thailand and the Philippines, union fragmentation and competition (often encouraged by competing affiliations with economic and governmental elites) have plagued efforts to bring unity to the labor movement. Further, union organizational efforts have often been met by employer intransigence and police repression. This is particularly the case in the Philippines, where antiunion violence, including assassinations of union organizers and leaders, has been a continuing problem.

It is true that Thai unions, especially in the state-enterprise sector, have been able to slow (but not halt) the drive to privatize public utilities and other sectors. And trade unions were able sufficiently to leverage their limited political influence at the height of the financial crisis to push a weakened government to enact the very important Labor Protection Act of 1998. But given the more general political and economic structural problems facing unions in these two countries, and their general exclusion from government policy circles, it is not surprising that they have sought to ally with social movements to pursue broader agendas of improved public services and social protections.

Those social-movement coalitions have in turn brought important gains, particularly for informal-sector workers and impoverished urban and rural families. Relatedly, labor-oriented NGOs and nonunion workers' associations have played a correspondingly important role in Thailand and the Philippines. In Thailand, they have sought to represent the needs of both unionized and nonunion workers, and of informal workers, the self-employed, contract workers, the unemployed, and home workers through street demonstrations and political rallies. It was noted that women workers in the rapidly growing manufacturing export sectors played a key role in linking industrial labor and women's organizations through their campaigns for improved safety and health in the workplace. NGOs, in particular, have been supported by international organizations and university activists in their ongoing effort to extend the protections that formal-sector workers enjoy to informal and non-regular workers. In the Philippines, union organizing efforts among unorganized workers have been somewhat more successful in gaining government concessions and legislative protections than in winning union recognition.

Social unionism and NGO activism have together played the lead role in pressing for the extension of social protections and services to previously marginalized groups of non-regular and informal workers. But the effectiveness of their social advocacy has been greatly augmented when they have been able to ally with labor-oriented or populist political movements or parties during periods of democratic reform. In Thailand, the beginning years of the twenty-first century saw the rise to power of a business-led neo-populist government that relied heavily on electoral support from national social movements, as well as from disgruntled rural populations who had suffered under growing regional inequalities between the urbanized central region and the poorer northern and northeastern provinces. In mobilizing this potential political base, the Thai Rak Thai government instituted new programs of village infrastructural funding, universal health care, SME support, and other social programs aimed in large part at informal-sector workers and rural populations.[5] This and other social policies enacted during the period speak not so much to the concerns of formal-sector or SOE workers as to those of a far broader range of informal-sector workers, families living in poverty, populations living in impoverished upcountry provinces, and migrant urban workers in Bangkok who retain strong social bonds with upcountry families, patrons, and friends.

The Thai case further illustrates the way in which policy changes or political accommodations may become institutionalized through the political support they generate among targeted beneficiaries. In part in response to Thaksin's efforts to assert greater control over the military through interference in internal promotions, and—more important—following growing complaints on the part of urban middle classes that the Thaksin government was turning to authoritarian measures and prioritizing rural villagers over urban constituents who had not supported him in the earlier elections, the army overturned the results of the 2006 elections won by the Thai Rak Thai Party. They appointed a caretaker government while preparing for new elections in December 2007, elections from which Thaksin and the Thai Rak Thai Party were barred from participating. The new government sought, among other things, to reverse a number of Thaksin's populist policies, including what they saw as a fiscally unsustainable national health program. The public outcry following this effort to undo the popular health-care program made clear the political price such a social-policy reversal could exact. The military government subsequently backed away from its efforts to rein in this program, even as it confronted renewed oppositional efforts to revive the Thai Rak Thai Party under a new name, the People Power Party. That party was subsequently able to win a plurality of the national vote in the newly scheduled elections. It set out to form a new government while beginning the legal process of bringing their exiled leader home. The new government was again forcibly displaced by the urban-based Democratic Party, whose leader and prime minister Abhisit Vejjajiva promised to continue existing populist policies and to bridge the economic divide between urban and rural

5. The widely popular universal health program was institutionally grounded in the new 1997 Thai Constitution, which established the principle of equity in health care for the whole population.

populations. In early 2011, in the run-up to July national elections, the ruling Democrats rolled out a comprehensive social welfare program (Pracha
Wiwat) that builds on and extends earlier-enacted populist programs.[6] Those
efforts proved insufficient, however, for the Democrats to retain power. In a
powerful and dramatic reassertion of electoral support for the populist programs initially established under Thai Rak Thai rule, Thaksin's younger sister
Yingluck Shinawatra won a seat in Parliamentary elections and, as head of
party, became Prime Minister, thus positioning an again renamed successor,
"Pheu Thai" (for Thais) party to form a new government. Among other
campaign promises, Yingluck pledged to raise the minimum wage by up to
40 percent. At the time of this writing, the military leadership has committed
to non-interference in this electoral outcome.

In the Philippines, social policy has been largely directed to poverty eradica-
tion, provision for minimum basic needs, day care, nutrition, primary health
care, improved access to potable water, and other social initiatives that target
both urban and rural poor.[7] Thus, for example, the primary thrust of the
Medium-Term Philippines Development Plan (2004–10) centered on poverty reduction, employment generation, village-level business development,
and community-based employment (Ramesh 2003; Sibal 2007, 307). While
workers in the relatively small formal sector have successfully defended existing insurance programs, these more prevalent informal-sector programs
have often been organized through public-private partnerships with NGOs,
churches, and a variety of community organizations. Most of these social
policies, broadly characterized by Ramesh (2003, 97) as policies of "social
development," have been instituted in response to political pressures from
NGO-led social movements of nonunionized impoverished workers and
their families, groups that had once provided the political base for the electoral victory of the populist president Joseph Estrada in 1998.[8]

To a lesser degree than elsewhere these policies have been informed by state
developmentalism. But having said this, it is clear that they have also been
institutionally disconnected from a third 'logic' of employment policy identified by Frenkel and Kuruvilla (2002): that of economic competitiveness.[9]
Here, I return to my earlier distinction between national developmentalism,
the form of competitiveness most centrally addressed by states, and firm-level

---

6. "Korn Touts Pracha Wiwat," *Bangkok Post,* January 8, 2011.
7. This paragraph draws heavily on Haggard and Kaufman (2008, 237–42).
8. The Thai experience under the Thai Rak Thai was in part paralleled by the populist interlude
of 1998–2001 under President Estrada, who suffered the same fate as Thailand's Thaksin in being
removed from office following accusations and conviction of corruption.
9. Also see Kuruvilla et al. 2000.

competiveness, the major focus of deregulatory reform. In the Philippine context, the relative absence of an effective development strategy,[10] a domestically strong (if externally dependent) national bourgeois, a weak state, a primary emphasis on attracting but not regulating foreign investment, and the presence of a weak, fragmented labor movement alongside strong grassroots social pressures, have together encouraged a two-track pursuit of a neoliberal version of competitiveness on the one hand, and a parallel, but developmentally decoupled, emphasis on social compensation, on the other.

Somewhat different has been the experience in China. Chinese leaders, confronting neither independent labor unions nor entrenched oppositional civil society organizations, have responded to public disturbances with police repression on the one hand, and, on the other, with concessions or social compensations to politically visible groups of protesting workers (especially former state-enterprise workers in the north, migrant workers in the costal export area, and impoverished populations in rural areas).

The Chinese case presents something of a paradox in its juxtaposition of an ineffectual trade union movement and disorganized worker and rural protests with a fairly robust state response to the privations and job losses facing workers. Labor and public disturbances (including internationally publicized worker suicides, ostensibly acts of desperation, not strength) have wrought significant wage gains from anxious employers and upward adjustments of the minimum wage on the part of local governments,[11] new programs of social insurance and livelihood support, and experimental programs to support migrant workers and their families in coastal export zones.[12] As regards state workers, Dorothy Solinger (2009, 208–9) offers one explanation for this paradox, noting first the ways in which a deep historical revolutionary heritage linking the ruling Communist Party with its worker base, along with growing fear of social instability and turmoil on the part of party leaders, has predisposed government to move quickly and preemptively to meet the demands of workers. Second, she notes that China's impotent national labor federation, the ACFTU, unable either to represent or to manage labor demands, creates an institutional void that frees workers to take to the streets to voice their demands. Moreover, the preemptive social reforms undertaken by the state respond not only to demonstrations by angry state workers, but

---

10. EABER Newsletter, October 2008, http://www.eaber.org.

11. Andrew Batson, "China's Shifting Jobs Keep Migrants Closer to Home," *Wall Street Journal,* June 17, 2010. Compare Chan and Ngai (2009, 302) on the influence of a wave of protest in 2004–5 in pushing up minimum wage levels and in bringing improvements in local enforcement of labor law.

12. "Migrant Workers Get Chance for Urban Residency," *South China Morning Post,* June 9, 2010.

as well to protests mounted by the even-more-disorganized and powerless migrant workers in urban industrial zones. For those workers, the 2008 Labor Contracts Law is particularly important in that it offers them unprecedented legal protections to compensate for their otherwise disempowering conditions of employment. Here, as in so many other cases, the reluctance and often inability of local and municipal governments to undertake important social protections has forced the central government to take the lead role.

A further observation relates to the role of labor politics in the emergence and shaping of the economic, rather than only social, regulatory strategies of states. Here, the influence of labor is somewhat less direct, in that workers' primary focus on employment and livelihood security rarely embraces larger, more strictly economic agendas. Nonetheless, even in this area, labor politics have played at least a modest role. The continuing institutional capacity of Korean trade unions, the growing influence of nonunion labor politics in Thailand and the Philippines, and the increasing threat to social stability posed by China's politics of social disorder, all have forced on government leaders a heightened acceptance of the need to reconcile social and economic agendas in national policy. Thus, labor politics has at a minimum been instrumental in forcing attention to the importance of attending to social agendas in the making of economic policy.

A third, and particularly important observation by Yongshun Cai (2007) relates less to structural and strategic determinants of labor's political influence than to the self-generated power of labor militancy itself. Based on a study of the responses of laid-off state-enterprise workers to their economic plight, Cai observes that:

> The power of Chinese laid-off workers thus lies in the fact that the impact of resistance goes beyond a single individual or collective action. In other works, constant pressure applied through many small-scale actions makes the government see the potential effect of a flood of resistance. James Scott describes the resistance of the weak: "[T]he aggregation of thousands upon thousands of such petty acts of resistance has dramatic economic and political effects." It is in this sense that the weak have power, though they may not realize that each of their acts contributes to the aggregate impact. In China, the resistance of laid-off workers has not only slowed some reform measures like privatization, it has also pushed the Chinese government to take layoffs seriously and to make great efforts to guarantee the payment of lay-off subsidies and pensions."... "Crucial industrial reforms are being slowed down as Beijing concentrates on warding off social unrest." (118–19)

Finally, the self-reinforcing correspondences between the modalities of labor politics expressed by workers and the social policies and agendas pursued by Asian governments lends support to the claim that labor politics has in fact played an important role in influencing the variety of social policies associated with evolving reform trajectories. This role, however, must be understood largely as a process of mutual conditioning, as new policies have in some cases acquired a degree of path dependence rooted in the social and political support generated by the subsequent flow of benefits and resources to targeted groups. A case in point is Thailand's "Red Shirt" supporters of former Prime Minister Thaksin and his populist programs. As beneficiaries of those programs, they have become a powerful political force that has survived continuing roll-back efforts by the military and urban elites.[13] This conclusion applies not only to workers who enjoy empowering economic structures and democratic institutions, as in Korea, but to workers who cannot so readily turn to trade unions or, more rarely, to labor-oriented political parties to augment their role in national policy debates.

---

13. "Many Thai Workers, Now Out of Poverty, Are in Dissent." *Washington Post,* June 9, 2010.

Conclusion

In this book I have sought to understand the implications of three decades of market-oriented economic reform for Asian workers. I have suggested a conceptual framework, centering on labor systems and their regulatory regimes, through which to draw together disparate literatures on institutional change, labor relations, social policy, and development that directly or indirectly help elucidate the labor implications of market reform. I have focused on the industrial sectors of four Asian countries that I have selected to exemplify contrasting contexts and trajectories of reform in this economically dynamic region.

Drawing on Polanyi's discussion of the social dislocations and "countermovement" following the attempted commodification of land, labor, and money in nineteenth-century England, I have suggested a more general analytical framework centering on the dynamic relationship between two dimensions, or faces, of reform: the first is that of market deregulation, and the second is made up of a host of reregulatory responses, both reactive and anticipatory, to the tensions thus fostered. From the standpoint of elites, the deregulatory face of reform was associated with a number of systemic tensions relating both to economic agendas and to the requirements for social and political stability. From the standpoint of workers, those and related tensions have varyingly compromised the conditions of their livelihood security. Those two sets of tensions, and the political conflicts they have produced, have eventuated in policy adaptations and social accommodations that have influenced national trajectories of regulatory reform. Those trajectories, driven by the dynamic interplay of regulatory change, problematic outcomes, and regulatory response, have displayed substantial variation across sectors, national jurisdictions, and world economic zones, even as they have together reflected long-term changes in the ideological and institutional character of the evolving project of global market reform.

National reform trajectories have been explained by reference to the interaction of the interests and strategies of dominant coalitions, economic constraints and opportunities, the requisites of political stability and legitimation, institutional path dependencies, and class politics. While it would seem that regulatory strategies cannot possibly attend simultaneously to so many often-conflicting pressures, I have noted that (1) social economies are composed of loosely coupled systems, which afford a degree of flexibility in the ways in which particular economic strategies and accumulation requirements may be pursued and systemic tensions addressed; and (2) the very success of economic growth strategies is predicated on adequate management of a range of social and political requirements, including at least minimal provision for the social and livelihood protections of the working population.

The divergent trajectories of labor reform in the four contrasting Asian countries have suggested a shared tendency toward deregulatory overreach, along with growing recognition of the need to accommodate the resultant dislocations by reregulating labor markets and by instituting new social protections that do not conflict with, and indeed may often correspond with, the institutional requirements of reform. These trajectories highlight the dynamic interdependencies among the primary phases of labor systems. Thus, for example, labor market deregulation has generated pressures for new policies of social protection and compensation in order to lubricate flexible labor markets and as well to provide a social safety net to ensure political order. The instituting of new social protections has in turn forced changes and accommodations in the labor process. Further, the potential *developmental* deficits of labor market reform, including those relating to an increased contingency of employment among skilled and technical workers, has given new impetus to the expansion of high-tech industrial zones and networks, not only to foster technology innovation and interfirm collaboration, but also to create career opportunities and encourage heightened organizational commitments among mobile technical workers.

While the institutional and economic tensions of Asian reform emerged gradually over many years, social and political dislocations escalated sharply during the late-1990's financial crisis.[1] These outcomes have had political repercussions that have been further reinforced by political reforms and democratization. New political pressures have in turn pushed governments to seek a greater balance between social and economic agendas (Cheung 2009). While these pressures might in principle be restrained by a return to a more controlled authoritarian politics, as is clearly preferred by China's ruling groups, and as indeed seems to have occurred under both populist and liberal governments in Thailand during the '00s, new international pressures, the international media, and a host of popular-sector organizations and NGOs render that an increasingly costly and problematic response.

The multiple, interacting strands of social policy transformation that have in part defined Asian reform trajectories (productivist, early neoliberal, compensatory, market inclusionary, and developmental) are best understood as overlapping logics and patterns that coexist in varying ways in particular sectoral and national settings. The last of these social-policy strands, development, stands out from the rest because of its reengagement with earlier reform-displaced economic policies. Given the prominence of labor productivism in Asia's earlier developmental states, I have suggested that later patterns of *labor* developmentalism, best seen in active labor market policy and microindustrial policies, offer the possibility of a relatively stable institutional ensemble that draws together the often-conflicting imperatives of social stability and economic growth, while also responding to new political and economic pressures.[2]

As in the case of earlier iterations of regulatory reform and consolidation, new tensions continue to emerge. This is especially apparent in the realm of labor politics. Insofar as new social policies and institutional accommodations have responded to the demands of particular groups, they then face oppositional pressures from excluded groups. Thus, Thailand's populist programs have provoked political opposition among urban elites and middle classes, including state-enterprise workers. China's developmentally less-favored rural sectors threaten that country's headlong rush to urban-based industrialization through political instability and disorganized protest. And, in South Korea, tripartite negotiations with powerful trade unions are challenged by

---

1. While the world recession of 2008–10 had similar consequences, its employment effects were both less severe and more effectively cushioned by existing social-policy accommodations instituted after the earlier crisis.

2. Zhu (2003) suggests in this regard that China increasingly resembles a developmental state, particularly at subnational levels.

the middle class and other groups who often see Korean trade unions as pursuing narrow sectoral interests.

As I have suggested, the Asian reform experience must be understood against the larger canvas of world-market reform. Indeed, the World Bank has transitioned from a narrow early focus on deregulation to a greater emphasis on institutional consolidation and social accommodation. In this context, Asian reform trajectories do not seem altogether remarkable, except in one critical respect. Contrary to the experience of many countries in other world regions, such as Latin America, where market reform has proven more politically vulnerable, Asian market reform has retained a generally privileged, if contested, place in national economic agendas. That the Asia-Pacific region has, with important exceptions, enjoyed long periods of economic growth has granted states the structural opportunity, political legitimacy, and material resources to continue reform programs, to address multiple tensions, and to experiment with alternative policies. Equally important, the relative economic autonomy most Asian states have generally enjoyed vis-à-vis international lenders has afforded them a degree of latitude to introduce market reform gradually rather than through socially disruptive and politically destabilizing programs of rushed economic restructuring. Conversely, the Philippines presents the negative case that further confirms this regional characterization.

Variation in regional trajectories suggests that a search for an "Asian" model of regulatory reform may be misdirected. On the other hand, a broader view of these diverse regional experiences points to their shared origin in strategic efforts on the part of dominant groups to realize their core interests and to consolidate their political position in ways that mitigate social outcomes, manage political tensions, and enhance the institutional possibilities for continued growth. But it is clear that these often conflicting pressures can never be fully reconciled, especially given the underlying and more fundamental contradictions between social and economic agendas. For this reason, one can only assume that the institutional accommodations discussed in this book will by necessity only give way to further and continuing institutional tensions, adaptations, and change.

REFERENCES

Adams, F. Gerard. 2006. *East Asia, Globalization, and the New Economy.* London: Routledge.

Agarwala, Rina. 2008. "Reshaping the Social Contract: Emergent Relations between the State and Informal Labor in India." *Theory and Society* 37: 375–408.

Aglietta, Michel. 1998. "Capitalism at the Turn of the Century: Regulation Theory and the Challenge of Social Change." *New Left Review* 232, 41–90.

Alpha Research Co. Ltd. 2005. *Thailand in Figures 2004–2005.* 10th edition. Bankok: Alpha Research Co.

Amin, Ash. 2002. "The Informal Sector in Asia from the Decent Work Perspective." International Labor Organization, Papers on the Informal Economy, No. 4. Geneva, ILO.

———. 2004. "Regulating Economic Globalization." In *Transactions of the Institute of British Geographers.* London: Royal Geographical Society.

Amsden, Alice. 1989. *Asia's Next Giant: South Korea and Late Industrialization.* New York: Oxford University Press.

Appelbaum, Richard P. 2009. "Big Suppliers in Greater China." In *China and the Transformation of Global Capitalism,* edited by Hung Ho-fung, 65–85. Baltimore: Johns Hopkins University Press.

Archibughi, Franco. 2000. *The Associative Economy: Insights beyond the Welfare State and into Post-Capitalism.* London: Macmillan.

Arrighi, Giovanni. 2009. "China's Market Economy in the Long Run." In *China and the Transformation of Global Capitalism,* edited by Hung Ho-fung, 22–49. Baltimore: Johns Hopkins University Press.

Asian Development Bank. 2003. *Key Indicators for Asia and the Pacific.* Special chapter: "Education for Global Participation."

———. 2005. *Key Indicators for Asia and the Pacific.* Special chapter: "Labor Markets in Asia: Promoting Full, Production, and Decent Employment."

Athukorala, Prema-Chandra, Chris Manning, and Piyasiri Wickramasekara, 2000. *Growth, Employment, and Migration: Structural Change in the Greater Mekong Countries.* Cheltenbam, UK: Edward Elgar.

Ativanichayapong, Napaporn. 2002. *Trade Unions and the Workers' Collective Action in Thailand: An Articulation of Social Movement Unionism and Economic Unionism.* PhD dissertation, Department of Economics, Chulalongkorn University, Bangkok.

Bain, George, and Hugh Clegg. 1974. "A Strategy for Industrial Relations Research in Great Britain." *British Journal of Industrial Relations* 12 (1): 91–113.

Beeson, Mark, and Iyanatul Islam. 2005. "Neo-Liberalism and East Asia: Resisting the Washington Consensus." *Journal of Development Studies* 41 (2): 197–219.

Behrman, Jere R., Anil Deolalikar, and Pranee Tinakorn, with Worawan Chandoev-wit. 2000. *The Effects of the Thai Economic Crisis and of Thai Labor Market Policies on Labor Market Outcomes.* Bangkok: Thailand Development Research Institute.

Belassa, Bela. 1981. *The Newly Industrialising Countries in the World Economy.* New York: Pergamon.

Bello, Walden, Herbert Docena, Marissa de Guzman, and Mary Lou Malig. 2006. *The Anti-Developmental State: The Political Economy of Permanent Crisis in the Philippines.* London: Zed Books.

Betcherman, Gordon, and Rizwanul Islam, eds. 2001. *Fast Asian Labor Markets and the Economic Crisis.* Washington, DC: World Bank, and Geneva: International Labour Office.

Birdsall, Nancy, and Stephan Haggard. 2002. "After the Crisis: The Social Contract and the Middle Class in East Asia." In *When Markets Fail: Social Policy and Economic Reform,* edited by Ethan Kapstein and Brouko Milanovic, 58–101. New York: Russell Sage Foundation.

Blomqvist, Ake, and JiWei Qian. 2008. "Health System Reform in China: An Assessment of Recent Trends." *Singapore Economic Review* 53 (1): 5–26.

Blyth, Mark. 2002. *Great Transformations: Economic Ideas and Institutional Change in the Twentieth Century.* Cambridge: Cambridge University Press.

Boyer, Robert. 2005. "How and Why Capitalisms Differ." *Economy and Society* 34 (4): 509–57.

Brecher, Jeremy, Tim Costello, and Brendan Smith. 2006. "Labor Rights in China." Washington, DC: Foreign Policy in Focus, December 19.

Brown, Andrew. 2004. *Labour, Politics, and the State in Industrializing Thailand.* London: RoutledgeCurzon.

Brown, Andrew, B. Thonachaisetavut, and Kevin Hewison. 2002. *Labour Relations and Regulation in Thailand: Theory and Practice.* Working Papers Series 27 (July). Hong Kong: Southeast Asia Research Centre, City University of Hong Kong.

Brown, Earl Jr. 2003. "Thailand: Labour and the Law." In *Asia Pacific Labour Law Review: Workers' Rights for the New Century,* edited by Stephen Frost, Omana George, and Ed Shepherd, 353–66. Hong Kong: Asia Monitor Resource Centre.

Brown, Philip H., Alan de Brauw, and Yang Du. 2009. "Understanding Variation in the Design of China's New Cooperative Medical System." *China Quarterly* (June): 198–207.

Buğra, Ayşe, and Kaan Ağartan, eds. 2007. *Reading Karl Polanyi for the Twenty-first Century: Market Economy as a Political Project.* London: Palgrave Macmillan.

Burawoy, Michael. 1985. *The Politics of Production: Factory Regimes under Capitalism and Socialism.* New York: Verso Books.

Cai, Yongshun. 2006. *State and Laid-off Workers in Reform China.* London: Routledge.

Cao, Cong. 2004. "Zhongguancun and China's High-Tech Parks in Transition: Growing Pains or Premature Senility?" *Asian Survey* 44 (5): 647–68.

Caraway, Teri. 2006. *Assembling Women*. Ithaca: Cornell University Press.

——. 2009. "Labor Rights in East Asia: Progress or Regress?" *Journal of East Asian Studies* 9:153–86.

——. 2010. "Labor Standards and Labor Market Flexibility." *Studies in Comparative International Development* 45:225–49.

Castells, Manuel. 2000. "Materials for an Exploratory Theory of the Network Society." *British Journal of Sociology* 51 (1).

——. 2000 [1996]. *The Rise of the Network Society*, 2nd edition. Volume I. Malden, MA: Blackwell Publishing.

Chan, Anita. 2001. *China's Workers under Assault: The Exploitation of Labor in a Globalizing Economy*. Armonk, NY: M. E. Sharpe.

Chan, Cris King-Chi. 2010. *The Challenge of Labor in China: Strikes and the Changing Labour Regime in Global Factories*. London: Routledge.

Chan, Chris King-Chi, and Pun Ngai. 2009. "The Making of a New Working Class? A Study of Collective Actions of Migrant Workers in South China." *China Quarterly* (June): 287–303.

Chandler, Alfred D. 1962. *Strategy and Structure: Chapters in the History of the Industrial Enterprise*. Cambridge: MIT Press.

Chandler, Alfred D. 1977. *The Visible Hand: The Managerial Revolution in American Business*. Cambridge: Harvard University Press.

Chang, Dae-oup. 2009. "Labour Politics Not As We Know It: Politics of Labour in East Asia." *Asian Labour Update*, issue 70 (January–March): 4–6, 23–28.

Chen, John. 2003. "Reflections on Labour Law in China." In *Asia Pacific Labour Law Review: Workers' Rights for the New Century*. Hong Kong: Asia Monitor Resource Centre.

Chen, Lan, and Bao-qin Hou. 2008. "China: Economic Transition, Employment Flexibility, and Security." In *Globalization, Flexibilization and Working Conditions in Asia and the Pacific*, edited by Sangheon Lee and François Eyraud, 347–83. Geneva: International Labour Office.

Cheung, Anthony B. L. 2009. "Interpreting East Asian Social Policy Development: Paradigm Shifts or Policy 'Steadiness'?" In *Changing Governance and Public Policy in East Asia*, edited by Ka Ho Mok and Ray Forrest, 25–48. London: Routledge.

Chiu, Catherine C. H. 2005. "Changing Experiences of Work in Reformed State-Owned Enterprises in China." *Organization Studies* 27 (5): 677–97.

Chiu, Stephen W. K., and Stephen J. Frenkel. 2000. *Globalization and Industrial Relations in China*. Bangkok: Regional Office for Asia and the Pacific, ILO.

Chun, Jennifer Jihye. 2009. *Organizing at the Margins*. Ithaca: Cornell University Press.

Corben, Ron. 2010. "Thailand''s New Migrant Labor Laws Spark Fear, Criticism." Bangkok: News.com, July 7. URL: http://www.printthis.clickability.com/pt/cpt?action=cpt&title=Thailand%27s+New+Migra.

Deyo, Frederic C. 1987. "Coalitions, Institutions, and Linkage Sequencing—Toward a Strategic Capacity Model of East Asian Development." In *The Political Economy of the New Asian Industrialism*, edited by Frederic C. Deyo, 227–47. Ithaca: Cornell University Press.

Deyo, Frederic C. 1989. *Beneath the Miracle*. Berkeley: University of California Press.

——. 1993. "Singapore: Developmental Paternalism." In *Minidragons: Hong Kong, Singapore, South Korea, Taiwan—Fragile Economic Miracles in the Pacific,* edited by Steven M. Goldstein, 64–103. Boulder, CO: Westview.

——. 1996. "Competition, Flexibility, and Industrial Ascent: The Thai Auto Industry." In *Social Reconstructions of the World Automobile Industry,* edited by Frederic C. Deyo, 136–56. New York: St. Martin's Press.

——. 2002. "The 'New Developmentalism' in Post-Crisis Asia: The Case of Thailand's SME Sector." In *New Challenges for Development and Modernization,* edited by Yeung You-man, 15–33. Hong Kong: Chinese University Press.

——. 2006. "Southeast Asian Industrial Labour: Structural Demobilization and Political Transformjation." In *The Political Economy of South-East Asia,* 3rd edition, edited by Garry Rodan, Kevin Hewison, and Richard Robison, 283–304. Melbourne: Oxford University Press.

Deyo, Frederic C., and Kaan Ağartan. 2007. "Reforming East Asian Labor Systems: China, Korea, and Thailand." In *Market Economy as a Political Project: Reading Karl Polanyi for the Twenty-first Century,* edited by Ayşe Buğra and Kaan Ağartan, 191–218. New York: Palgrave Macmillan.

Deyo, Frederic C., and Richard F. Doner, 2001. "Dynamic Flexibility and Sectoral Governance in the Thai Auto Industry: The Enclave Problem." In *Economic Governance and the Challenge of Flexibility in East Asia,* edited by Frederic C. Deyo, Richard F. Doner, and Eric Hershberg, 107–35. New York: Rowman and Littlefield.

Dollar, David. 2003. "Eyes Wide Open: On the Targeted Use of Foreign Aid." *Harvard International Review* (Spring): 48–52.

Doner, Richard F. 2009. *The Politics of Uneven Development: Thailand's Economic Growth in Comparative Perspective.* New York: Cambridge University Press.

Doner, Richard F., and Eric Hershberg. 1999. "Flexible Production and Political Decentralization: Elective Affinities in the Pursuit of Competitiveness?" *Studies in Comparative and International Development* 34 (1).

Doner, Richard F., and Ansil Ramsay. 2003. "The Challenges of Economic Upgrading in Liberalising Thailand." In *States in the Global Economy: Bringing Domestic Institutions Back In,* edited by Linda Weiss, 121–41. Cambridge: Cambridge University Press.

Dong, Bauhua. 2002. "Labor Law and Reform in China." Stanford Law School: International Labor Standards Conference (May 19–21). URL: http://ils.stanford.edu/conference/papers/Dong%20Baohua.pdf.

Dressel, Bjorn. 2009. "Thailand's Elusive Quest for a Workable Constitution, 1997–2007." *Contemporary Southeast Asia* 31 (2): 296–325.

Dunlop, John. 1958. *Industrial Relations Systems.* Carbondale: Southern Illinois University Press.

[EABER] East Asian Bureau of Economic Research. Newsletter (monthly). Australian National University. URL: http://www.eaber.org.

Economist. 2009. *Pocket World in Figures: 2009 Edition.* London: Profile Books.

Erickson, Christopher, Sarosh Kuruvilla, and Rene Offreneo. 2003. *Industrial Relations* (April).

Evans, Peter. 1989. "Predatory, Developmental, and other Apparatuses: A Comparative Political Economy Perspective on the Third World State." *Sociological Forum* 4:561–87.

———. 1995. *Embedded Autonomy: States and Industrial Transformation.* Princeton: Princeton University Press.

Everling, Clark. 1997. *Social Economy: The Logic of Capitalist Development.* London: Routledge.

Fligstein, Neil. 2001. *The Architecture of Markets: An Economic Sociology of Twenty-first–Century Capitalist Societies.* Princeton: Princeton University Press.

Fontan, Jean-Marc, and Eric Shragge. 2000. "Tendencies, Tensions and Visions in the Social Economy." In *Social Economy: International Debates and Perspectives,* edited by Eric Shragge and Jean-Marc Fontan. Montreal: Black Rose Books.

Freeman, Richard. 1992. "Labor Market Institutions and Policies: Help or Hindrance to Economic Development?" Washington, DC: World Bank: World Bank Annual Conference on Development Economics, 117–44.

Frenkel, Stephen. 1993. "Variations in Patterns of Trade Unionism." In *Organized Labor in the Asia-Pacific Region,* edited by Stephen Frenkel. Ithaca: ILR Press, 309–46.

Frenkel, Stephen, and Sarosh Kuruvilla. 2002. "Logics of Action, Globalization, and Changing Employment Relations in China, India, Malaysia, and the Philippines." *Industrial and Labour Relations Review* 55 (3): 387–412.

Gaelle, Pierre, and Stefano Scarpetta. 2004. "How Labor Market Policy Can Combine Workers' Protection and Job Creation." Background paper for the World Bank, partially reproduced in World Bank, *World Development Report 2005.*

Gereffi, Gary. 1994. "The Organization of Buyer-Driven Global Commodity Chains: How U.S. Retailers Shape Overseas Production Networks." In *Commodity Chains and Global Capitalism,* edited by Gary Gereffi and Miguel Korzeniewicz, 95–122. Westport, CT: Praeger.

Goodman, Roger, Gordon White, and Huck-ju Kwon, eds. 1998. *The East Asian Welfare Model: Welfare Orientalism and the State.* London: Routledge.

Gordon, David. 1994a. "The Global Economy: New Edifice or Crumbling Foundations." In *Social Structures of Accumulation: The Political Economy of Growth and Crisis,* edited by David Kotz, Terrence McDonough, and Michael Reich, 292–305. Cambridge: Cambridge University Press.

Gordon, David. 1994b. "Long Swings and Stages of Capitalism." In *Social Structures of Accumulation: The Political Economy of Growth and Crisis,* edited by David M. Kotz, Terrence McDonough, and Michael Reich, 1–28. Cambridge: Cambridge University Press.

Gordon, David, Richard Edwards, and Michael Reich. 1982. *Segmented Work, Divided Workers: The Historical Transformation of Labor in the United States.* Cambridge: Cambridge University Press.

Green, Duncan. 2003. *Silent Revolution: The Rise and Crisis of Market Economies in Latin America.* New York: Monthly Review Press.

Grootaert, Christiaan, and Thierry van Bastelaer, eds. 2002. *The Role of Social Capital in Development.* Cambridge: Cambridge University Press.

Guan, Xinping. 2000. "China's Social Policy: Reform and Development in the Context of Marketization and Globalization." *Social Policy and Administration* 34 (1) (March).

Gunn, Christopher. 2004. *Third Sector Development: Making Up for the Market.* Ithaca: Cornell University Press.

Gutman, Herbert. 1977. *Work, Culture, and Society in Industrializing America.* New York: Vintage.

Haggard, Stephan. 1995. *Developing Nations and the Politics of Global Integration.* Washington, DC: Brookings Institution.

Haggard, Stephan, and Robert Dohner. 1994. *The Political Feasibility of Adjustment in the Philippines.* Paris: Development Centre of the Organisation for Economic Co-operation and Development.

Haggard, Stephan, and Robert R. Kaufman. 2008. *Development, Democracy, and Welfare States.* Princeton: Princeton University Press.

Hall, Peter A., and David Soskice. 2001. "An Introduction to Varieties of Capitalism." In *Varieties of Capitalism,* edited by Peter Hall and David Soskice, 1–70. Oxford: Oxford University Press.

Han, Ji-wan. 2009. "Dynamics of Unionism and the Movement for a Labour Party." *Asian Labour Update,* issue 70 (January–March). Hong Kong: Asia Monitor Resource Centre.

Hare, Denise. 1999. "'Push' versus 'Pull' Factors in Migration Outflows and Returns: Determinants of Migration Status and Spell Duration among China's Rural Population." *Journal of Development Studies* 35 (3).

Harvey, David. 2005. *A Brief History of Neoliberalism.* New York: Oxford University Press.

———. 2010. *The Enigma of Capital.* Oxford: Oxford University Press.

Haworth, Nigel, and H. Ramsay. 1984. "Grapsing the Nettle: Problems with the Theory of International Trade Union Solidarity." In *The New Labour Internationalism,* edited by P. Waterman. The Hague: ILERI.

Herrin, Alejandro N., and Ernesto M. Pernia. 2003. "Population, Human Resources, and Employment." In *The Philippine Economy: Development, Policies, and Challenges,* edited by Arsenio Balisacan and Hal Hill. New York: Oxford University Press.

Hewison, Kevin. 2006a. "Outcomes of the Thai Economic Crisis." In *East Asia and the Trials of Neo-Liberalism,* edited by Kevin Hewison and Richard Robison, 114–34. London: Routledge.

———. 2006b. "Thailand: Boom, Bust, and Recovery." In *The Political Economy of South-East Asia: Markets, Power, and Contestation,* 3rd edition, edited by Garry Rodan, Kevin Hewison, and Richard Robison, 74–108. Melbourne: Oxford University Press.

Hill, Hal. 2003. "Manufacturing." In *The Philippine Economy: Development, Policies, and Challenges,* edited by Arsenio Balisacan and Hal Hill. New York: Oxford University Press.

Ho, Lup Fung. 2007. "Between Idealism and Realism." In *The Crisis of Welfare in East Asia,* edited by James Lee and Kam-Wah Chan, 203–21. Plymouth, UK: Lexington Books.

Holliday, Ian. 2000. "Productivist Welfare Capitalism." *Political Studies* 48 (4): 706–23.

Holliday, Ian, and P. Wilding, eds. 2003. *Welfare Capitalism in East Asia: Social Policy in the Tiger Economies.* Houndmills, UK: Palgrave Macmillan.

Hsu, Jennifer. 2009. "Quietly, Quietly, Quietly: Beijing's Migrant Civil Society Organisations." In *Dissent and Cultural Resistance in Asia's Cities,* edited by Melissa Butcher and Selvaraj Velayutham, 53–71. London: Routledge.

———. Forthcoming 2012. "Spaces of Civil Society: The Role of Migrant Non-Governmental Organizations in Beijing and Shanghai." *Progress in Development Studies* 12 (1).

Hutchison, Jane. 2006. "Poverty of Politics in the Philippines." In *The Political Economy of South-East Asia: Markets, Power, and Contestation,* 3rd edition, edited by Garry Rodan, Kevin Hewison, and Richard Robison, 39–73. Melbourne: Oxford University Press.

Hyman, Richard. 1975. *Industrial Relations: A Marxist Introduction.* London: Macmillan.

Ignacio-Esteban, M. Angelina. 2003. "The Dynamics of Illegal Migration: The Philippines-South Korea Case." *Philippine Labor Review* 27 (1): 22–81.

Imperial, M. Luisa Gigette S. 2003. "Overseas Employment: A Growth Strategy?" *Philippine Labor Review* 27 (1): 1–21.

Imudom, Waranagkana 2000. "The Role of Minimum Wage in Thailand." UN Public Administration Network. URL: http://Unpan1.un.org.

Islam, Iyanatul, and Anis Chowdhury. 2000. "Governing East Asia in the 21st Century: Toward a Post-Washington Consensus?" In *The Political Economy of East Asia: Post-Crisis Debates,* edited by Iyanatul Islam and Anis Chowdhury, 208–39. Oxford: Oxford University Press.

Itzigson, Jose. 2000. *Developing Poverty: The State, Labor Market Deregulation, and the Informal Economy in Costa Rica and the Dominican Republic.* University Park: Pennsylvania State University Press.

Jaffee, David. 2001. *Organization Theory: Tension and Change.* Columbus, OH: McGraw Hill.

Jayasuriya, Kanishka. 2006. *Statecraft, Welfare and the Politics of Inclusion.* Houndmills, UK: Palgrave Macmillan.

Jeorges, Christian, Bo Strath, and Peter Wagner, eds. 2005. *The Economy as a Polity: the Political Construction of Contemporary Capitalism.* London: UCL Press.

Jessop, Bob. 2002. *The Future of the Capitalist State.* London: Polity Press.

Jessop, Bob, and Ngai-Ling Sum. 2006. *Beyond the Regulation Approach: Putting Capitalist Economies in their Place.* Cheltenham, UK: Edward Elgar.

Johnson, Chalmers A. 1982. *MITI and the Japanese Miracle: The Growth of Industrial Policy, 1925–1975.* Palo Alto: Stanford University Press.

——. 1989. "Political Institutions and Economic Performance: The Government-Business Relationship in Japan, South Korea, and Taiwan." In *The Political Economy of the New Asian Industrialism,* edited by Frederic C. Deyo, 136–64. Ithaca: Cornell University Press.

Kalleberg, Arne L. 2007. "Flexible Firms and Labor Market Segmentation: Effects of Workplace Restructuring on Jobs and Workers." In *The Transformation of Work in the New Economy,* edited by Robert Perrucci and Carolyn C. Perrucci, 166–79. Los Angeles: Roxbury Publishing Company.

Kang, Soon-Hie, Jaeho Keum, Dong-Heon Kim, and Donggyun Shin. 2001. "Korea: Labor Market Outcomes and Policy Responses after the Crisis." In *East Asian Labor Markets and the Economic Crisis,* edited by Gordon Betcherman and Rizwanul Islam, 97 139. Washington, DC: World Bank, and Geneva: the International Labour Office.

Kapstein, Ethan B. 1999. *Sharing the Wealth.* New York: W. W. Norton and Company.

Kapstein, Ethan B., and Branko Milanovic, eds. 2002. *When Markets Fail: Social Policy and Economic Reform.* New York: Russell Sage Foundation.

Kelly, Philip F. 2001. "The Political Economy of Local Labor Control in the Philippines." *Economic Geography* 77 (1): 1–22.

Kerr, Clark, John Dunlop, Frederick Harbison, and Charles Meyers. 1960. *Industrialism and Industrial Man*. Cambridge: Harvard University Press.

Kim, Dong-One, Johngseok Bae, and Changwon Lee. 2000. "Globalization and Labour Rights: The Case of Korea." In *Globalization and Labour in the Asia Pacific Region*, edited by Chris Rowley and John Benson, 133–53. London: Frank Cass.

Kim, Yoo-Sun. 2007. *Working Korea 2007*. Seoul: Korea Labor and Society Institute.

King, Victor. 2008. *The Sociology of Southeast Asia*. Honolulu: University of Hawaii Press.

Klotzbucher, Sascha, Peter Lassig, Qin Jiangmei, and Susanne Weigelin-Schwiedrzik. 2010. "What Is New in the 'New Rural Cooperative Medical System'?: An Assessment in One Kazak County of the Xinjiang Uyghur Autonomous Region." *China Quarterly* 201 (March): 20–37.

Koo, Hagen. 2001. *Korean Workers: The Culture and Politics of Class Formation*. Ithaca: Cornell University Press.

Korea, Republic of, Ministry of Finance. 1997. *Vocational Training Promotion Act*.

Kotz, David. 1994. "The Regulation Theory and the Social Structure of Accumulation Approach." In *Structures of Accumulation: The Political Economy of Growth and Crisis*, edited by David Kotz, Terrence McDonough, and Michael Reich, 85–97. Cambridge: Cambridge University Press.

Kuczynski, Pedro-Pablo, and John Williamson, eds. 2003. *After the Washington Consensus: Restarting Growth and Reform in Latin America*. Washington, DC: Institute for International Economics.

Kuravilla, Sarosh, Christoper Erickson, Mark Anner, Maragtas V. Amante, and Ina Ortiz. 2000. *Globalization and Industrial Relations in the Philippines*. Bangkok: Regional Office for Asia and the Pacific, ILO.

Kuruvilla, Sarosh, and Mingwei Liu. 2010. "Tripartism and Economic Reforms in Singapore and Korea." In *Blunting Neoliberalism: Tripartism and Economic Reforms in the Developing World*, edited by Lydia Fraile, 39–64. New York: Palgrave Macmillan.

Kwon, Huck-ju. 2002. "Welfare Reform and Future Challenges in the Republic of Korea: Beyond the Developmental Welfare State?" *Development and Change* 55 (4).

——. 2005a. "An Overview of the Study: The Developmental Welfare State and Policy Reforms in East Asia." In *Transforming the Developmental Welfare State in East Asia*, edited by Huck-ju Kwon, 1–23. New York: Palgrave Macmillan.

——. 2005b. "Transforming the Developmental Welfare State in East Asia." *Development and Change* 36 (3): 477–97.

Lange, Peter. 1985. "Semiperiphery and Core in the European Context: Reflections on the Postwar Italian Experience." In *Semiperipheral Development: The Politics of Southern Europe in the Twentieth Century*, edited by Giovanni Arrighi, 179–214. Beverly Hills, CA: SAGE.

Laquian, Aprodicio A. 2005. "The Philippines: Poor and Unequal but Free." In *Getting Globalization Right: The Dilemmas of Inequality*, edited by Joseph S. Tulchin and Gary Bland, 93–124. Boulder, CO: Lynne Rienner.

Lawler, John J., and Chokechai Suttawet. 2000. "Labour Unions, Globalization, and Deregulation in Thailand." In *Globalization and Labour in the Asia Pacific Region*, edited by Chris Rowley and John Benson, 214–38. London: Frank Cass.

Lee, Byung-Hee, and Bum-Sang Yoo. 2008. "The Republic of Korea: From Flexibility to Segmentation." In *Globalization, Flexibilization and Working Conditions in Asia and the Pacific,* edited by Sangheon Lee and François Eyraud, 187–233. Geneva: International Labour Office.

Lee, Ching-kwan. 1998. *Gender and the South China Miracle: Two Worlds of Factory Women.* Berkeley: University of California Press.

——. 2007. *Against the Law: Labor Protests in China's Rustbelt and Sunbelt.* Berkeley: University of California Press.

Lee, James. 2007. "Deciphering Productivism and Developmentism." In *The Crisis of Welfare in East Asia,* edited by James Lee and Kam-Wah Chan, 1–26. Plymouth, UK: Lexington Books.

Lee, Yoonkyung. 2006. "Varieties of Labor Politics in Northeast Asian Democracies." *Asian Survey* 46 (5): 721–40.

——. 2011. *Militants or Partisans: Labor Unions and Democratic Politics in Korea and Taiwan.* Stanford, CA: Stanford University Press.

Levi-Faur, David, and Jacint Jordana, eds. 2005. "The Rise of Regulatory Capitalism: The Global Diffusion of a New Order." *Annals of the American Academy of Political and Social Science* 598 (March).

Lim, Young-il, Dae-sook Kim, and Young-hee Kim. 2003. "South Korea." In *Asia Pacific Labour Law Review: Workers' Rights for the New Century,* edited by Stephen Frost, Omana George, and Ed Shephard, 313–26. Hong Kong: Asia Monitor Resource Centre.

Lin, Chien-ju. 2010. Institutions, Local Politics and Firm Strategies: Two Labor Systems in Taiwan. PhD dissertation, Binghamton University, State University of New York.

Lin, Nan. 2001. *Social Capital: A Theory of Social Structure and Action.* New York: Cambridge University Press.

Lipietz, Alain. 1992. *Towards a New Economic Order: Postfordism, Ecology, and Democracy.* New York: Oxford University Press.

Lippit, Victor D. 2005. *Capitalism.* London: Routledge.

——. 2010. "Social Structure of Accumulation Theory." In *Contemporary Capitalism and Its Crises,* edited by Terrence McDonough, Michael Reich, and David M. Kotz, 45–71. Cambridge: Cambridge University Press.

Liu, Yang, Lianjun Wang, and Shengxi Wenku. 2010. "The Urban Informal Sector in China." *View,* November 18.

Lü, Xiaobo, and Elizabeth J. Perry. 1997. "Introduction: The Changing Chinese Workplace in Historical and Comparative Perspective." In *Danwei: The Changing Chinese Workplace in Historical and Comparative Perspective,* edited by Xiaobo Lü and Elizabeth J. Perry, 3–17. Armonk NY: M. E. Sharpe.

Luce, Stephanie, and Edna Bonacich. 2009. "China and the U.S. Labor Movement." In *China and the Transformation of Global Capitalism,* edited by Hung Ho-fung, 153–73. Baltimore: Johns Hopkins University Press.

Majone, Giandomenico. 1997. "From the Positive to the Regulatory State: Causes and Consequences of Changes in the Mode of Governance." *Journal of Public Policy* 17 (2): 139–67.

McDonough, Terrence. 2010. "The State of the Art of Social Structure of Accumulation Theory." In *Contemporary Capitalism and Its Crisis: Social Structure of*

Accumulation Theory for the 21st Century, edited by Terrence McDonough, Michael Reich, and David M. Kotz, 23–71. Cambridge: Cambridge University Press.

McKay, Steven. 2006. *Satanic Mills or Silicon Islands: The Politics of High-Tech Production in the Philippines.* Ithaca: Cornell University Press.

McMichael, Philip. 2008. *Development and Social Change: A Global Perspective,* 4th edition. Thousand Oaks, CA: Pine Forge Press.

Meng, Jianjun. 2002. "Economic Structural Reform and Labor Market Formation in China." Paper published by the Research Institute of Economy, Trade and Industry (April). URL: http://www.rieti.go.jp/en/columns/a01_0037.html.

Milkman, Ruth. 1998. "The New American Workplace: High Road or Low Road." In *Workplaces of the Future,* edited by Paul Thompson and Chris Warhurst. London: Macmillan.

Mok, Ka Ho, and Ray Forrest. 2009. "Introduction: The Search for Good Governance in Asia." In *Changing Governance and Public Policy in East Asia,* edited by Ka Ho Mok, and Ray Forrest, 1–22. London: Routledge.

Montgomery, David. 1979. *Workers' Control in America.* New York: Cambridge University Press.

Moore, Phoebe. 2007. *Globalization and Labour Struggle in Asia: A Neo-Gramscian Critique of South Korea's Political Economy.* London: I. B. Tauris.

Moore, Wilbert. 1965. *The Impact of Industry.* Englewood Cliffs, NJ: Prentice-Hall.

Moran, Michael. 2001. "The Rise of the Regulatory State in Britain." *Parliamentary Affairs* 54:19–34.

Mun, Young Cho. 2010. "The Population: Ethnographic Research on the Minimum Livelihood Guarantee." *China Quarterly* 201 (March): 20–37.

Munck, Ronaldo. 2002. *Globalization and Labour: The New "Great Transformation."* London: Zed Books.

Murillo, M. Victoria. 2000. "From Populism to Neoliberalism." *World Politics* 52 (January): 135–74.

Nair, C. V. Devan, ed. 1976. *Socialism That Works: The Singapore Way.* Singapore: Federal Publications.

Naughton, Barry. 1995. *Growing Out of the Plan: Chinese Economic Reform 1978–1993.* New York: Cambridge University Press.

Nevins, Joseph, and Nancy Lee Peluso. 2008. "Introduction: Commoditization in Southeast Asia." In *Taking Southeast Asia to Market,* edited by Joseph Nevins and Nancy Lee Peluso. Ithaca: Cornell University Press.

Ngai, Pun. 2005. *Made in China: Women Factory Workers in a Global Workplace.* Durham: Duke University Press.

North, Douglas. 1990. *Institutions, Institutional Change, and Economic Performance.* Cambridge: Cambridge University Press.

Ofreneo, Rene E. 1995a. "The Changing Terrains for Trade Union Organising." Unpublished manuscript. Quezon City: University of the Philippines, School of Labour and Industrial Relations.

——. 1995b. "Philippine Industrialization and Industrial Relations." In *Employment Relations in the Asian Economies,* edited by Anil Verma, Thomas Kochan, and Russell Lansbury, 194–247. London: Routledge.

———. 2009. "Development Choices for Philippine Textiles and Garments in the Post-MFA Era." *Journal of Contemporary Asia* 39 (4): 543–61.

Olson, Mancur. 1971. *The Logic of Collective Action: Special Interests and Economic Policy.* Cambridge: Harvard University Press.

Ong, Aihwa. 2006. *Neoliberalism as Exception: Mutations in Citizenship and Sovereignty.* Chapel Hill: Duke University Press.

Palat, Ravi. 2007. *Capitalist Restructuring and the Pacific Rim.* London: RoutledgeCurzon.

———. 2010. "World Turned Upside Down?" *Third World Quarterly* 31 (3): 365–84.

Parish, William. 1985. "Introduction: Historical Background and Current Issues." In *Chinese Rural Development: The Great Transformation,* edited by William Parish, 3–29. Armonk, NY: M. E. Sharpe.

Peck, Jamie, and Adam Tickell. 2002. "Neoliberalizing Space." *Antipode* 24 (3): 380–404.

Pereira, Alexius A. 2003. *State Collaboration and Development Strategies in China: The Case of the China-Singapore Suzhou Industrial Park (1992–2002).* London: RoutledgeCurzon.

Piore, Michael, and Charles Sabel. 1984. *The Second Industrial Divide: Possibilities for Prosperity.* New York: Basic Books.

Polanyi, Karl. 2001 [1944]. *The Great Transformation: The Political and Economic Origins of Our Time.* Boston: Beacon Hill Press.

Portes, Alejandro. 1994. "The Informal Economy and Its Paradoxes." In *The Handbook of Economic Sociology,* edited by Neil Smelser and Richard Swedberg, 426–49. Princeton: Princeton University Press.

Portes, Alejandro, Manuel Castells, and Lauren Benton, eds. 1989. *The Informal Economy: Studies in Advanced and Developing Countries.* Baltimore, MD: Johns Hopkins University Press.

Putnam, Robert. 1993. *Making Democracy Work: Civic Traditions in Modern Italy.* Princeton: Princeton University Press.

Quintos, Paul L. 2003. "A Century of Labour Rights and Wrongs in the Philippines." In *Asia Pacific Labour Law Review: Workers' Rights for the New Century,* 277–91. Hong Kong: Asia Monitor Resource Centre.

Ramesh, M. 2000. *Welfare Capitalism in Southeast Asia.* New York: Saint Martin's Press.

———. 2003. "Globalisation and Social Security Expansion in East Asia." In *States in the Global Economy: Bringing Domestic Institutions Back In,* edited by Linda Weiss, 83–98. Cambridge: Cambridge University Press.

———. 2004. *Social Policy in East and Southeast Asia: Education, Health, Housing, and Income Maintenance.* London: RoutledgeCurzon.

Reutersward, Anders. 2002. "Labour Market and Social Benefit Policies." In *China in the World Economy: The Domestic Policy Challenges.* Paris: OECD.

Robinson, William. 2004. *A Theory of Global Capitalism.* Baltimore: Johns Hopkins University Press.

Robison, Richard. 2004. "Neoliberalism and the Future World: Markets and the End of Politics." *Critical Asian Studies* 36 (3): 405–23.

Rodrik, Dani. 2002. "After Neoliberalism, What?" Paper presented at a conference on "Alternatives to Neoliberalism." Organized by Harvard University, Washington, DC. May 23.

Rodriquez, Robyn Magalit. 2010. *Migrants for Export: How the Philippine State Brokers Labor to the World.* Minneapolis: University of Minnesota Press.

Rudnycky, Daromir. 2008. "Worshipping Work." In *Taking Southeast Asia to Market,* edited by Joseph Nevins and Nancy Lee Peluso, 73–87. Ithaca: Cornell University Press.

Ruggie, John. 1982. "International Regimes, Transactions and Change: Embedded Liberalism in the Postwar Economic Order." *International Organization* 36 (Spring): 379–415.

Sachs, Jeffrey D. 2000. "A New Map of the World." *Economist* (June 22): 81–83.

——. 2003. "Institutions Matter, but Not for Everything." *Finance and Development* (June): 38–41.

——. 2005. *The End of Poverty: Economic Possibilities for Our Time.* New York: Penguin.

Saunders, P., and F. Ping. 2000. "Social Security Development in a Context of Economic Reform and Social Change: The Case of Rural Social Insurance Program in China." Paper presented at the conference Social Transformation in the Asia Pacific Region. CAPSTRANS–UNESCO-MOST. University Of Wollongong, Australia. December 4–6.

Saxenian, Annalee. 1994. *Regional Advantage: Culture and Competition in Silicon Valley and Route 128.* Cambridge: Harvard University Press.

Scott, Solomon. 2009. "State-Led Migration, Democratic Legitimacy, and Deterritorialization: The Philippines' Labour Export Model." *European Journal of East Asian Studies* 8 (2): 275–300.

Seidman, Gay. 1994. *Manufacturing Militance: Workers' Movements in Brazil and South Africa, 1970–1985.* Berkeley: University of California Press.

Selden, Mark. 1985. "Income Inequalities and the State." In *Chinese Rural Development: The Great Transformation,* edited by William L. Parish, 193–218. Armonk, NY: M. E. Sharpe.

Seo Dong Jin. 2005. "The Will to Self-Empowerment, the Will to Freedom: An Understanding of the Transition of Korean Capitalism and the Transformation of Subjectivity through the Self-Empowerment Discourses." PhD dissertation, Yonsei University, Seoul.

Shin, Dong-Ho. 2001. "An Alternative Approach to Developing Science Parks: A Case Study from Korea." *Regional Science* 80 (1), 103–11.

Shragge, Eric, and Jean-Marc Fontan, eds. 2000. *Social Economy: International Debates and Perspectives.* Montreal: Black Rose Books.

Sibal, Jorge V. 2007. "Social Partnership Between the Civil Society, Government and the Private Sector in Improving Working Conditions in the Informal Sector." *Philippine Journal of Labor and Industrial Relations* 27 (1–2): 20–41.

Sibal, Jorge V., Maragtas S. V. Amante, and M. Catalina Tolentino. 2008. "The Philippines: Changes at the Workplace." In *Globalization, Flexibilization and Working Conditions in Asia and the Pacific,* edited by Sangheon Lee and François Eyraud, 279–312. Geneva: International Labour Office.

Sicat, Geradro P., and Rahimaisa D. Abdula. 2003. "Public Finance." In *The Philippine Economy: Development, Policies, and Challenges,* edited by Arsenio M. Balisacan and Hal Hill. Oxford: Oxford University Press.

Siengthai, Sununta. 2008. "Thailand: Globalization and Unprotected Workers." In *Globalization, Flexibilization and Working Conditions in Asia and the Pacific,* edited by Sangheon Lee and François Eyraud, 313–43. Geneva: International Labour Office.

Silver, Beverly J. 2003. *Forces of Labor.* Cambridge: Cambridge University Press.

Silver, Beverly J., and Lu Zhang. 2009. "China as an Epicenter of World Labor Unrest." In *China and the Transformation of Global Capitalism,* edited by Hung Ho-fung, 174–87. Baltimore: Johns Hopkins University Press.

Smith, Brendan, Jeremy Brocher, and Tim Costello. 2006. "China's Emerging Labor Movement." (October 9). URL: http://www.zmag.org/content/print.

So, Alvin Y. 2009. "Rethinking the Chinese Development Miracle." In *China and the Transformation of Global Capitalism,* edited by Hung Ho-fung Hung, 50–63. Baltimore: Johns Hopkins University Press.

Solinger, Dorothy. 1997. "The Impact of the Floating Population on the Danwei: Shifts in the Pattern of Labor Mobility Control and Entitlement Provision." In *Danwei: The Changing Chinese Workplace in Historical and Comparative Perspective,* edited by Xiaobo Lü and Elizabeth J. Perry, 195–222. Armonk NY: M. E. Sharpe.

——. 1999. *Contesting Citizenship in Urban China: Peasant Migrants, the State, and the Logic of the Market.* Berkeley: University of California Press.

——. 2009. *States' Gains, Labor's Losses.* Ithaca: Cornell University Press, 2009.

Song, Jesook. 2009. *South Koreans in the Debt Crisis: The Creation of a Neoliberal Welfare Society.* Durham: Duke University Press.

Soto, Hernando de. 1989. *The Other Path: The Invisible Revolution in the Third World.* New York: Harper and Row.

Stiglitz, Joseph. 2000. *Globalization and Its Discontents.* Washington, DC: World Bank.

——. 2001 [1944]. Foreword to *The Great Transformation: The Political and Economic Origins of Our Time,* Karl Polanyi, vii–xvii. 2nd edition. Boston: Beacon Hill Press.

——. 2010. *Freefall: America, Free Markets, and the Sinking of the World Economy.* New York: W. W. Norton.

Sumano, Boonwara. 2010. *East Asia Forum.* July 9 (online).

Sundaram, Jomo Kwame. 1998. *Tigers in Trouble: Financial Governance, Liberalisation and Crises in East Asia.* London: Zed Books.

——. 2009. "Export-Oriented Industrialization, Female Employment, and Gender Wage Equity in East Asia." *Economic and Political Weekly.* January 3, 41–54.

Suttawet, Chokchai. 1999. [Philanthropic labor organizations in Thailand]. *Raengngan Poritha*t 13 (12): 4–9.

Tang, K. I. 2000. *Social Welfare Development in East Asia.* Houndmills, UK: Palgrave Macmillan.

Taylor, Bill. 1999. "Patterns of Control within Japanese Manufacturing Plants in China: Doubts about Japanization in Asia." *Journal of Management Studies* 36 (6).

Taylor, Bill. 2002. "Privatization, Markets and Industrial Relations in China." *British Journal of Industrial Relations* 40 (2): 249–72.

Thailand Development Research Institute Foundation (TDRI). 2002. *Employment Policy Framework under National Development Plan.* Bangkok: Thailand Development Research Institute Foundation.

Thompson, Paul. 2010. "The Capitalist Labour Process: Concepts and Connections." *Capital and Class* 34 (1): 7–14.

Tipton, Frank. 1998. *The Rise of Asia: Economics, Society, and Politics in Contemporary Asia*. Honolulu: University of Hawaii Press.

Tolentino, Catalina M. 2007. "Job Satisfaction of SME Workers in Select Cities of Mindanao." *Philippine Journal of Labor and Industrial Relations* 27 (1–2): 42.

Trubeck, David, Jim Mosher, and Jeffrey Rothstein. 2000. "Transnationalism in the Regulation of Labor Relations: International Regimes and Transnational Advocacy Networks." *Law and Social Inquiry* 25 (4) (Fall).

United Nations, Division for the Advancement of Women. 1999. 1999. "Employment and Displacement Effects of Globalization." In *1999 World Survey on the Role of Women in Development: Globalization, Gender, and Work*. New York: United Nations.

United States, Department of Labor. 2003a. *Foreign Labor Trends, Korea*. Washington, DC.

United States, Department of Labor. 2003b. *Foreign Labor Trends, Philippines*. Washington, DC.

Wade, Robert. 1990. *Governing the Market: Economic Theory and the Role of Government in East Asian Industrialization*. Princeton: Princeton University Press.

——. 2003. "The Disturbing Rise in Poverty and Inequality: Is It All a Big Lie?" In *Taming Globalization: Frontiers of Governance*, edited by David Held and Mathias Koenig-Archibugi, 18–46. Cambridge: Polity Press.

Wade, Robert. 2007. "The WTO and the Shrinking of Development Space." In *The Globalization and Development Reader*, edited by J. Timmons Roberts and Amy Bellone Hite, 277–94. Malden, MA: Blackwell Publishing.

Wang, Shaoguang. 2002. "Openness, Distributive Conflict, and Social Insurance: The Social and Political Implications of China's WTO Membership." In *New Challenges for Development and Modernization*, edited by Yeung You-man, 35–73. Hong Kong: Chinese University Press.

Weiss, Linda. 2003. "Is the State Being Transformed by Globalization?" In *States in the Global Economy: Bringing Domestic Institutions Back In,* edited by Linda Weiss, 293–317. Cambridge: Cambridge University Press.

Weiss, Linda, and John Hobson, 1995. *States and Economic Development*. Cambridge: Polity Press.

Whyte, Martin King, and William L. Parish. 1984. *Urban Life in Contemporary China*. Chicago: University of Chicago Press.

Williamson, John. 1990. "What Washington Means by Policy Reforms." Chap. 1 in *The Progress of Policy Reform in Latin America*. Washington, DC: Institute for International Economics.

Williamson, Oliver E. 1975. *Markets and Hierarchies: Analysis and Antitrust Implications*. New York: Free Press.

Wolf, Diane. 1992. *Factory Daughters: Gender, Household Dynamics, and Rural Industrialization in Java*. Berkeley: University of California Press.

Wolfson, Martin, and David Kotz. 2010. "A Reconceptualization of Social Structures of Accumulation Theory." In *Contemporary Capitalism and Its Crises*, edited by Terrence McDonough, Michael Reich, and David Kotz, 72–90. Cambridge: Cambridge University Press.

Wong, Joseph. 2004. *Healthy Democracies: Welfare Politics in Taiwan and South Korea.* Ithaca: Cornell University Press.

World Bank. 1993. *World Development Report: The East Asian Miracle.* Oxford: Oxford University Press.

———. 2002a. *Globalization, Growth, and Poverty.* New York: Oxford University Press.

———. 2002b. *World Development Report: Building Institutions for Markets.* New York: Oxford University Press.

———. 2005. *World Development Indicators* special chapter: "Workers and Labor Markets." New York: Oxford University Press.

———. 2006. *Doing Business 2007: How to Reform.* New York: Oxford University Press.

World Bank. Website on social capital, URL: http://go.worldbank.org/ COQTRW4QFO.

Yang, Jae-jin, and Chung-in Moon. 2005. "South Korea: Globalization, Neoliberal Labor Reform, and the Trilemma of an Emerging Welfare State." In *Getting Globalization Right: The Dilemmas of Inequality,* edited by Joseph S. Tulchin and Gary Bland, 71–91. Boulder, CO: Lynne Rienner.

Yu, Wei. 1999. "Financing Unemployment and Pension Insurance." In *Dilemmas of Reform in Jiang Zemin's China,* edited by Andrew J. Nathan, Zhaohui Hong, and Steven R. Smith. Boulder, CO: Lynne Rienner.

Zhao, Yaohui. 1999. "Labor Migration and Earnings Differences: The Case of Rural China." *Economic Development and Cultural Change* 47 (4).

Zhu, Tianbiao. 2003. "Building Institutional Capacity for China's New Economic Opening." In *States in the Global Economy: Bringing Domestic Institutions Back In,* edited by Linda Weiss, 142–60. Cambridge: Cambridge University Press.

Zhu, Xiao, and Anita Chan. 2005. "Staff and Workers' Representative Congress— An Institutional Channel for Expression of Employees' Interests?" *Chinese Sociology and Anthropology* (Summer).

Official and Statistical Sources

In-text references noted in parentheses; see preceding reference list for key issues of several of these statistical series used extensively in this book.

Asian Development Bank (ADB), Manila

    Asian Development Outlook (Outlook), annual
    Key Indicators for Asia and the Pacific (KI), annual; Online at http://www.abd.org/statistics

International Bank for Reconstruction and Development
(World Bank), Washington, DC.

    Global Development Finance (GDF), annual
    World Development Indicators (WDI), annual; Online at http://data.worldbank.org/ indicator
    World Development Report (WDR), annual

International Labour Organization (ILO), Geneva

    Key Indicators of the Labour Market (KI), periodic
    Statistical Update on Employment in the Informal Sector

World Employment (WE), annual
World Labour Report (WLR)
Yearbook of Labour Statistics (YLS), annual; Online at laborsta.ilo.org

International Monetary Fund (IMF), Washington, DC

   International Financial Statistics (IFS), annual
   Government Finance Statistics Yearbook (GFS), annual

Kingdom of Thailand (KOT)

   Statistical Yearbook of Thailand (SY), annual; National Statistical Office.
   Yearbook of Labor Statistics (YLS), annual; Ministry of Labor and Social Welfare.
   Report of the Thai *Laborforce Survey* (quarterly); Bangkok: National Statistical
      Office

People's Republic of China (PRC)

   China Labor Statistics Yearbook (LSY), annual; National Bureau of Statistics of China
   China Population and Employment Statistics Yearbook (2008); Department of Popu-
      lation and Employment Statistics
   China Statistical Yearbook (CSY), annual; China Statistical Press
   Industrial Economy Statistical Yearbook (2006); National Bureau of Statistics of China

Republic of Korea (ROK)

   KLI Quarterly Labor Review. Seoul: Korea Labor Institute
   Korea Statistical Yearbook (SY), annual; National Bureau of Statistics
   Report on the Economically Active Population; Ministry of Employment and
      Labor
   Report on Mining and Manufacturing (periodic)
   Yearbook of Labor Statistics(YLS), annual; Ministry of Employment and Labor

Republic of the Philippines (ROP)

   Annual Survey of Philippine Business and Industry (annual survey); National Statis-
      tics Office
   Economic Indicators. Manila: Philippine Economic Zone Authority (PEZA)
   Philippine Census of Business and Industry 2004; National Statistical Coordina-
      tion Board.
   Philippine Industry Yearbook of Labor Statistics (Industry Labor Yearbook), annual.
      Philippine Labor Statistical Service.
   Philippine Statistical Yearbook (SY), annual. National Statistical Coordination Board
   Yearbook of Labor Statistics (YLS); Department of Labor and Employment

United Nations

   Comtrade, annual
   United Nations Development Program (UNDP)
   Human Development Report (HDR), annual
   United Nations Economic and Social Commission for Asia and the Pacific (ESCAP)

Economic and Social Survey of Asia and the Pacific (Survey), annual
United Nations Educational, Scientific and Cultural Organization (UNESCO)
Statistical Yearbook (SY), annual
United Nations Industrial Development Organization (UNIDO)
International Yearbook of Industrial Statistics (Yearbook), annual
Industrial Development Report, annual

INDEX